The Traffic Systems of Pompeii

The Traffic Systems
of Pompeii

ERIC E. POEHLER

OXFORD
UNIVERSITY PRESS

OXFORD
UNIVERSITY PRESS

Oxford University Press is a department of the University of Oxford. It furthers
the University's objective of excellence in research, scholarship, and education
by publishing worldwide. Oxford is a registered trade mark of Oxford University
Press in the UK and certain other countries.

Published in the United States of America by Oxford University Press
198 Madison Avenue, New York, NY 10016, United States of America.

Library of Congress Cataloging-in-Publication Data
Name: Poehler, Eric, author.
Title: The traffic systems of Pompeii / Eric E. Poehler.
Description: New York, NY : Oxford University Press, 2017. |
Includes bibliographical references and index.
Identifiers: LCCN 2016036974 | ISBN 9780190614676 (hardcover) |
9780197541395 (paperback) | ISBN 9780190614683 (PDF) |
ISBN 9780190614690 (online resource) | ISBN 9780190668709 (ePub)
Subjects: LCSH: Traffic engineering—Italy—Pompeii (Extinct city)—History. |
City and town life—Italy—Pompeii (Extinct city)—History. |
Streets—Italy—Pompeii (Extinct city)—History. |
Infrastructure (Economics)—Italy—Pompeii (Extinct city)—History. |
Pompeii (Extinct city)—Social conditions. | Pompeii (Extinct city)—Economic conditions.
Classification: LCC HE347 .P64 2017 | DDC 388.10937/72568—dc23
LC record available at https://lccn.loc.gov/2016036974

1 3 5 7 9 8 6 4 2
Printed by Sheridan Books, Inc., United States of America

CONTENTS

FIGURES

NOTE TO READERS: An online mapping application for the figures in this
book can be seen here: https://arcg.is/1mK510.

TABLES

PREFACE

This book is a project nearly two decades in the making. It began in July 1998, while I was a field school student. As we sat on the high curb of via Consolare waiting for our site to be opened, a group of students speculated on the purpose of the small stones (guard stones) placed along the edge of the road. Perhaps they were to keep the tall curbstones from falling over or maybe to prevent parked carts from rolling down the sloping street? When the project director walked up, his answer to this question of function was at once a deflection and an invitation: "I don't know, Eric. Why don't you go find out?" It was good advice. Since that day in 1998, I have made traffic and the streets of Pompeii the subject of eighteen seasons of fieldwork, two master's theses (1999, 2003), a PhD dissertation (2009), and three published articles (2006, 2011a, 2016). These works document a long-term communion with Pompeii and the evolution of a process to identify the directional evidence for traffic, to develop a method to analyze it, and finally to interpret it as a system. *The Traffic Systems of Pompeii* is the culmination of those archaeological efforts.

One project of this book, therefore, is to champion archaeology as the only avenue to certain aspects of the Roman world. Indeed, traffic systems, at Pompeii and beyond, are (so far) uniquely archaeological phenomena. Thus, the first chapters are meant to document my attempt to find an archaeological solution to an archaeological puzzle. They are also meant to serve as a testament to the value of sustained and repeated engagement with a problem and with a site, especially at Pompeii. Pompeii is not a site that one can "do" in a short survey. One must be confronted by the site, build up understanding and expectations, then use the city to confront those conceptions and preconceptions. But this is the joy of Pompeii. The city is an instrument, in the musical sense, that must continually be practiced, and although it can be mastered, it can never be completed. Even after more than seven hundred days at Pompeii, I am still nowhere near "done."

The second half of the book, however, pushes beyond the physical to under-stand the traffic systems as larger historical phenomena. It is here that art, epig-raphy, history, literature, and ethnographic analogy are brought to bear upon the same puzzle to fill in the many still-missing pieces. It is here that the history of traffic becomes richer and broader as the subject slips from traffic to urban-ism. But as the book shifts from microscope to macroscope, new gaps appear, and bigger puzzles need bigger pieces. These are beyond the scope of this book but squarely in the purview of the growing interest in movement in the ancient world. There are, however, a number of tools and approaches within this book that I hope will inspire one reader to see such gaps in the history as an invitation to her or his own "why don't you find out" moment.

July 16, 2016
Pompei

ACKNOWLEDGMENTS

No one does archaeology alone. It is fundamentally a collaborative project and requires the cooperation of many people over many years. Consequently there are many people to thank. First, are the very many people who have helped me document evidence for traffic and challenged my understanding of it: Mike Burns, Kevin Cole, Eills Cox, Ben Crowther, Orit Darwish, Cindy Drakeman, Janet Dunkelbarger, Jarrett Lobell, Jennifer and Arthur Stevens, Tom Tolley, Jason Urbanus, Claire Weiss, Juliana van Roggen, and Walter van Roggen. Special thanks belong to Caity Bogdan who brought her engineering skills to the problem of how wearing forms and helped me to redefine cyclical wear. I am forever grateful to the superintendency and the custodians of Pompeii who watch over the site and whose aid was essential to this research. Special thanks go to Pier Guzzo, who made so much of the site open to me for many years, and to Massimo Osanna, who continues that support.

Many other people helped me in the writing of this book, especially in grappling with areas beyond my expertise and training. Beth Greene and Kristina Kilgrove gave bibliography and analysis on Roman shoes and feet, and Ken Kitchell offered his learned perspective on the word *plaustrum*. Chapter 7 benefited from Jason Moralee's suggested reading, and Ginna Closs's edits saved me from several errors. I thank Mark Robinson and Ivo van der Graaff for their many discussions of the earliest settlements and fortifications. Jeremy Hartnett shared many important suggestions and citations over the years. I'm also indebted to the anonymous reviewers whose engagement with the early manuscript was remarkably thoughtful and generous. Deep appreciation belongs to Sarah Pirovitz for helping me bring this book to Oxford University Press and for shepherding it though the entire editorial and production process.

I have many mentors to thank as well. Deep appreciation goes to Rick Jones for first teaching me Pompeian archaeology and to Damian Robinson for teaching me to love its architecture; to Mickey Deitler for helping me to keep one eye on theory and to Ingrid Rowland for keeping the other on art while at the University of Chicago; to John Dobbins for taking a chance on me and this research at the University of Virginia and to Tyler Jo Smith for sowing the seeds of Sabinus's trip across Pompeii; to John Humphrey for his diligence in publishing the early results in his journal; and to Lisa Fentress and Andrew Wilson, who brought me to Algeria and introduced me to Roman North Africa. Finally, Andrew Wallace-Hadrill deserves special mention for his faith and his friendship when it really mattered.

Two people, above all others, were fundamental to this research. From even before I was looking for traffic at Pompeii, Steven Ellis was a true friend and colleague. His enthusiasm built my confidence in the value of this research, and his critiques always pushed me to fit the results into an ever larger historical context. Most important is Wenona Rymond-Richmond, a brilliant scholar in her own right and my wife, who has unfailingly given me love and who endured my absence over these eighteen years.

Finally, although no one does archaeology alone (and who would want to?), all mistakes remain mine alone.

1

Introduction

In February 1863, Giuseppe Fiorelli, the recently appointed superintendent of Pompeii under the new Italian government, reported that he had made a remarkable discovery, one that he described as a revelation:

> On the third of this month, while digging in the small street that begins opposite one of the secondary doors of the Stabian Baths and issues in the vicinity of the Building of Eumachia, were found, at the height of five meters above the soil, about a hundred silver coins, four earrings, and a small finger ring of gold, with two iron keys and some traces of cloth in which the coins had been wrapped. In a close search of the earth, lest any of this precious treasure be missed, we came to a place where the earth gave way under the trowel, revealing a hollow cavity deep enough to reach in at arm's length and remove some bones. I realized immediately that this was the impression of a human body, and I thought that by quickly pouring in scagliola, the cast of an entire person would be obtained. The result surpassed my every expectation.[1]

After expressing the considerable effort required to release the casts of the victims from the ash, Fiorelli describes in intimate detail their bodies, dress, and their contortions in death. The conclusion of his account makes it clear that neither the historical value nor the horror of his new method of recovering the dead at Pompeii was lost upon Fiorelli:

> If I shall be fortunate enough to encounter new bodies among the ashes, being better equipped with all the means necessary for obtaining good results in a work of such importance, my casts will come out more perfectly. For now it is a satisfactory compensation for the most exacting

[1] Translation by Dwyer (2010, 45) of Fiorelli's letter published in the *Giornale di Napoli* on February 12, 1863.

1

labors to have opened the way to obtaining an unknown class of monuments, through which archaeology will be pursued not in marbles or
in bronzes but over the very bodies of the ancients, stolen from death,
after eighteen centuries of oblivion.[2]

In these few sentences, Fiorelli established the origin of the Pompeian body cast
technique, painting it not only as a kind of personal epiphany but also as a pivot
in the history of archaeology toward a more personal kind of relationship with
the past. His is an enduring hope embodied in these monuments, these people,
and not least in the vicolo degli Scheletri, the small street whose name still com-
memorates their discovery.

  Yet we know that Fiorelli was not the first to notice the voids in the ash or the
impressions they left behind. Nearly a century before, Francisco La Vega had
noticed the imprint of people and objects, sending an impression of a woman's
breast—a contemporaneously famous object—to the museum in Portici. Nor
did Fiorelli first imagine the use of plaster as a molding technique. Only four
years before, casts of a set of doors were made and housed in the museum at
Pompeii.[3] It seems impossible that Fiorelli could have been unaware of these
finds. On the other hand, he did institute a new method of vertical excavation
that made the discovery of the voids and the use of plaster possible. Additionally,
he was in fact the first to create a cast of a person. Perhaps it did feel like an epiphany to Fiorelli. Upon finding the cavities filled with bones, the idea of casting
these people, like those doors in the museum might have come to him in a flash.
Not having it on hand, the plaster was hastily fetched, mixed up, and poured in.
Even if he had always planned to cast the bodies when he found the voids, no
one had ever excavated around a body cast before, and doubtless Fiorelli did
have to invent that method on his own.

  No matter the reality of the technique's invention, one thing is inarguably
true: Pompeii, an archaeological site already more than one hundred years
old, shocked the world with an entirely new and exceptionally rich, moving,
and informative kind of evidence that fundamentally altered the way we saw
the Romans who lived in Pompeii and beyond.[4] This is the greater truth of
Pompeii, that as archaeologists and historians change their methods, the ancient
city opens up new forms of evidence and new lines of inquiry. And when this
happens at Pompeii, more than any other site, there is a chance that our understanding of the Romans themselves will be enriched if not substantially altered.

---

  [2] Dwyer 2010, 46.
  [3] Dwyer 2010, 10–11, 29.
  [4] Dwyer (2010, 12, 35) reports the excavators' sense of relief that the Pompeians were clothed, as
they considered the ancients to have been a debauched people.

Indeed, soon after Fiorelli gave the casts of actual Romans to Roman archaeology, August Mau synthesized the painting styles at Pompeii and gave a typology applicable at the *Domus Aurea*.[5] At the beginning of the twentieth century, Vittorio Spinazzola's careful recovery of roofs along via dell'Abbondanza allowed scholars to know for certain the variety of ways that any atrium house could be covered.[6] Amedeo Maiuri's mid-century interest in the prehistory of Pompeii lit a long fuse that fifty years later led to an explosion of excavation below the 79 CE levels, challenging notions of Campania's history in the sixth to fourth centuries BCE.[7] At the end of the twentieth century, Ray Laurence and Andrew Wallace-Hadrill, following Richard Raper, understood that the preservation and the extent of Pompeii made it an ideal location to explore the social texture of a Roman city.[8] These studies were in the vanguard of a new wave of interest in Roman urbanism and urban movement, buoyed by concomitant advances in mapping tools and the adoption of sociological theories. Importantly, the studies of Roman painting and urbanism demonstrate that there is always much to learn from Pompeii in the extant ruins of 79 CE, even without excavation.

It was within the city's final landscape (fig. 1.1) that in 1999 I had my own moment of epiphany. While walking on via Consolare, a street I had used already at least four times a day for several weeks that summer, I suddenly noticed the odd shape of a curbstone (fig. 5.18). Just as suddenly, I knew what it meant: it was possible to see that ancient carts, hundreds of them, had traveled westbound on this street and then turned to the north. That moment certainly felt like an epiphany to me. Yet if that moment was the birth of a search for traffic, its conception was much earlier and its gestation fully a year in duration. The previous summer I had conducted a survey to map the distribution of guard stones, which had taken me to every one of Pompeii's excavated streets. Already during that research I recognized that vehicles had continually impacted the guard stones and one in particular (fig. 5.10) was overridden in such a way that, by the shape of its wearing and its position on the west curb, it was possible to surmise (wrongly) that Pompeian drivers preferred the left side of the street. The results of the guard stone survey were underwhelming, but they pushed me to change focus in 1999 and search for any traces of the ancient traffic that could be found in the scratches from hubs on curbs, hitching holes, and the position of ruts.[9] It was with these ideas and experiences percolating

[5] Mau 1882.
[6] Spinazzola 1953.
[7] Maiuri 1973; Ellis 2011.
[8] Raper 1977; Laurence 1994; Wallace-Hadrill 1994.
[9] Poehler 1999.

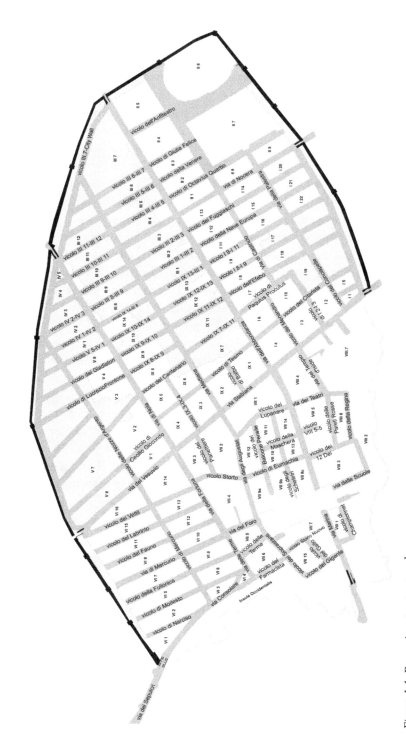

Figure 1.1 Pompeian street network.

unacknowledged in the background that, in a flash, I saw (and felt) for the first time the cyclical pattern of wear at the end of vicolo di Mercurio and understood its form as the result of thousands of vehicles following the same pattern and possibly the same rule.

The point of this reminiscence is at once to recount the early history of the methodology developed for this research and to personalize the much larger idea that for those lucky enough to be in the right place, at the right time and, crucially, with the right question, Pompeii still has much with which to surprise and to delight us. Far more than Fiorelli, and to distance myself from his comparison, I cannot overstate how the invention of a method for studying traffic and how the broader research in this book has relied on the work of generations of scholars. In fact, although academic interest in movement is relatively new, even the early visitors to Pompeii recognized and lingered on the hints of motion embedded in the city's physical fabric. Artists and authors saw Pompeii's potential to put people in motion and used the architectures of passage to give life to their subjects. Many early artistic representations not only illustrate the ruined city but also show people on tour who engage with Pompeii in ways similar to how the ancient inhabitants might have done. Figures stroll the colonnades, rest in the schola tombs outside the gates, and drive carts across the forum, leaving ruts in the ash (fig. 1.2).[10] Other artists take a direct interest in the streets themselves. Giovanni Battista Piranesi's drawing of via Consolare, for example, focuses as much upon the architecture of the street—the irregular paving stones, the curbs, and even the street-side bench and the ramp leading off the street—as the painting of the facades or the decoration of the bar counter.[11] Moreover, the image recalls Piranesi's careful study of the via Appia's paving in which each element is labeled to explain how such ancient marvels for movement were made.[12]

How such marvels were used in daily life was a question taken up by modern authors who visited, or imagined visiting, the ancient city. Both Gautier's *Arria Marcella* and Jensen's *Gradiva* take the emotional encounter with the vestiges of Pompeian bodies (La Vega's imprint and Fiorelli's casts) as their conceit to cast characters back through the streets and over the ruts and the stepping stones that serve as stage for their pursuit of a woman and an imagined past.[13] So vivid were these voyages that Freud used *Gradiva* to explore the psychology of repression, memory, and desire.[14] Yet it is Mark Twain's twist of irony that brings together

[10] Købke 1841. *The Forum, Pompeii, with Vesuvius in the Distance.* Image courtesy of the J. Paul Getty Museum.

[11] Piranesi 1804 [ca. 1778]. *Vue de la rue en entrant sous la porte de la ville di Pompeïa, avec les trottoirs et boutiques.*

[12] Piranesi, n.d. *Vedutta dell'antica via Appia.*

[13] Gautier 1890, 159–60; Jensen 1918, 7, 21, 46–48. See also Liveley 2011.

[14] Freud 1907.

Figure 1.2 "The Forum, Pompeii, with Vesuvius in the Distance," by C. S. Købke.

these two most iconic of Pompeii's relics, deep ruts and human remains, each a powerful symbol of life, motion, and intent.

> But no—the sun shines as brightly down on old Pompeii to-day as it did when Christ was born in Bethlehem, and its streets are cleaner a hundred times than ever Pompeiian saw them in her prime. I know whereof I speak—for in the great, chief thorough-fares (Merchant street and the Street of Fortune) have I not seen with my own eyes how for two hundred years at least the pavements were not repaired!—how ruts five and even ten inches deep were worn into the thick flagstones by the chariot-wheels of generations of swindled tax-payers? And do I not know by these signs that Street Commissioners of Pompeii never attended to their business, and that if they never mended the pavements they never cleaned them? And, besides, is it not the inborn nature of Street Commissioners to avoid their duty whenever they get a chance? I wish I knew the name of the last one that held office in Pompeii so that I could give him a blast. I speak with feeling on this subject, because I caught my foot in one of those ruts, and the sadness that came over me

when I saw the first poor skeleton, with ashes and lava sticking to it, was tempered by the reflection that maybe that party was the Street Commissioner.[15]

Beyond its clever composition, there are two aspects of Twain's description that are relevant here. First is his bodily experience of the ruts. Due to the millions of tourists who walk the Pompeian streets each year, twisting an ankle is one experience the city produces common to both ancient inhabitant and modern visitor. A second point to take away from Twain's passage is the many great misconceptions he has absorbed and repeats. The age of the pavements and their forms, the chariot as a regular means of transport, the filth expected in the streets, and the corruption in civic governance that left Pompeii to ruin all are ideas now debunked by modern scholarship.

Modern Scholarship

Modern interest in Roman roads and the traffic that plied them goes back at least to 1570, when Palladio described two types of roads and offered explanations for how they functioned.[16] While popular interest in the Roman road grew throughout the eighteenth and nineteenth centuries, particularly in English-language publications, sustained academic interest would not take hold until the latter half of the twentieth century, when works by Nigel Sitwell, Raymond Chevalier, and Lorenzo Quilici became standard references on the subject in English, French, and Italian.[17] Yet the subjects of these works remained largely descriptive and technical, focusing on the construction of the most sophisticated examples of Roman engineering. By the 1990s, historians like Ray Laurence had begun to shift the approach to the Roman roads and streets from descriptive to social, using their histories as a way to explore social change in Republican and Imperial Italy.[18] Research by Colin Adams brought greater detail to lives of Romans in Egypt and how transportation and mobility fit into it, while Anne Kolb and others re-examined the history and function of state transport, such as *cursus publicus* or the Roman army.[19] Interest grew also in pedestrian traffic at the turn of the millennium, with publications focusing on walking in cities, gardens, and dedicated architectural spaces.

[15] Twain 1869, 328–29.
[16] Codrington 1918, 11–12.
[17] Chevallier 1976; Sitwell 1981; Quilici 1990.
[18] Laurence 1999; cf. descriptive approach of Davies (2002) or Gesemann (1995).
[19] Adams 2001; Coulston 2001; Kolb 2000, 2001.

These subjects have engendered a still wider interest in movement in the ancient world. The topic of movement in the classical world has taken its theoretical origins from sociological thinkers such as Michel De Certeau, Anthony Giddens, Jane Jacobs, Henri Lefebvre, and Kevin Lynch on architecture, space, and cities, and scholars have borrowed much of their methodological toolkit from urban geographers especially Bill Hillier and Julienne Hanson.[20] From that foundation, however, a broad array of subjects abound: the grid plan as a structuring force,[21] control (or absence) and superstition at thresholds,[22] directionality and function in passage architecture,[23] walking for purpose and for pleasure,[24] pausing and interrupting movement,[25] and movement as a variable in analyses.[26] Many of these topics are now explored in a single book, *Rome, Ostia, Pompeii: Movement and Space*, though earlier, more disparate publications contributed to its foundation.[27] In this, Diane Favro and Barbara Kellum were pioneers.[28]

On the topic of traffic specifically, the state of the question largely has been defined over the last decade by two books with markedly different approaches. Cornelius van Tilburg's *Traffic and Congestion in the Roman Empire* is a densely documented philological discussion of the character of ancient traffic, particularly wheeled traffic, with many useful additions of archaeological material. Though not a synthetic historical treatment, van Tilburg's book is and will remain an essential reference for anyone interested in the variety and conditions within which Roman traffic operated. *Roman Street Networks*, by Alan Kaiser, also resting atop a solid historical and literary foundation, takes a different approach. Kaiser applies basic space syntax tools to four urban street systems (Pompeii, Ostia, Silchester, Empúries), comparing the way in which those networks generate the social texture of Roman urban space.[29] The results of these two approaches, however, could hardly be farther apart. Thus, while van Tilburg offers detail and anecdote, Kaiser presents breadth and comparative history. What is missing between these two books is the actual circulation of vehicles in the ancient world.

---

[20] Lynch 1960; Jacobs 1961; De Certeau 1984; Giddens 1984; Hillier and Hanson 1984; Lefebvre 1991.

[21] Laurence 1994; Newsome 2007, 2011; Stöger 2008, 2011; Kaiser 2011a, 2011b.

[22] Ellis 2011; Malmburg and Bjur 2011; Lauritsen 2013.

[23] Frakes 2009; Zarmakoupi 2011.

[24] Macaulay-Lewis 2011; O'Sullivan 2011.

[25] Hartnett 2008; 2011; Trifilò 2011.

[26] Anderson 2011.

[27] Bjur and Frizell 2005; Laurence and Newsome 2011.

[28] Favro 1996; Kellum 1999.

[29] For a recent critique, see Poehler 2016, 168–80.

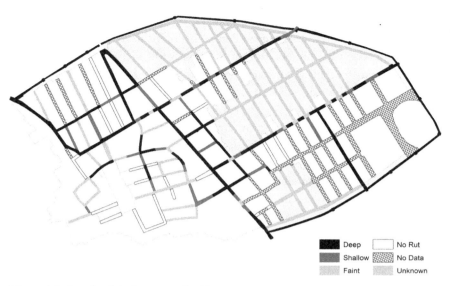

Figure 1.3 Rut depth in Pompeii, after Tsujimura.

Pompeii has been the place scholars have expected to find such evidence of traffic circulation.[30] The birth of the modern study of Roman traffic can be identified in the remarkable work, led by Sumiyo Tsujimura, to clear the streets of sand and grit and study the location and depth of ruts across 11 kilometers of Pompeii's paved streets (fig. 1.3).[31] Her research established for the first time not only where ancient vehicles were present and where they were absent but also defined a range of intensity that could be used to gauge the comparative volumes of traffic. Tsujimura went further still to classify the ruts into types—straight and curved—with the latter, she believed, revealing the organizing philosophy behind traffic flow. Although her conclusions were flawed, Tsujimura's contributions to the intellectual history of ancient traffic are of seminal importance.

Indeed, scholars immediately took notice of her work and attempted to apply it. In the early 1990s, the social texture of Pompeii's urban form was the premier research question, and the relative (though not complete) absence of ruts on the western section of via dell'Abbondanza convinced some that a "moral geography" could be identified within the city.[32] Although insufficiently critical of the rutting data, these publications pushed Tsujimura's research to a wider audience, fostered an interest in the historical potential of movement, and drove

---

[30] e.g., Ciprotti 1961.

[31] Tsujimura 1991.

[32] Wallace-Hadrill 1995.

the search for archaeological proxies to identify it.[33] For example, when Steven Ellis published his research on bars in Pompeii, he considered the position of the masonry counters not only as a form of advertising but also as a reflection of the dominant trends in pedestrian traffic. Similarly, Jeremy Hartnett's examination of benches along the sidewalks documented the places of potential pedestrian congregation and the congestion they might cause.[34] Most directly influenced by Tsujimura, of course, has been my own research found in this book and in earlier attempts at understanding the directional movement of wheeled traffic.[35] Twenty-five years after her research was published, the image of people walking and driving through Pompeii is immeasurably richer because Tsujimura simply measured (and published) how deep the ruts are. Today there is a marketplace of ideas about traffic and the methods to measure it. Like any good consumer, however, we must enter that marketplace with a critical mind.

The New Myths of Ancient Traffic

A common story told about the Roman street, the ruts worn into it, and the carts that made them is that the modern railroad gauge was derived from these ruts. The story goes like this: modern American train gauges are set at the curious distance of 4 feet 8.5 inches because they are derived from the English standards, the nation that supplied America with equipment and possibly the experts to build its rail lines. The English chose this specific dimension from standards already in use by wainwrights, who built wagons and carts to fit into the ruts left in many long-distance roads built by the Romans. The Romans, a belligerent but also meticulous people, had specified this distance for their axles because it matched the width of the two draft animals pulling the vehicle. The story ends with a satisfying quip, simultaneously curious and vulgar, about this historical impact of the horse's ass.

Stories such as this one become popular legends because they purport to inform but actually intend to entertain. The story has an avuncular feel to it and is arranged in such a way as to pay off with a punch line. Perhaps as important, however, are the underlying assumptions about human nature and the sources of culture that are subtly reinforced. To those who want to see us in the best light, we're a resourceful species, recognizing the folly in reinventing the wheel (rut) and at worst, we're just lazy. Likewise, for those who wish to see the best in the constancy of human existence, the story has a *plus ça change* moral to it, and for

---

[33] The premier movement proxies are doorways. Laurence 1994; Poehler 2016.
[34] Hartnett 2008, 2011.
[35] Poehler 2003, 2006, 2009.

those resistant to the pace of change in the modern world, there's a proof of the relevance of ancient ideas. There's something here for everyone, so long as you don't think too hard about it. In fact, stories such as this one also stay popular legends because of their trivial nature; no one ever has reason to check.

When a skeptical mind is turned to the story, however, the many assumptions glossed over by its pace begin to unmake it. Even if we consider only the Roman aspects, obvious questions abound: how did Roman roads survive uninterrupted use into the nineteenth century without repair? How did wainwrights find this standard when most people lived nowhere near a Roman road? How did they take this standard from the varied ruts on Roman roads when some are unrutted and some have multiple pairs of ruts? Most importantly, did Romans actually have a single standard for their axle gauges?[36] These simple inquiries begin to unravel the yarn, showing how little truth there was in such a satisfying story. Yet the stories persist. When Mark Twain wrote about how the ruts in Pompeii had formed, how long they had existed, and how long they had been ignored by the "Street Commissioner," he imagined Pompeians riding in chariots through the city. One can still hear tour guides at Pompeii explain the ruts in the same way or find books that illustrate a chariot rolling through the ruts in the street.

While it is unfortunate that modern conceptions of ancient traffic are filled with misbelief, these are largely popular notions with little opportunity for application beyond one's collection of trivia. Where it might matter, in academic discourse that seeks the most accurate image of the ancient world possible, these legends have largely been dispelled. Largely but not entirely. In fact, the basis for the train gauge myth, the belief in a single standard Roman vehicle gauge of 1.40 meters, continues to draw support. A modern study of a road in Bulgaria repeats the finding of a 1.40-meter-wide pair of ruts seven times in order to date the road surface to the Roman period.[37] What can plainly be seen from the published images, however, is that each rut is 10 to 15 centimeters wide, a dimension sufficient to accommodate wagons with a gauge up to 1.60 meters. As Chapter 5 will demonstrate, there was not a single standard but rather a variety of standard vehicle gauges, several of which would easily fit within the ruts on this Bulgarian road.

The growth in interest in the subject of ancient traffic has had the curious effect of creating a new set of untested assumptions and undercritiqued assertions. Some are factually wrong, but most are merely in need of better contextualization. These new myths of ancient traffic are equally in need of examination

---

[36] Chapter 5, 114–23.

[37] Lang 2003; Kaiser (2011a, 181–83, table 7.1) also relies on Greiner (1934) and Pike (1967) in order to typologize the size of carts by the size of the draft animals.

because, although they are based on solid research in many cases, they often possess the same satisfying elision between explanation and expectation or else do the opposite and play upon the power of the counterintuitive answer. These myths fall into three broad categories: the surface of the street and the creation of ruts, ancient vehicles and the laws and attitudes concerning them, and streets as an element of ancient cities.

The Street Surface and Rut Creation

It has been claimed and oft repeated that ruts were cut into some roads deliberately in order to guide carts on particular paths. In some cases, such as the famous rock-cut consular road near Donnas, Italy, this idea seems to be a logical solution to the danger of accidentally driving your wagon off the cliff. In nearly all other cases, however, there are good reasons to assume this was an exceptionally rare endeavor, which is supported by the physical evidence of ruts themselves. In the first instance, the cutting of ruts is antithetical to the creation of the surface; paving is meant to resist such deformations that lead to the destruction of the roadway. Second, one must ask which vehicle gauge or how many gauges would those cutting the ruts choose to accommodate? Removing even an additional 5 centimeters of stone from each guiding rut would as much as double the effort to build the ruts. Most importantly, actual ruts are most often discontinuous, off alignment and show no evidence of ever having been cut into the pavement. Even the ruts at Donnas can be seen to obviously vacillate in depth and width, indicating they were created by thousands of iterations of similar behaviors rather than a single moment of deliberate action. Other examples from mountainous regions purporting to be cut in are equally irregular.[38]

Ruts were thus always worn into the hard surface of the road or street, which, depending on the type of surface, had only a few names in Latin. When covered in gravel or created in beaten earth, the surface was called *glarea*, but when paved in harder stones, the term *silex* was applied.[39] Apart from bare earth, no other Latin terms describe the varieties of surface form, nor is there a vocabulary for the subsurface layers of the road.[40] Two inventions of the seventeenth and nineteenth centuries, however, continue to percolate through modern descriptions of Roman road construction. The first of these is the application of Vitruvius's terminology for laying pavement in a building—*stratum, rudus,*

---

[38] Van Tilburg 2007, 17.

[39] "Silex" refers to any hard stone, but in the context of road pavements the term has become synonymous with lava stone.

[40] D.43.2.1.2; D.54.42.27.

nucleus, pavimentum—to the layers of roads known from excavation and litera-ture.[41] It is ironic that this terminology should persist so long, as it was adopted by Nicholas Bergier in 1622 as a direct response to the absence of such words in Latin about roads.[42] A second misapplication of terms comes from the modern use of the word "metalling" to describe the durable surface of a Roman road. The term derives from the nineteenth-century practice of using the crushed cinders and slag of industrial iron furnaces to gravel the roads (and railroads) of the time. Since then, it has become a broader term, particularly in Britain, denoting the solid top surface of a road. Thus, as a synonym, metalling has slipped into the descriptions of ancient road surfaces, bleeding its modern con-notations into the ancient constructions. Ironically and despite this misnomer's etymology, recent research at Pompeii has shown that molten iron and iron slag was poured into the streets as a mechanism of repair.[43] There were streets that were genuinely metalled, and so now it behooves one to know the histories of both the general and specific uses of that term.

Vehicles, Laws, and Attitudes

Ancient carts and wagons are the subject of a number of underexamined ideas. At the broadest scale, the inefficiency of land transport in comparison to water transport was blamed for having stunted the Roman economy. This idea became the consensus opinion until Laurence showed the comparison to be mislead-ing.[44] One of the most oft-cited ideas about ancient vehicles is the notion that with only a few exceptions, they were banned from cities during the daytime, leaving urban areas to pedestrians. The idea comes from the (so-called) Lex Iulia Municipalis, a set of civic regulations on bronze tablets, known as the Tabula Heracleensis. Among many other rules about the proper administration of a town,[45] one brief regulation on traffic stands out:

> Whatever roads shall lie within the city of Rome within those areas
> where there shall be continuous habitation, no-one, after the Kalends

---

[41] Vit. *De Arch* 7.1.

[42] Codrington 1918, 8–9.

[43] Chapter 7, 204.

[44] Harris 1993, 27; Laurence 1998, 126–32.

[45] The rules charge the aedile to compel building owners to repair streets (ll. 20–23) and to pay for that repair in full or in part (ll. 29–31, 46–49); to make both public disclosure and private notice of needed repair; in the case of a failure to repair the street, to let a contract for repair by government authority and, after thirty days, to indemnify the city against the cost of the contract by giving legal possession of the debt to the contractor plus a penalty of half of the initial cost (ll. 32–45).

of January, in the day-time, after sunrise or before the tenth hour of the day, is to lead or drive a cart on those roads, except insofar as it shall be appropriate for anything to be brought or conveyed, for the purpose of building sacred temples of the immortal gods or carrying out work (on them), or insofar as it shall be appropriate for any of those things, for which a contract shall have been let for their public demolition, to be publicly removed from the city or from those areas (mentioned above), and in those cases where it shall be lawful under this statute of specified persons for specified reasons to lead or drive carts.[46]

The text is unequivocal: except on certain types of official business, no one may enter Rome with a wagon during daylight hours. Yet if the text shines clarity on the mandate, one must admit that same light only deepens the shadows around the truth of its application. Was it a model adopted (even required) in other towns? How long was this law in effect? To the first question, we must admit to having almost no evidence to go on save for the fact that the inscriptions that preserve the law were found not at Rome but instead at Heraclea, a newly chartered *municipium*. Still, the text is specific to Rome and its environs, and if Heraclea (or any other town) adopted the statute as its own, we are in the dark. As to how long the law lasted, we are better informed. Agrippina's notable dispensation to ride in an ornate *carpentum* and Juvenal's complaints of the night traffic's noise indicate the law's enforcement likely continued into the second century CE.[47] Yet there is room for doubt among these anecdotes and the law. Could Rome really enforce such a rule in a city of a million people? One recent, though not original, argument purports a way forward.[48] By reading the word "wagon" (*plostrum*) narrowly, this general term becomes an appellation, a specific kind of heavy, ox-drawn wagon. Such a reading resolves the conflict between the law and the paucity of evidence for its enforcement, painting a picture of Rome (and beyond) as "devoid of some oxcarts hauling goods, but dotted with carts for personal transport as well as some heavy wagons hauling construction materials, debris, or religious paraphernalia."[49]

It is an appealing solution and image of the ancient street scene, but unfortunately it is equally problematic. The idea that the writers of the Lex Iulia Municipalis used the word *plostrum* to mean only a vehicle for haulage and not for passenger transport is undermined three lines later by the exception carved out for carrying Vestals, Flamines, and the Rex Sacrum. Such an exception

[46] Crawford 1996, 374.
[47] Tac. *Ann.* xii. 42; Juv. 3. 232–38.
[48] Robinson 1992, 64; Kaiser 2011a, 174–75.
[49] Kaiser 2011a, 175.

should not be necessary if passenger traffic were allowed. Moreover, if *plostrum* indicates only a specific vehicle, then we must imagine it appropriate in form, which in the same sentence the writer of the *lex* did, to carry both these most important religious officials and the trash—and if we read the word *stercoris* narrowly, shit—that amassed in the city. There are also many other vehicles that could and were used for heavy haulage—the *angaria, carruca, clabula, raeda*— yet these vehicles are not mentioned. Should we thus imagine these transport vehicles were free to circulate during the day, or do we nudge the specific name *plostrum* toward the more general term "truck," as Alan Kaiser does to incorporate all heavy haulage vehicles? Beyond beginning to dissolve the distinction being made by a narrow reading, this otherwise reasonable compromise raises its own problems. Which of the vehicles named above (and those not named) would be considered *plostra*? How do we know and, more importantly, how would a Roman reading, told of, or enforcing the statute know? Once the meaning is put on a spectrum, there is no more reason to believe that *plostrum* is a general term for a class of vehicle than an umbrella term for all vehicles.

Finally and despite assertions to the contrary, there are instances in which it is clearly preferable to read *plostrum* (and other vehicles)[50] as referring to all vehicles. For example, an inscription from Cliternia announces that "the lower road is the private road of T. Umbrenus c. f. Passage is by permission. No one is to drive a flock or a cart."[51] Here *pecus* and *plostru* are operating in the most general of senses not to ban specific types of animals or forms of travel but instead to assert the complete control of the road. Another inscription records the construction of a *viam plostralem*, which we are hard pressed to imagine was built to carry only one specific type of vehicle.[52] When Cato uses *plostrum*, he assumes that any variety of draft animal—oxen, mules, even donkeys—could be used to pull what must therefore be different varieties of vehicles.[53] Similarly, when Ulpian opines on fault for stones falling from a *plostrum*, he does not mean to exclude operators of passenger vehicles from liability by using this term.[54] For all these reasons, it is clearly better to see the language of the Lex Iulia Municipalis as being general, referring to all carts and wagons, and the language of the exceptions being narrow and specific.

The language the Romans used to describe their attitudes toward vehicles in general has also been misunderstood. Based on a dozen ancient

---

[50] Stefani (2003, 209) claims *cisium* is used so often as to be a general word for vehicle, citing Mart. IV, 64, 19, Verg., *Georg.*, III, 204.

[51] CIL IX 4171; translation by Crawford (2005, 166).

[52] Campedelli 2014, 116, n. 5.

[53] Cato *Agr.* 62. See also White 1975, 79–80.

[54] D.9.2.27.33. I am grateful to Professor Ken Kitchell for alerting me to some of these references.

references to carts having negative qualities—from damaging architectures to injuring people—Kaiser has argued that Romans not only recognized these dangers but also were possessed of a genuine fear of vehicles. In many cases, however, such as the complaints of Horace, Juvenal, Pliny, and Seneca, the author is merely describing the nuisances of traffic: the dust, noise of the carts, and the foul language of the drivers.[55] Fear is not the same as annoyance. Nor is disdain. Referring to an account of Aurelian entering Antioch, it is claimed that the stigma of riding in a wagon was so great that the emperor chose to change to riding on horseback despite his serious wounds. As the rest of the context makes clear, the story is not about the means of the transport but about the condition of the emperor and the perception of his health.

These examples show the oblique nature of references toward the attitudes that Romans held for wheeled transport and the interpretive distance one must span to cross from nuisance to fear. Moreover, the Republican ban on the sumptuary uses of vehicles and the lengths Roman matrons went to regain that right as well as the permissions granted to high-status Romans contradicts such a notion of a fear of vehicles.[56] Of course, some authors do mention serious and real harm that could come from wagons or their loads. Plautus even reveals the phrase "the wagon is overturned" was a euphemism for misfortune.[57] To make these statements into a general fear of vehicles, however, requires both shifting the focus of the story to the vehicle and confusing calamity for fear. Thus, when Pliny recounts concern that a transport of columns might collapse the sewer below, it is not the cart but the cargo that is to blame.[58] Similarly, in Juvenal's account of the poor man being crushed by a load of marble, the calamity is but one of many that are used to satirize the difficulties and dangers of the street, not carts in particular.[59] Moreover, it is the load not the vehicle that crushes the man. Even the expression "the cart is overturned" does not show a specific fear of carts but instead expresses the suddenness and immutability of calamity in general. To read Plautus's text this specifically is to both miss the broader point and mischaracterize the content. "The cart is overturned" is no more about the Roman fear of carts than the American euphemism for death, "bought the farm," is about Americans' fear of farms. These phrases use a real and serious set of negative connotations in the context of wagons and farms to express calamity but are not evidence for how people actually felt about or behaved around them.

[55] Kaiser 2011a, 188–90.
[56] Livy 34.1.
[57] Plaut. *Epid* 591.
[58] Pliny *HN* 36.2.6.
[59] Juv. 3.260–61.

Control of Urban Streets

A final misconception concerning traffic stems from a more general presumption about how Romans cities were governed. Put simply, the absence of an invasive Imperial system with an extensive bureaucratic apparatus[60] has convinced some that because the state did not engage in the day-to-day operations of civic management, local municipal authorities would be equally uninterested. Examining legal expressions of municipal power in civic charters and the jurists' opinions in relation to streets and traffic, Kaiser has gone a step further to argue that those rights and powers not seized by the state were therefore legally invested in the individual: these "laws have virtually no intent to facilitate cart traffic flow. Indeed, some laws gave Rome's residents the right to control the traffic that passed along their streets, taking the possibility of creating a coherent city-wide traffic policy away from civic individuals."[61] Unfortunately, none of the laws Kaiser offers in his survey actually makes such a claim.[62] Instead, these selected laws and decrees are only obliquely related to traffic control, a fact that is then transformed into the argument that there were no laws intended to facilitate traffic. Moreover, the many other legal codes Kaiser excluded from his discussion (though not completely from his bibliography, however) clearly do express governmental interest not only to protect the right of public movement but also to facilitate the ease of such traffic. The language of statues concerning public thoroughfares in the Lex Tarentina, Lex Coloniae Genetivae, Lex Iulia Municipalis, and in the Digest all follow a nearly identical formulation in which public officials are charged with the protection of public streets both against the actions of private individuals and for their benefit.[63]

The presumption that individuals were invested in de iure freedoms (even if they did make de facto claims occasionally) also leads to misreading archeological evidence. That is, if one starts with the premise that "with the responsibility to maintain a street came the right to control it,"[64] then the origin and purpose

---

[60] Garnsey and Saller 1987, 20–40.

[61] Kaiser 2011a, 184. It is surprising to see how differently Kaiser describes these same laws in his book (2011b, 21–23) published in the same year: "civic officials promulgated laws to keep streets clean specifically so that wheeled vehicles might pass."

[62] Kaiser (2011, 186, n. 48) cites D.43.8.2.25 and D.43.10.3 to assert street blockages can be instituted, but the purpose of both of these statutes is to charge magistrates and property owners with removing such impediments, not to permit them. Similarly, in claiming that restrictions to city streets can be applied by citizens day or night, Kaiser (2011, 186, n. 51–52) cites D.8.4.14, D.18.1.66, and D.8.6.11. These statutes, however, describe private servitudes and contracts, not public streets. Moreover, two of these express that the right of way is *not* lost by misuse or by time of day.

[63] Crawford 1996; D.43.10.1.

[64] Kaiser 2011a, 186.

of traffic-control mechanisms found in the street must be ascribed to private individuals. Thus, the impediments to traffic at many intersections in Pompeii and their apparently unsystematic distribution are evidence that Pompeian citizens willfully and individually disrupted the proper functioning of the street. Unfortunately, this idea and even the evidence it rests upon are deeply flawed.[65] In fact, Kaiser's desire to conclude that it was private individuals who must have instituted almost all these impediments requires him to steadfastly dismiss both the work of others and his own observations. Neither Koga's (correct) idea that these blockages related to a city-wide drainage system[66] nor Kaiser's own admission that some "impediments" did not actually bar traffic[67] (but did block water) could dissuade him from the perverse conclusion that Pompeians individually and intentionally made the circulation of traffic more difficult.

The fallacy of this ideology is revealed in still other examples of tortured logic that are required to maintain it. Thus, in discussing the legal widths of Roman *viae*, Kaiser again takes a narrow, textualist approach to argue that because some streets were smaller than the minimum required for a cart to pass, Romans did not care about the free circulation of traffic. But surely these exceptions are the point of the regulation. That is, because some streets were too narrow for wheeled traffic, the width of others needed to be mandated such that traffic could be facilitated. These "narrow" streets, together with the existence of bottlenecks and the failure to use less expensive materials to pave side streets are interpreted by Kaiser as "missed opportunities" that by their inefficiency reveal a lack of Roman municipal interest in traffic.[68]

The idea that because lava stone surfaces were used uniformly on both main thoroughfares and side streets indicates that the city government was not invested in their construction is particularly unconvincing, not least for being factually wrong. Almost half of Pompeii is not paved in silex, including two back streets in Region VI that remained as battuti despite the stone pavements across the rest of the region.[69] Furthermore, if it were true that paving style was ignored by civic officials and was solely the discretion of the property owner facing onto that street, then we are at a loss to explain why he could fashion his own curb and sidewalk to his liking and (according to Kaiser) block carts from the street beside his house but could change neither the materials nor the format

---

[65] Kaiser's (2011a, 178) map 7.1 is replete with errors. The most important to this argument are the identification of impediments where none exist and claims that ramps specifically designed to permit traffic are impediments.

[66] Koga 1991. My article on drainage (Poehler 2012) appeared a year after Kaiser published his article (2011a), and therefore he cannot be faulted for not considering it.

[67] Kaiser 2011a, 179.

[68] Kaiser 2011a, 179–81.

[69] Chapter 3, 58–60.

of the silex street surface he paid for. Similarly, if it were more efficient to pave side streets in less expensive materials, why did so many frontagers not make this more economical choice? The parsimonious answer is that municipal governments, together with property owners, defined and created the form of the streets, and while certain aspects were negotiable (e.g., curb materials, stepping stones, sidewalk pavements), others were not (e.g., minimum height of curbs, format of silex surfaces, placement of blockages).

The Shape of the Book

Beyond dispelling these new myths of ancient traffic, the purpose of the preceding discussion is to establish the notion of an ongoing negotiation of control in the Pompeian street. Indeed, it is impossible to explain the complexity of the archaeological remains without acknowledging that each instance of variable street width, paving style, or vehicle type allowed was the product of the tension (and cooperation) between private initiative and varying levels of governmental oversight (in both senses of the word). Control is always complicated in reality with de facto rights sometimes claimed and de iure rights sometimes deferred. Nonetheless, such distinctions are very often visible archaeologically. The identification of the systematic organization of traffic at Pompeii and its separation from the "natural" flows of an uncontrolled network depend on it. This notion of complex and constantly renegotiated relations to power is threaded throughout this book, though seldom is it expressed as explicitly.

Certainly, control and compromise are present in Chapter 2, which explores the evolution of the Pompeian street network from the archaic age through the final alterations in the post-earthquake(s) period. This chapter relies on the explosion of excavations below the 79 CE surfaces over the last thirty years to complement more formal analyses of the shape of the grid itself. The following three chapters offer a deep archaeological description and analysis of the Pompeian street, telescoping in detail from surface treatment to the individual architectural components that make up the final street form to the shapes worn into those architectures by the repeated impact of vehicles. Chapter 3 examines the evolution of the Pompeian street surface, describing six different surface treatments, from beaten ash surfaces to the adoption of stone pavements to the construction of streets above debris piles on the edges of the city. The curbstones that separated and elevated these sidewalks from the paving stones, the stepping stones that allowed level crossings between them, and the guard stones that protected pedestrians on the sidewalks are the subject of Chapter 4. Like the street surface, these features are considered within a social and evolutionary framework, revealing that even as curbstones, stepping stones, and guard stones were adopted in one part of the city, they were already being removed and superseded in another.

Chapter 5 then explores how vehicles interacted with the horizontal surface of the street to form Pompeii's famous ruts. More important are the more than six hundred examples of wearing from the vertical faces of its architectures that reveal the direction of traffic that once passed each location. Divided into a typology of three forms and described at several levels of clarity, Chapter 5 outlines the methodology used to identify, evaluate, and aggregate the evidence for traffic. Beyond grounding the argument at the center of this book, these pages are conceived of as a species of handbook, suitable for consultation while in the field and applicable to the wider Roman world or anywhere and at any time that cart's wheels eroded the surfaces of the street.

Chapter 6 is the archaeological heart of the book as well as the transition from the description of Pompeii's traffic systems as an archaeological fact to its discussion as a historical phenomenon. The first half of the chapter looks back to the discussion of the street network's evolution (Chapter 2) to consider the effects of its shape on the origins and basic operation of the traffic system. Together with the directional evidence from curbs and from stepping stone crossings, the first rule and the first norm of the traffic systems can be documented: Pompeians drove on the right side of the street, unless there was room to drive in the center. It is in the identification and analysis of one-way streets, however, that the traffic systems come clearly into focus, as the directional evidence is carefully parsed chronologically to reveal four periods of Pompeii's vehicular governance.

Despite the archaeological clarity of the traffic systems' existence and maintenance, we lack direct epigraphic, literary, or historical evidence for how it was implemented and enacted. Chapter 7 is therefore an exploration of three interrelated scenarios for how Pompeians might have solved what was essentially an issue of information transfer from magistrate to *mulio*. Due to the speculative (though thoroughly researched and documented) nature of these discussions, a fictional character—a Pompeian revival of Sabinus the Muleteer—is tasked with a trip across the city and through a series of interactions so that the reader might explore not only the means by which traffic rules were materialized and shared but also encounter a number of rich, if minor, details of the Pompeian cart driver's daily life.

Writ large, however, such daily details at Pompeii and beyond make up the social history of traffic in the Roman world. That history and the evidence for it is the subject of Chapter 8. Having surveyed the streets of more than thirty cities around the Mediterranean allows me to situate the systems of traffic at Pompeii archaeologically within the wider world of Roman urbanism and to make meaningful comparison with the solutions that Romans attempted at other times and other places. Thus, by looking for not only whole systems but their components—for example, restricting driving to one side of a two-way street, the use of one-way streets, and the evidence for reversals of direction—a wider range of municipal solutions and experiments can be detected. Finally, these solutions, known only from archaeology, are themselves contextualized within a brief history of traffic from legal, literary, epigraphic, historical, and art-historical perspectives. At last, the book is summarized and reconsidered in Chapter 9, bringing discussion back to some of the messy realities of urban behavior, which in aggregate made up the traffic systems of Pompeii.

2

The Development of Pompeii's
Urban Street Network

The first network of streets and the earliest road surfaces in Pompeii bear little resemblance to the city's familiar streetscape of the first century CE. Trackways of compacted ash that led (at least) between the gates of the town and its prominent and sacred landmarks through these thoroughfares can hardly be called urban. Although research on the archaic and early Samnite periods of Pompeii's development have naturally focused on the monumental, sacred, and residential structures, it is the layout of the streets—their presence, alignments, and intersections—that defines the shape of the city at each period of its development. In earlier periods of sparse settlement, without the definite existence of the streets, one is left to speculate on the formal organization of space. Once established, however, the street network (or networks) serves as the warp and weft of the urban fabric, prescribing the sizes, shapes, orientations, and arrangements of the city's architectural and infrastructural development. Like textiles, sections of urban form can be altered—threads or streets removed or inserted—but only with ramifications that reverberate far beyond the location of change. And if the grid is a textile, then Pompeii of 79 CE appears as a patchwork quilt, with irregular cuts of differently woven cloth awkwardly stitched together.

The goal of this dense chapter is to examine the present understanding of Pompeii's evolution by disassembling this patchwork and reconsidering the presumed awkwardness in its adhesion. To do this, the traditional tools of formal analysis—street alignments and block shapes—are employed with and critiqued by the stratigraphic evidence recovered in the last three decades of excavation below the 79 CE levels. The chapter therefore begins by deconstructing the prevailing theories of Pompeii's development as well as recounting a brief history of the current model's own evolution. The result is an outline of the development of Pompeii's urban form as a series of street networks: from the archaic age through the period of the "hiatus" of the fifth to fourth century BCE to a reorganization of the city's space so profound that it can genuinely be considered a refoundation and finally to the adjustments of the refounded city in the Colonial, Augustan, and post-earthquake(s) periods.

A Brief History of the Current Model

The idea I offer here of a fourth century BCE refoundation is controversial, though hardly novel, and strikes against a century of scholarship that has argued for a linear model of Pompeii's evolution. That model derives from Francis Haverfield, whose articulation of the "patchwork quilt" of grid plans, though not the earliest investigation of this type, was certainly the most influential. In *Ancient Town Planning*, Haverfield[70] proposed the now well-known idea that an older settlement, an Altstadt,[71] was embedded within the fabric of later development that would come to be called, in opposition, the Neustadt. This model challenged Mau's conception that the city's grid was laid out in a single event based on the axes of via di Mercurio and via della Fortuna / via di Nola. According to Mau, via Stabiana took advantage of the natural cut through the volcanic promontory upon which Pompeii sits and the irregularly shaped insulae along it are explained by the need to adjust to its line.[72] Haverfield, in contrast, explained the lack of symmetry across the entire city plan as the effect of successive phases of outward growth from the Altstadt.[73]

Throughout the twentieth century the concept of the Altstadt was the *communis opinio* for the origin of Pompeii, and the same chronological, topographical, and cultural explanations continue to be employed to debate the development of the eastern half of the city.[74] In 1940, Armin von Gerkan further developed the model, defending the Neustadt as the product of a single, later event but reviving Mau's appeal to topography.[75] Other scholars identified cultural factors as having had the strongest influence on the design and therefore the date of the

---

[70] Haverfield 1913, 65–68. See Castagnoli (1971, 25–35) for an expansive discussion of the early theories about Pompeii's evolution. Also, Fiorelli 2001, 29–30, and Mau 1899, 32–33.

[71] I will use the term Altstadt to indicate its traditional geographical definition though not its chronology.

[72] Mau 1899, 32–33.

[73] Haverfield 1913, 67.

[74] The unitary plan thesis was still upheld by Sogliano until 1937. With new evidence it has been revived as a master plan for Region VI and the east by De Caro (1991) and supported by Wallace-Hadrill (2013, 77–78), who, however, reconstructed an archaic date for the plan.

[75] The articulation of a "Neustadt" is attributed to von Gerkan (1940), who used the idea formally. By contrast, Haverfield's (1913, 66) use of "Altstadt" is more referential than definitive: "this area has all the appearance of an 'Altstadt.'" Carrington's research (1936, 21–27), which preceded von Gerkan, is often overlooked. See also, Laurence 1994, 16.

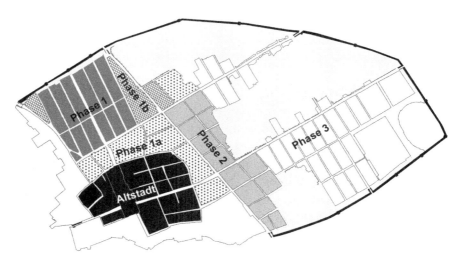

Figure 2.1 Evolution of the Pompeian street network, after Geertman.

Neustadt.[76] Nearly a century after Haverfield, Herman Geertman further refined the multiphase model of planned urban growth. Through an examination of how groups of insulae that represent individual grid plans articulate with one another, Geertman constructed a relative chronology to explain the sequence of their construction (fig. 2.1).[77] In this model, the first growth out of the Altstadt occurred on the axis of via di Mercurio in Regio VI shortly after 300 BCE with a group of long, rectangular blocks (Phase 1). Following these were the square insulae along via Stabiana, which formally bounded the edge of the Altstadt (Phase 2). The area between the Altstadt and the new quarters to the north and east is made up of irregular, even nongeometrical shapes (Phases 1a, 1b), which Geertman saw as the result of pre-existing streets in the peri-urban area surrounding the Altstadt. Finally, the eastern half of the city (Phase 3) was later cast in sets of long, rectangular insulae.

   In this formulation, irregularities in the street network and changes in insula shape are explained by appealing to a distinction in chronology: they must be different because they are the products of different events of planning. And while he acknowledged the impact of topography, Geertman gave it no real power to explain the shapes of the insulae. Considering these challenges and the radical new picture emerging from recent excavations, that traditional model is ripe for reconsideration. The following period-by-period examination of Pompeii's evolution attempts such a re-evaluation.

---

[76] E.g., Castagnoli (1971, 30–32) saw Greek influence in the plan, while Sommella (1989, 17–26) assumed Roman influence.

[77] Fig. 2.1 is based on Geertman 2007, 89, fig. 7.6, and Geertman 1998, 19, fig. 16.

Archaic Pompeii

Despite Pompeii's prosperity during the archaic period—a time when two great temples were surrounded by a wide ring of fortifications[78] and sparse but regular occupation—we have only a few traces of the network of streets that divided the oldest urban landscape (fig. 2.2).[79] The extent of the sixth-century-BCE city was defined by a circuit of pappamonte walls built on essentially the same alignment as the later fortifications.[80] A second set of walls, built in large blocks of local travertine and carefully arranged as orthostates (thus, the orthostat walls), replaced the pappamonte walls sometime in the early fifth century BCE.[81] The gates cutting through these walls at Porta Vesuvio and Tower XI provide most of the information about the archaic street network, attesting to a route on the alignment with the via del Vesuvio / via Stabiana and another on alignment with via di Mercurio.[82] That these routes continued on these alignments is supported by their connection to important monuments of the period: one could reach the Quadrivio di' Orfeo[83] and Temple

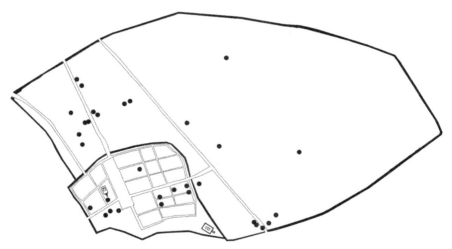

Figure 2.2 Archaic-era street network, with locations of archaic structures.

[78] De Caro 1985. See also Maiuri 1929, 151–63, 233; Arthur 1986, 30–44; Etani et al. 1998, 119–20; Curti 2008, 50–52.

[79] Carafa (2007, 65 and n. 30), following De Caro (1992, 72), imagines a sparse agricultural landscape, while Coarelli (2008, 174) reconstructs a more fully urbanized archaic town.

[80] Robinson (2011, 24) defines pappamonte as "a local grey, soft gritty tuff." See Esposito, Kastenmeier, and Imperatore (2011, 121–33) on pappamonte structures at Pompeii.

[81] van der Graaf 2013, 53–56.

[82] Maiuri 1929, 168; De Caro 1985, 104–6; Carocci et al. 1990, 217–26.

[83] Mau 1875, 261–68; Coarelli et al. 2001–2, 227–28.

of Minerva from Porta Vesuvio and the sacred grove[84] and Temple of Apollo from the Tower of Mercury gate. Via Consolare also is expected to have been an important archaic route,[85] as is a street represented by via dell'Abbondanza, which intersected the main north–south routes to form the primary axes of archaic Pompeii.

The network outside these major thoroughfares is elusive and the subject of speculation. At the beginning of the fifth century BCE an inner pomerial road existed near the Porta Nocera associated with the orthostat walls.[86] Other sections of a pomerial street have been identified at Porta Stabia,[87] Porta Ercolano,[88] and at Tower IX.[89] While the via di Nola and the eastern section of the via dell'Abbondanza seem natural extensions of the western archaic street network, both Maiuri and Chiaramonte Treré failed to find any surviving traces of an archaic gate at the Porta Nola.[90] Claims that the street grid of Region VI originated in the archaic period are not supported by the excavations into these streets (vicolo della Fullonica and vicolo del Fauno) even as the density of archaic finds here is the highest outside of the Altstadt.[91] The recent discovery of two constructions at the Casa dei Gladiatori (V 5, 3) and Casa di Amarantus (I 9, 12) have been used to argue for the existence of streets on essentially the same alignment as via di Nola and the eastern section of via dell'Abbondanza.[92] Wallace-Hadrill has even gone so far as to ask if the basic framework of the street network was an archaic invention.[93] While these constructions do align with the primary eastern streets and some network of streets must have existed, the absence of eastern gates gives greater weight to the interpretation that the alignments made by via di Nola and eastern via dell'Abbondanza are products of a much later period.

[84] Bonghi Jovino 1984, 364–65; De Caro 1992, 72; Coarelli and Pesando 2011, 41; Guzzo 2011, 14, n. 10.

[85] Carocci et al. 1990, 193–207.

[86] De Caro 1985, 76; Chiaramonte 2007, 142. Coarelli and Pesando (2011, 38–39) hesitate on the date of this pomerial route, but not its existence.

[87] Maiuri 1929, 200.

[88] De Caro 1985, 89.

[89] Etani 2010, 55–60.

[90] Maiuri 1929, 206–18; Chiaramonte Treré 1986, 13–19; See also Esposito, Kastenmeier, and Imperatore 2011, 114, n. 17, for a brief discussion of these excavations.

[91] Coarelli and Pesando 2011, 40–46. See also Anniboletti et al. 2007, 5; Befani 2008, 3; Sorriento 2008, 2.

[92] Fulford et al. 1999, 47–50, 105–12; Esposito, Kastenmeier, and Imperatore 2011; Wallace-Hadrill 2005, 103.

[93] Wallace-Hadrill 2013.

Hiatus

From the latter half of the fifth century BCE until the middle of the fourth, the urban space of Pompeii appears to have contracted into a small, nucleated settlement (fig. 2.3). Occupation ended beyond the Altstadt, and even within it, offerings at the primary temples ceased.[94] The recent discovery of a set of defensive walls built in large blocks of Sarno limestone and tuff north of via degli Augustali (VII 2, 27, 30) and of a wide ditch beneath the Stabian Baths and the insula of the Postumii now strongly suggests that a ring of fortifications once surrounded the so-called Altstadt, as Haverfield had long ago suspected.[95] His notion that the Altstadt was the embryonic urban form of Pompeii, however, is not sustained by these finds. Indeed, for reasons that are still unclear, following the archaic age Pompeii entered a period now commonly called the hiatus but is more accurately called a regression.

Though considerably smaller in size (ca. 8.6 hectares), the fifth century BCE town had a complete network of streets that were organized around a set of logical principles, though ones that, after two millennia of orthogonal planning, appear to us as a backward kind of logic. Although there is little stratigraphic evidence of the streets themselves, their relationship to the Altstadt's fortification

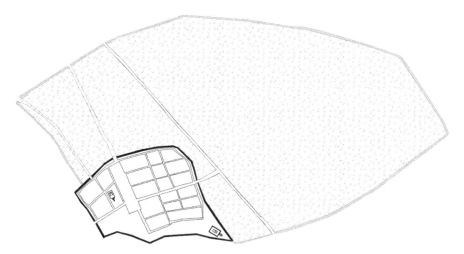

Figure 2.3 Hiatus-era street network.

[94] Wallace-Hadrill 2013, 47, n. 45.

[95] Dickmann and Pirson 2002a, 2002b; Pedroni 2011, 162–63. Ribera i Lacomba et al. (2009, 95–96) place the wall closer to via degli Augustali. Ongoing excavations in the Stabian Baths, however, may once again cast doubt on the existence of these walls. I thank Mark Robinson for alerting me to this research.

walls provides a clear formal relationship that sets the network in the fifth century rather than in preceding or following periods. Even if, as some have argued, the Altstadt were entirely formed and laid out in the sixth century BCE, by the fifth century these are the only remaining urban routes of the much-reduced town.[96] Additionally, as we will see, the logic inherent in the plan can also be recognized in contemporary Italian towns.

It is likely that the archaic crossroads of via Marina / via dell'Abbondanza and the southern extension of via di Mercurio / via delle Scuole remained in place and defined the location of the town's forum or at very least would determine where it would evolve. These routes divided the reduced urban area into quadrants, but the axes they offered did not become the basis of the fifth-century street network. Instead, the roughly circular route along the interior perimeter of the Altstadt fortifications—now represented by vicolo del Gigante / vicolo dei Soprastanti / via degli Augustali / vicolo del Lupanare / via dei Teatri / vicolo della Regina—provided the underlying geometry, to which the rest of the network responded. Streets were planned to intersect this ring road at right angles, creating parallel alignments within each quadrant but meeting the archaic north–south axis at opposing low angles. The streets surrounding insula VII 15 offer a clear example: leaving vicolo del Gigante to the east at a right angle, vicolo del Gallo once continued at least as far as its intersection with vicolo Storto Nuovo, the angle of which was defined by the latter street's right-angle intersection with the northern section of the ring road (vicolo dei Soprastanti). These street alignments created insula VII 15 as a rough parallelogram, a basic geometry that is replicated throughout the Altstadt, even as the different number of streets cut the insulae into different sizes on different alignments. This arrangement of streets has been described by scholars as a "herringbone" pattern, which assumes that there must be a central spine to which these secondary "ribs" attach. Yet no north–south or east–west street can genuinely serve this function. For example, the regularizing effect of via dell'Abbondanza gives shape to the many insulae that touch it, but the notion that this street was the basis of a once regular but now deformed orthogonal grid is undermined by the other side of these same blocks, which often take a strikingly different alignment (e.g., VII 15 and VIII 5).[97] Moreover, the earlier via Marina shared an alignment much closer to that of vicolo del Gallo than via dell'Abbondanza.

---

[96] Here I follow the model put forward by Esposito, Kastenmeier, and Imperatore (2011, 128–33), offered earlier by Guzzo (2007, 57–62), of a new spatial organization for the Altstadt arriving with the fortifications. These authors argue persuasively against a more traditional theory, supported by Coarelli and Pesando, which suggests the Altstadt had its well-developed urban form—including pappamonte fortifications and herringbone street network—already in the archaic period.

[97] Laurence 1994, 112–3.

Contemporary comparanda for the logic of this street network is found at Gabii in Latium, where long streets intersect a primary road curving along the edge of Lake Castiglione. At Gabii, all streets radiate from this trunk road at right angles, creating long and narrow wedge-shaped blocks in two modules (approximately 42 and 20–21 meters in width). As at Pompeii, neither block shape nor true orthogonality were at the heart of these urban designs. Instead, in each case a consistent set of relationships (right-angle intersections) was created with a primary route in the town, itself shaped by an even more important topographic feature (i.e., the lake or the fortifications). Pompeii's herringbone pattern is simply an inverted expression of Gabii's plan, compressed into a much smaller and previously occupied area but built upon the same basic principles of fifth-century-BCE urban design.

Though still rare, the results of excavation in the Altstadt streets supports this organization of space, showing agreement between the fifth century and final street network. Investigations below the northern sidewalk via degli Augustali uncovered the edge of a beaten ash street dating to the late sixth–early fifth century BCE. Although clearly a beaten ash street, including a ledge demarcating the street and sidewalk, it was initially interpreted as an agger associated with the Altstadt fortifications (fig. 2.4).[98] Across the street in a shop north of the Macellum (VII 9, 25), excavators found no trace of this street, but instead uncovered a north–south oriented wall of the fifth or fourth century BCE, the existence of which limits the width of the first surface of via degli Augustali to less than 3 meters.[99] Both sides of this same street were discovered in 1981 below the same northern sidewalk where via degli Augustali meets via del Foro. Interpreted as a defensive ditch, this east–west running feature was 2.5 meters wide rim to rim and was put out of use sometime after the fourth century BCE. Ditches of equal dimension defining the eastern edge of the Sanctuary of Apollo were found in the same excavations along the west side of the forum and are reminiscent of the surface found under via degli Augustali. These are described as flat-bottomed, with ledges cut into either slope.[100]

It is easy to understand how the small size and inward sloping shapes of early beaten ash streets can be confused for ditches or an agger,[101] but there are several reasons why these interpretations are unlikely. First, they are found in locations

---

[98] Bustamante et al. 2010, 13–15, figs. 23–25, 30. The excavators also discovered a thin (4 cm), waterborne gravel layer on the surface of this street. Chapter 3, 55–60.

[99] Bustamante et al. 2010, 7–8, figs. 19–20.

[100] Arthur 1986, 34–35.

[101] Nearly contemporary (late fifth-century) streets at Gabii are also narrow, ranging from 2.0 to 2.8 meters wide; Mogetta 2014, 151. The Crustumerium road was also once confused for an agger; Attema et al. 2014, 185–87, n. 48.

Figure 2.4 Beaten ash street below via degli Augustali, from Bustamente et al. 2010, fig. 23.

where or on alignments on which fifth-century streets are expected: two segments parallel the Altstadt fortifications, and a long feature in the forum, perpendicular to via degli Augustali, matches the alignment of vicolo Storto Nuovo. These alignments are supported by excavations below vicolo di Eumachia, which was founded on its current orientation and included a pair of ruts worn into the bedrock.[102] Additionally, if the feature along via degli Augustali was indeed a fosse, then it is on the wrong side of the fortification wall and only half the size of the defensive ditch revealed under the insula of the Postumii, outside the Altstadt fortifications.[103] Moreover, by recognizing features below via degli Augustali as a street, the inner fortifications now match the organization of

---

[102] Eschebach and Eschebach 1995, 23, fig. 12. Despite what their drawing shows, Eschebach and Eschebach claim the earlier street was wide enough for two lanes and was given a lateral gutter. To date the street, they rely on depth (1.1 m down, at "oppidum level") and comparanda: "The same road technology can be seen in the Etruscan road in S. Giovenale that in the end of the 7th century. v. BC". See Hanell 1962, 277.

[103] Dickmann and Pirson 2002a, 2002b; Pedroni 2011, 162–63.

the external fortifications: external fosse, fortification walls, and inner pomerial street.[104] Indeed, the entire city has a more coherent and familiar structure in the fifth and fourth centuries, appearing much more like the fortified urban enclosures of contemporary Samnium, of which Pompeii was a part.[105]

Refoundation: Pompeii's Fourth-Century-BCE Master Plan

For nearly the next two centuries, Pompeii's only formal street network comprised those routes inside the Altstadt, even as occupation beyond it began again in the fourth century BCE. The two major buildings known from this century are either off alignment with the later street grid or were suppressed by it (fig. 2.5). This new network of streets was instituted at the end of the fourth century BCE, and its design would dominate the organization of space outside the Altstadt for the rest of Pompeii's existence. Indeed, from its complexity, scope, and ambition, this new city plan can be described without exaggeration as the blueprint of Pompeii's refoundation. In the same moment a new set of fortification walls were built upon the outline of the archaic city, establishing the position of the final seven gates and anchoring a city-wide street network within which developed revitalized cult spaces and residential areas.

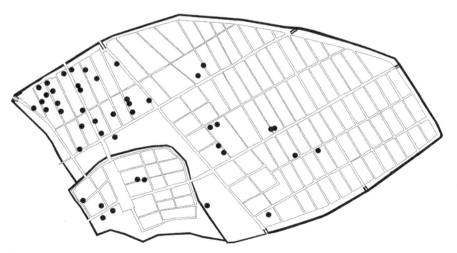

Figure 2.5 Refoundation street network, with locations of third-century-BCE structures.

[104] Esposito, Kastenmeier, and Imperatore 2011, 133.
[105] Guzzo 2011, 15–16; Robinson 2014, 199–200.

The date for the refoundation and its master plan now can be firmly established by excavation. Nowhere amongst the westernmost streets of Region VI, the central areas of Region IX, or the southernmost routes of Region I can any street be dated by excavation earlier than approximately 300 BCE. For example, investigations below vicolo del Fauno and vicolo della Fullonica offered a detailed glimpse into the history of streets in this part of the city but no stratified evidence of early streets in Region VI parallel to via di Mercurio.[106] Excavations along the vicolo di Narciso and along vicolo dei Vettii have found that no building occupied the spaces these streets defined before the end of the third century BCE.[107] Crossing into Region V, research in insula I and below the paving stones of the vicolo delle Nozze d'Argento found a beaten ash surface 50 centimeters below the final street with a clear pair of ruts of the same gauge as was worn into the lava pavers. Although no datable ceramic evidence was uncovered, the ruts in the earlier street were filled at least once with second-century-BCE material, while the first building at the insula's northwest corner (V 1, 13) was also founded on the paleosol in the second century.[108]

Similarly, a trench sunk in the blocked and truncated street between the unfinished Central Baths and insula IX 3 revealed that the first street surface belongs to the late fourth or early third century BCE.[109] The north wall of insula IX 3 cuts through this surface and, like the earliest deposits within the Casa di Marcus Lucrezio (IX 3, 5), dates the earliest occupation of these blocks to the beginning of the third century BCE. Farther south, via Mediana was constructed over the remains of an earlier building dating to the sixth and fifth centuries BCE. New buildings immediately took on this alignment of via Mediana and vicolo di Tesmo: the first walls of XI 7, 21–22 as well as the atrium and impluvium foundations at IX 1, 29 were completed in the last decades of the fourth to the first decades of the third century BCE. Vicolo di Balbo connects via Stabiana to vicolo di Tesmo but terminates at the western facade of insula IX 7. Surprisingly, excavations within the shop at IX 7, 18 have found no evidence that vicolo di Balbo ever continued eastward.[110]

---

[106] Chapter 3, 58–60.

[107] Jones and Schoonhoven 2003, 128–29. Seiler et al. 2005, 217–18.

[108] The Swedish Pompeii Project has published its excavation of vicolo delle Nozze d'Argento; Nilsson 2014. The nails recovered from between the lava pavers, however, might have been from a number of sources, including shoes (Rodríguez Morales 2014), the studs of cart's wheels (Crouwel 2012, 82–83), and wedged or poured iron used to repair the street (Poehler, van Roggen, and Crowther 2019).

[109] Castrén et al. (2008, 334) called this surface a sidewalk.

[110] Gallo 2005, 207–8, 2008, 323; Giglio 2005, 204, 2008, 342–48.

Formal Analyses of the Master Plan

As Mau understood long ago (ideas most effectively revived by Stefano De Caro), the strongest arguments for such a master plan come from the plan itself and the unity of the final layout of streets.[111] The creation of via di Nola and eastern via dell'Abbondanza around 300 BCE divided Pompeii into three roughly equal parts, each leading to one of the gates along the new fortification walls.[112] Via delle Terme / via della Fortuna extends this division to the west, separating the Altstadt area from the new quarters in Region VI and meeting the western fortifications at a smaller pedestrian gate, a postern. Subdividing Region VI is vicolo di Mercurio, which continues eastward across via del Vesuvio as vicolo delle Nozze d'Argento all the way to the eastern fortification wall, where it aligns with a defensive tower. Via Mediana makes the same subdivision for the middle section of Pompeii, while vicolo I 2–I 3 equally divides the south, each aligning with an eastern defensive tower. At the same time, several north–south streets in the eastern orthogonal grid also align with towers, including one street (vicolo del Anfiteatro) that aligns with two towers. While the current construction of the towers is later than the walls, the discovery of the postern within Casa M. Fabius Rufus lends support to the idea that the towers replaced pedestrian passages in the original design.[113] So too does the location of the towers: if the grid plan had been later than the towers, it would have been exceptionally difficult to both align with these towers and maintain the regular width of the eastern insulae. If the towers had been later than the grid, aligning with streets would have been easier, but surely the placement of the towers would have been influenced more by questions of defense than urban design.

The most rudimentary formal elements of this unified urban design—the city-wide axes that led to gates and towers—can thus be directly connected to the Sarno limestone enceinte around 300 BCE. These aspects of design alone, however, do not explain the curious changes in block shape and orientation across the city, which scholars have taken as markers of chronological distinction and thus multiple periods of urban growth. Yet the changes in shape and alignment can be incorporated within a single master plan by understanding the tension of two opposing forces: sloping topography and a desire for orthogonality.

---

[111] Mau 1899, 327–33; De Caro 1991, 1992.

[112] See Geertman 2007, 86–87, fig.7.4; Nappo 2007, 348, n. 2. Measurements taken from GIS, however, refute or at least complicate the belief in the equality of these sections. One finds different results measuring north to south from the middle of the fortification wall to the middle of an intersection (259 m, 248 m, and 250 m), from the corner of the sidewalks of the insulae (233 m, 242 m, 235 m), and from the corner of buildings of the insulae (241 m, 239 m, and 230 m).

[113] Eschebach and Eschebach 1995, 77; Grimaldi 2014, 23–26.

Figure 2.6 Pompeian topography.

The first of these forces can be analyzed by mapping and calculating the average slope of the ground within each insula (fig. 2.6),[114] the results of which lead to an important observation: on flat ground Pompeians preferred rectangular shaped blocks, but once the slope reached 3%, they shortened and widened those rectangles until the blocks became squares and in one case (I 3) even becoming a squat rectangle perpendicular to the rest of the grid.

Topography (together with the greater size of the area) also explains why Regions I and II were divided into three parts rather than two, like the other regions to the north. The northern row of blocks in this tripartite division of Regions I and II are commensurate in size with the southern blocks in Region VI (ca. 89 m) at approximately 87 meters in length, while the middle blocks shrink to 82 meters and the southern blocks are truncated still further, to 79 meters.[115] Salvatore Nappo, following Satoshi Sakai, offered an ingenious explanation for these different lengths involving the middle and southern row of blocks, each yielding slightly more of their area to roadways between them. Still, this hypothesis explains only *how* the unequal division might have been envisioned and accomplished rather than *why* such a division was deemed necessary in the first place. Additionally, it is puzzling that the streets seem to have been such an afterthought in the plan that insulae had to suffer for their creation.

Awkward design decisions would appear to be the hallmarks of a retrofit, and these discontinuities have been used as evidence of a later date for the layout of

---

[114] Slope calculations used elevation data from Eschebach and Eschebach (1995) and van der Poel (1984).

[115] Sakai 1991, 35; Nappo 1997, 97.

this part of Region I and even for the entire eastern orthogonal grid. The change in design in Region I, however, is not reactionary but rather a rational adaptation to different geographical conditions: this area is simply larger and more steeply sloped than the other sections of the orthogonal grid. Because the southern for-tification wall bent southward east of Porta Stabia, it created an area 30 meters longer along its north–south axis than the corresponding southern section of via Stabiana.[116] Dividing this area in half would have produced exceptionally long blocks, over 120 meters in length, longer even than the equivalent insulae north of via dell'Abbondanza.

Considering the slope south of via dell'Abbondanza, such long blocks would be impractical to build upon. In the northwest of Region I, where the first blocks of orthogonal grid (I 8, I 9, and I 11) adjoin the square blocks along via Stabiana (I 4 and I 6), the terrain slopes steeply southward, though it is flatter than within the square blocks, and continues to flatten toward the intersection of via dell'Abbondanza and via di Nocera. At the southern end of via di Nocera, how-ever, the slope increases again, reaching a 4% grade in the final section between via della Palestra and Porta Nocera. Thus, we can now see that the shape of Region I was influenced by terrain on both edges, with the difference in form being a response to its intensity: the difference in length between via Stabiana (shorter) and via di Nocera (longer) south of via dell'Abbondanza combined with areas of steeply sloping ground to require the use of squares in the west and three rows of foreshortened rectangles farther east.

Intersection Shape and Urban Aesthetics

Contemporary with this preference for block shape is another cultural choice, one that determined how streets would form intersections in different parts of the city.[117] In the eastern orthogonal grid, streets meet one another at right angles, and each street continues through the intersection on the same alignment. With a few necessary exceptions almost every intersection east of the vicolo di Cecilio Giocondo / vicolo di Tesmo / vicolo del Citarista line shares this form. In the west, the situation is radically different.[118] Where the archaic and fifth-century

---

[116] From northern to southern extent of insulae, via Stabiana measures 229.8 meters and via di Nocera measures 260.1 meters. Note also that this disparity in length is despite the via Stabiana's longer diagonal path to its intersection with via dell'Abbondanza.

[117] Chapter 6, 140–44.

[118] The exceptions are the intersections at the Porta Nola and Porta Sarno, where the pomerial road meets via di Nola and via dell'Abbondanza. At Porta Nocera, however, the change in elevation creates a dead end for the southern pomerial route at via di Nocera, at least by the Augustan era. Finally, the blocked off area of Region II creates six T intersections for wheeled traffic, but for pedes-trians (and determined drivers) these remain orthogonal.

roads imperfectly join with those of the later fourth-century master plan, only three intersections meet in an orthogonal arrangement. Instead, many form Y or T shapes. Region VI shows this clearly: the archaic streets of via Consolare and via del Vesuvio are intersected at high angles, creating Y intersections, while the streets of the northern grid terminate in T intersections along via delle Terme / via della Fortuna. A similar set of bifurcating intersections exists along the pomerial road of the old fifth-century town. Both periods of urban design, however, share a revealing preference for narrower streets to cross larger thoroughfares so that the two sections of the narrower street are offset from one another on either side of the junction. Again, Region VI offers a clear example: as vicolo di Mercurio crosses via di Mercurio from east to west, it shifts southward by 95 centimeters. Similarly, three of the five north–south streets that cross vicolo di Mercurio shift to the west on the south side of the intersection. The situation inside the Altstadt and along via del Vesuvio / via Stabiana is the same: every intersection where four streets come together is offset in some way.

Examining the precise manner in which these intersections are formed shows that there was even a hierarchy of the streets encoded within these intersections (fig. 2.5). In such a system the archaic-era route of via del Vesuvio / via Stabiana is a primary street, as it makes no adjustment for any other street over its 723 meters length. A later but equally broad street, the via della Fortuna, shifts to the south as it crosses via del Vesuvio / via Stabiana and continues east as via di Nola. Likewise, via dell'Abbondanza adjusts as it crosses via Stabiana, taking on a slightly more northerly alignment in the east.[119] Via di Mercurio, another archaic street, can also be recognized as a primary street from the way that via delle Terme shifts to the north as it becomes via della Fortuna.[120] Indeed, all the east–west routes that meet via del Vesuvio / via Stabiana are secondary routes: vicolo di Mercurio / vicolo delle Nozze d'Argento; via degli Augustali / via Mediana; via del Tempio d'Iside / vicolo del Menandro, vicolo I 2–I 3. To this we should also add the blocked street on the south side of the Central Baths, vicolo IX 3–IX 4. The addition is warranted not only because it shifts far to the north as vicolo del Panettiere but also because vicolo di Tesmo adjusts to the east as it crosses vicolo IX 3–IX 4. In fact, the long line of vicolo di Tesmo / vicolo del Citarista shifts eastward at every intersection but two, further demonstrating the tertiary rank of these lesser north–south streets already seen in Region VI. Like the fourth-century design surrounding it, the fifth-century grid in the Altstadt also

[119] The offset of via dell'Abbondanza is made by the southern curb taking a more southerly course, creating a triangular plaza. On the north side of the street, however, the facade of the Stabian Baths is on alignment with that of insula IX 1 across via Stabiana.
[120] The unusual width and slightly skewed orientation of via del Foro makes it difficult to determine its relationship to via di Mercurio.

had its own hierarchy of streets, the order of which is likewise expressed in the asymmetries of offset intersections. Though there are far fewer examples from which to judge, via dell'Abbondanza east of the forum was denoted as the primary street, while vicolo di Eumachia was secondary, and vicoli Scheletri and Balcone pensile ranked third. In all these cases the oldest streets were given deference, and in general east–west streets were preferred over those north–south streets crossing them.

The use of the offset intersection was clearly a conscious choice and seems to encode some hierarchical and even chronological relationships between the streets. This system may have survived or been reinvented by later Romans surveyors who ensconced a similar hierarchy of rural roads—from public to local to private—in both continuous and discontinuous centuriation systems.[121] What influenced the Pompeians to create such forms and apply them in such regular ways is not known with certainty. We know that the fourth-century-BCE street system was laid out with the new limestone fortifications, which themselves indicate a renewed interest in the defense of the city. These offset intersections might also have been included in the plan for reasons of defense. Aristotle, whose writings were only a generation old when Pompeii's master plan was devised, conceived of the ideal city's design as a balance between desires and needs, between salubriousness and governmental form, between beauty and defense. To balance the desired aesthetic and the needs of internal defense, Aristotle thought a hybridity of modern and ancient plans was best, which he conceived of and expressed through the metaphor of the "well planted vineyard":

> As to the form of private houses, those are thought to be best and most useful for their different purposes which are distinct and separate from each other, and built in the modern manner, after the plan of Hippodamus: but for safety in time of war, on the contrary, they should be built as they formerly were; for they were such that strangers could not easily find their way out of them, and the method of access to them such as an enemy could with difficulty find out if he proposed to besiege them. A city therefore should have both these sorts of buildings, which may easily be contrived if anyone will so regulate them as the planters do their rows of vines; not that the buildings throughout the city should be detached from each other, only in some parts of it; thus elegance and safety will be equally consulted.[122]

---

[121] Campbell 2000, 93–95, 119–21 (text), and 366–67, 373–75. Laurence, Esmonde Cleary, and Sears 2011, 139.

[122] Aristotle 1913, 221 (1330b).

The design of a city is thus meant to be cultivated in a particular manner, but what shape did Aristotle suggest by comparing it to a row of vines?

Nicholas Cahill's translation of this garden metaphor to the more familiar Roman quincunx offers the best way to understand what Aristotle had envisioned. The quincunx is a series of vertical columns in which each crossing row crossing shifts slightly to fit between the columns, creating a series of parallel-stepped "zigzag" paths. Cahill saw a contemporary application of this idea at the Thessalian town of Goritsa, where the two sections of the northern grid shift orientation from north–south to east–west, creating a number of discontinuities in the street grid.[123] Mostly these disruptions are formed by T-shaped intersections, though there is at least one offset intersection as well. At Pompeii, the quincunx concept is nearly perfectly represented by the route dividing the square blocks along via Stabiana from the orthogonal grid to the east. Thus, vicolo di Cecilio Giocondo shifts eastward as it crosses vicolo delle Nozze d'Argento before taking a wide detour to meet vicolo di Tesmo and its further continuance as vicolo del Citarista south of via dell'Abbondanza. As mentioned, every intersection but two (the orthogonal junctions at via dell'Abbondanza and vicolo del Conciapelle) along this 433-meter line makes a slight eastward shift, accurately representing a vineyard's organization and offering the important physical and visual disruptions suggested by Aristotle.

Even as a defensive argument for the offset intersection type ties the street system in the west more tightly to the creation of the Sarno limestone fortifications and thus the entire street network to its chronology, the absence of these intersections in the east might seem to undermine the unity of the overall plan. In fact, the change in the use of offset intersections in favor of orthogonal intersections falls precisely on the change of insula shape and orientation of the so-called Neustadt. Because it is not credible to imagine that intersection shape can change so dramatically through the vagaries of occupation and inhabitation (requiring both sides to change in the same way), the use of offset or orthogonal intersection types must have been a part of the original design. But if these different street junctions were part of the same design and offset intersections were in fact intended to facilitate the internal defense of the city, it becomes more difficult to understand the reason for adopting orthogonal intersections. If the new fortification walls were contemporary with the entire post-hiatus street network, then why should the internal defense of the eastern half of Pompeii be deemed unnecessary?

Returning to Aristotle, the best answer may in fact be the aesthetic desires of Pompeians to have a beautiful and modern city, a city worth defending. In fact, if

---

[123] Cahill 2002, 15–18.

we reverse the formulation and imagine that contemporary aesthetics were the primary concern of the urban designers, then the internal defense of the city, like the varying shape of insulae due to the sloping ground, becomes the compromise. Indeed, this is the very way Aristotle approached the question, of modern ideals compromised by ancient practicalities. The ideal of beauty is inseparable from even the construction of purely defensive structures. Aristotle says of fortification walls that "it is not only necessary to have walls, but care must be taken that they may be a proper ornament to the city, as well as a defense in time of war; not according to the old methods, but the modern improvements also."[124]

Recently, Ivo van der Graaff has demonstrated that Pompeii's fourth-century fortifications do precisely that. Not only are the fortifications a defense for a properly ornamented city, the design of the walls themselves has a built in chromatic effect: a rusticated lower three courses of yellow Sarno limestone blocks was paired with upper courses in gray tuff to create a two-tone appearance for the walls.[125] Additionally, the image of Minerva became prevalent at the gates and fortifications at the same time that her temple was refurbished, invoking her role as the protectress of cities.[126] Even private houses took on this two-tone civic aesthetic (fig. 2.7).[127] Applying this argument to the offset intersections in the west, it becomes possible to understand them as a conscious attempt to allow parts of the new grid to fit and "feel" better with the older center of the city. Laid beside (rather than on top, as in the fortifications) the rusticated western section of the fourth-century master plan is the modern eastern orthogonal plan, with its rectangular blocks and long, uninterrupted vistas. Like the topography of Pompeii, which decreases in steepness from west to east, permitting the long rectangular blocks, so too does the aesthetic expression flow and flux in the street network from west to east, from archaic and practical to modern and beautiful.

Excavation of the Neustadt

Excavation in the so-called Neustadt, at first blush, would seem to complicate the idea of contemporaneity of east and west in the fourth-century-BCE master plan (fig. 2.5). On average, occupation of the east is demonstratively later and seems to have been driven by a particular burst of construction near the end of the third century BCE, perhaps in response to the Carthaginian presence in Italy.

---

[124] Aristotle 1913, 222 (1331a).

[125] van der Graaff 2013, 74–81.

[126] van der Graaff 2013, 83; van der Graaff and Ellis, 2018.

[127] E.g., the facade of Domus M. Spurius Mesor (VII 3, 29). Contemporary houses using a Sarno limestone ashlar facade are more common. See van der Graaff 2013, 84–85.

Figure 2.7 Limestone and tuff facade, Domus M. Spurius Mesor (VII 2, 29).

There is, on the other hand, good evidence for occupation of the Regions I and II prior to this building boom. For example, the wells found in the area all preceded the construction of the current architectures, suggesting that they served earlier agricultural functions.[128] It is important to note that no agricultural feature was found to precede a street, so these wells are only indirect evidence for the date of the eastern grid. If Nappo's expansion of Fausto Zevi's idea that a kind of "osmosis" through the fortifications links the rectangular blocks inside the city to the external cadastral system is correct, then an early agricultural occupation

---

[128] Nappo 1997, 96, n. 18; Nappo 2007, 348. Fulford et al. (1999, 51) found pits and postholes dating to the "fourth or fourth–third centuries" below the Casa di Amarantus (I 9, 12).

and later architectural development of the same plots of land—a transition not in shape or design but in function from *iugera* to *insula*—fits perfectly with the unified-plan thesis and its delayed occupation.[129]

There are also, however, a handful of houses that date to earlier than 200 BCE: the earliest walls of the Casa di Amarantus (I 9, 11–12)[130] are placed at the end of the fourth century BCE, the Casa della Soffitta (V 3, 4) is dated as early as 250 BCE,[131] as is the Casa della Nave Europa (I 15, 2)[132] in the far southeast, and the Casa di Giulio Polibio (IX 13, 3)[133] in the center of the Neustadt, which is dated slightly later. Near the Porta Stabia, the earliest structures in insula I 5 were constructed immediately following the new limestone fortifications.[134] Most importantly, the excavations below the streets flanking the Casa dei Casti Amanti (IX 12, 6) and in the vicolo di Lucrezio Frontone has found that the first surfaces on these street were laid on sloping paleosol after the first half of the third century BCE. Additionally, the first surface on vicolo del Centenario was founded on filing materials dated to no later than the mid-second century BCE.[135] Again, the evidence offers no contradiction to a complete street network designed and executed at the end of the fourth century.

Compared to the clearer picture of the occupation of the western insulae, the evidence from excavation in the Neustadt remains thin. Still, although on average occupation was earlier in the west than in the east, it was not completely or uniformly so. As we've seen, construction along via Stabiana is as old if not older than that found in the northwest. For example, in insula VI 1 the earliest grid-aligned structures are from the mid-third century BCE,[136] but the vicolo di Narciso has been dated to circa 200 BCE, and the northwest corner of insula V 1 was not built until the second century BCE. Yet these anomalies, for surely they are that, should not trouble our interpretation of the unity of Region VI. Indeed, they demonstrate in the west as well as in the east that the invention of an urban design, its execution, and its occupation are necessarily sequential events but have no other necessary chronological relationships. Execution can lag behind design, and its physical manifestations—likely ephemeral and

[129] Zevi (1982) suggests a date of the second half of the third century BCE for this event. Nappo (1997, 93) extends Zevi's idea for Region VI into Regions I and II.

[130] Fulford et al. 1999, 51–61.

[131] Pucci et al. 2008, 231–32.

[132] Nappo (1997,109) has suggested a date closer to 200 than 250, which its excavator, Aoyagi (1977), claimed.

[133] Casa di Giulio Polibio is dated by coin finds from under the atrium to the last decades of the third century BCE; De Franciscis 1988, 32.

[134] Brun 2008, 63.

[135] Anniboletti (2008b, 6–9) called this surface a sidewalk.

[136] Jones and Robinson 2007, 392.

difficult to recognize archaeologically—are often erased by the area's occupation, which itself might take centuries to realize fully, if ever.

The greatest, and most surprising lag in occupation in Pompeii appears to have been in the southern and western portions of Region I. Insulae I 6 and I 10 were built up for the first time at the very end of the third century BCE, and the neighboring house at I 3, 25 is dated to the third century BCE based on typological grounds.[137] Investigations of insula I 4 and the Casa del Citarista (I 4, 5.25) specifically have shown its earliest occupations to have been in the second half of the second century BCE.[138] The first orthogonal block in Region I (insula I 8), contains the Casa della Statuetta Indiana, which the excavators date to after 150 BCE.[139] Farther east, the buildings in I 9 are equivalent in date or even later still. The Casa del Bell'Impluvio (I 9, 1) was built in the second century BCE, and the current Casa di Amarantus cannot be dated to earlier than the mid-first century.[140] Such late dates are found even as far west as via Stabiana, where the perimeter wall of insula I 1 was not constructed until the last quarter of the first century BCE.

Excavation has found that a quarry was actively extracting the lava bedrock in the north of this block. Wedge cuttings, cracked faces on parallel ridges, and masonry work platforms were all discovered below the courtyard of the final period inn at I 1, 6–9. Exposed bedrock only 24 meters to the north in I 2, 3 shows that quarrying once occurred here as well and was likely in operation about the same time as in I 1, 6–9.[141] Support for this conclusion comes from the existence of a nearly identical masonry platform on the edge of vicolo del Conciapelle that is partially blocking a rut in the bedrock and which was built over by the new northern curbstones of the final street.[142]

Across via Stabiana, there is additional evidence for quarrying. A trench cut in the alley connecting via Stabiana to the Quadriporticus building revealed a deep linear escarpment in the bedrock with obvious quarry fracturing on its vertical face.[143] Farther west, inside the Quadriporticus, the results of a geophysical survey show the same characteristic ridges of bedrock—in places nearly 4

---

[137] On insula I 6, Ling (1997, 7–8) cites Michel (1990, 65, fig. 49) on the Casa dei Cei (I 6, 15). See Miele (1989, 167) on I 3, 25.

[138] Nappo 1998, 27.

[139] Carrillo, Lloris, and Jiménez Salvador 1998, 41–43.

[140] Fulford 1998, 52, 63–65; Fulford et al. (1999, 61) notes that continuity between the early and final house is in doubt.

[141] The outcrop in I 2, 3 has been sampled for comparison to building stones at Pompeii and beyond; Kastenmeier et al. 2010; Seiler et al 2011.

[142] Ellis et al. 2015, 16–17.

[143] Trench 20000, Pompeii Archaeological Research Project: Porta Stabia. I thank S. Ellis for allowing me to report this observation in advance of the project's final publications.

meters below the 79 CE surface—strongly suggesting the area was used for quarrying before the creation of the building.[144] With the Quadriporticus's (and theater's) initial construction dated to the second half of the second century BCE, this new entertainment structure fits neatly with the needs and expectations of a city experiencing both economic and a demographic growth. At the same time, the creation of the Quadriporticus also provides a date for the end of the western quarry and heralds an eastward shift in quarrying activity: stone could be extracted at the site of the Teatrum Tectum until its completion in 78 BCE, while quarrying in I 1, 6–9 continued approximately another half-century.

The long history of quarrying in the south of Pompeii is especially useful in explaining the lag in the occupation of southern and western parts of Region I.[145] In part, the steeply sloping nature of the area was a disincentive to inhabitation, especially when fertile, flatter ground was abundant farther east. Moreover, the land was valuable as a source of raw materials to supply the rapid urbanization of that eastern half of the city. Only when the rest of Pompeii had been given architectural shape did the quarries close. Quarrying in the south of Regions VIII and I also helps to counter the argument that the slow pace of inhabitation is evidence for the orthogonal grid to have been the product of a different design. Instead, the construction of the landscape within that eastern orthogonal grid was the very reason why the southernmost square blocks along via Stabiana (I 1–I 4) lagged in occupation as much as two centuries behind those blocks north of via dell'Abbondanza (IX 1—IX 4).

To summarize, the weight of all the available evidence and the strength of the arguments that tie them together point to the existence of a single master plan for all of Pompeii at the beginning of the fourth century BCE. As Mau articulated a century ago, formal principles connect the arrangement of the streets through shared alignments with the new fortification walls. Such formal analyses are supported by the results of excavation, whether it is providing direct evidence for the chronology of the streets' creation or showing that the lag in occupation between those streets was reasonable (in the east) and necessary (in the south). Moreover, the incongruities of form that once suggested discontinuities in time now can be explained as compromises for both practical (topography, defense) and theoretical (aesthetics) purposes. Indeed, where once scholars sought recourse in the scalpel of chronology to explain these differences in the plan, we now can see such inconsistencies as a realistic balancing act of convergent forces, both cultural and natural, and not the dividing incisions in a landscape filled with separate but equally idealized expressions of urban form. The impact of this

---

[144] Poehler and Ellis 2012, 3–4.

[145] Contrast this with Pesando and Guidobaldi's (2006, 167) suggestion that the extensive terracing in Region VI may have provided source material for the fourth-century-BCE agger.

formulation is to give up the conception of the staccato of grids rapidly appearing in the course of a century in favor of a richer understanding of Pompeii's history as a series of nonlinear and overlapping pulses of occupation within a landscape ordered by a singular design.

Changes to the Master Plan

The complete architectural delineation of Pompeii's landscape into blocks and streets, houses and shops, monuments and gardens, would take generations from the time of the initial design and execution of the master plan. Thus, while occupation was only beginning in some areas, it was intensifying to such a degree in others that changes to the original plan were required. Overall, changes to the street network were piecemeal and rare, with nearly all such changes caused by the construction of new monumental structures. Three conical periods of Pompeii's history—the advent of the Colonia Veneria Cornelia Pompeii, the Augustan floruit, and the post-63 earthquake(s) recovery—would provide Pompeii with its final arrangements of streets and outfit the town with a civic infrastructure appropriate for each era.

Some of the most important changes to Pompeii's new fourth-century urban form occurred in the next century (fig. 2.8) with the dismantling of the Altstadt fortifications and the contemporaneous construction of a major entertainment complex: the Stabian Baths, Samnite Palestra, and the Large Theater with its Quadriporticus, along with the great Altstadt sewer that connected them. In place of the previous fortifications, new houses were built infused with the latest

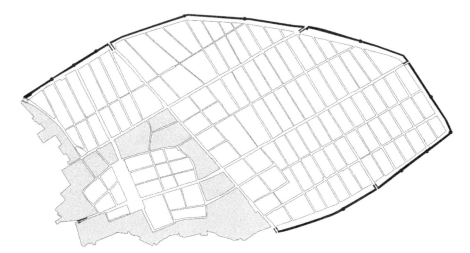

Figure 2.8 Second-century-BCE street network. Areas of change in gray.

Hellenistic styles, and irregular streets were created between them to connect the Altstadt to the new quarters in the north and east. By the mid-second century BCE, the curving course of vicolo Storto had been established, along with vicolo del Panettiere,[146] while insula VII 6 was built up, likely defining vicolo delle Terme at this same time.[147] Near the forum, the boundary routes surrounding the Temple of Apollo (i.e., the "ditches") were filled in, and via Marina was given its current course by the late second century BCE,[148] a reorientation linked to the repositioning of the Porta Marina.

Whatever earlier street network was present in the southeast of Region VIII was overtaken by the creation of the theater and its portico, but there may be some hint of that earlier network in the remaining architectures of passage into the entertainment district. For example, the double corridor from via Stabiana (VIII 7, 19–20), leading both up into the cava and directly to the orchestra, might record the position of a previous street. This street could have connected to vicolo della Regina on one end, though with a bend across the area of the later Triangular Forum, and connected through an offset intersection to via I 2–I 3, a street oriented to Tower VI on the eastern fortification wall. Paolo Carafa reports a "shallow ditch," like those found around the early Temple of Apollo, ran north of the Doric Temple.[149] Similarly, the alley leading to the Quadriporticus's Ionic Propylon from via Stabiana is a good candidate to preserve the alignment of an earlier street, perhaps going back even to the archaic period, leading up to the Doric Temple. The importance of this route can be seen by its monumental-ization within the Quadriporticus, between the Ionic Propylon and the monumental stairs.[150] Alternatively or in addition, a westward extension of the vicolo del Conciapelle might be suggested by the presence of dividing walls that pre-cede the construction of the Quadriporticus, but excavation has found that if this street existed, it was obliterated by later occupation. One passage is known to have existed, however, beyond the southern boundary wall of insula VIII

---

[146] Excavations by Fiel, Pedroni, and Tassar (2005, 256–57) demonstrate that the Domus of N. Popidius Priscus (VII 2, 20) was originally built ca. 190–180 BCE to be oriented to via degli Augustali and only turns to face vicolo del Panettiere ca. 130 BCE. Pedroni and Ribera i Lacomba (2005, 259) report similar dates for the construction and revision of the Casa di Arianna (VII 4, 31.51).

[147] Anderson et al. 2012, 4–5, n. 8; 14, nn. 36–37; Anderson 2015, 76–80. Earlier architecture, typologically dated to the fifth century BCE, could not be confirmed stratigraphically. I concur with Anderson's hypothesis of a mid-third-century date for the earliest architectures as well as its implica-tion for the existence of vicolo del Farmacista by this same period.

[148] The first surface on the current alignment of via Marina was a "hard packed and almost sterile soil, overlying the natural subsoil"; Arthur 1986, 35–37.

[149] Carafa 2011, 92.

[150] Poehler and Ellis 2012, 11.

7. Because of the blockage of the space, first by a wall abutting the Porta Stabia in the Augustan period and then later by sealing the remaining doorway, it is unknown if and for how long this pomerial route leading farther west was open.[151]

Colonia Veneria Cornelia Pompeii

Changes to the street network at the time of the colony were few, but their impact is hard to judge because new buildings obscure the previous routes (fig. 2.9). Still later developments further muddy the water. For example, the southwestern fifth-century pomerial road, if it ever existed in Region VIII, was buried by the addition of a row of houses south of the basilica.[152] The construction of the Basilica and Temple of Venus[153] left vicolo di Championnet as the only route in the extreme southwest of Pompeii.[154] At the forum, the construction of the Popidian colonnade was the first step in a long-term project to regularize the forum and insulate it from vehicular traffic.[155] This tufa colonnade barred carts from the south end of the forum and turned both vicolo di

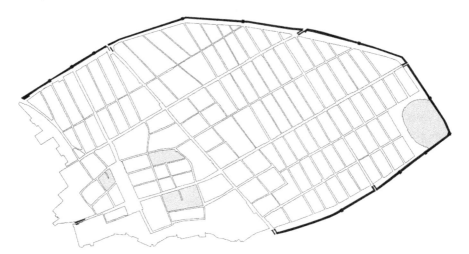

Figure 2.9 Colonial-era street network. Areas of change in gray.

[151] Devore and Ellis (2005, 8–9) believe the doorway blockage is modern.

[152] Zanella 2014.

[153] Curti 2008, 53–56; Carroll 2010.

[154] Ball and Dobbins 2013, 480–82, n. 106, 116–17. On the isolation of this street and a possible southern extension of the vicolo di Basilica, see Poehler 2011b, 157–59; Poehler 2012, 107, n. 65.

[155] Ball and Dobbins 2013, 473–87. Additionally, Cole (2009) conducted a comprehensive study of the architecture of the surrounding buildings.

Championnet and vicolo del Foro into vestigial appendages in the street network, while via delle Scuole became a dead end. East of the forum, vicolo della
Maschera's connection to via degli Augustali was severed by the expansion of
the Casa di L. Cornelius Diadumenus (VII 12, 26).[156] At the opposite end of
Region VIII, the Teatrum Tectum stepped into the space between the theater
and via Stabiana and extended southward into the broad route that connected
the Quadriporticus's Ionic Propylon to via Stabiana. While the route was only
narrowed, by the final period this alley would have mechanisms of closure that
indicate it was not always an open public thoroughfare.[157] The biggest change
the colonists made to the street network at Pompeii probably had the least
effect on circulation in the city. The construction of the amphitheater required
four city blocks to be sacrificed in the very southeast corner of Pompeii, but
the two streets destroyed with them served only those four blocks, and their
removal had no impact on movement anywhere else in the city.[158]

The Augustan Floruit

At the beginning of the Augustan age the changes sweeping the Roman world
left an indelible mark on Pompeii (fig. 2.10). Economic growth fueled transfor-
mations across the urban landscape, from humble garum workshops transform-
ing into the ubiquitous food and drink shops[159] to new monumental buildings
being erected on the latest Roman blueprint.[160] Once again, the forum was the
focal point for the city's new Imperial identity. The Macellum was renovated,
and new constructions—the Sanctuary of Augustus, the Porticus of Eumachia,
and the south buildings—were added to the east and south of the forum.[161] On
the west side of the forum, the Sanctuary of Apollo expanded westward, taking
over the space of the vicolo Storto Nuovo and narrowing its intersection with
vicolo del Gallo.[162] On the opposite side of the city, the Grand Palestra was built
beside the amphitheater, occupying six more blocks of Region II.

---

[156] Newsome 2007, 39.

[157] The insertion of a row of rooms in the final period between the Ionic Propylon and monumental stairway further interrupted this path across the city; Poehler and Ellis 2012, 11.

[158] It is likely that an inner pomerial road also previously existed under the east side of the amphitheater based on the spaces between insula II 5 and the Grand Palestra and the fortification walls.

[159] Ellis 2004, 2011.

[160] Richardson 1978.

[161] Richardson 1978, 191–202; Dobbins 1994; Poehler 2011b.

[162] Dobbins et al. 1998. If the vicolo del Gallo once extended to the forum it was removed at least
by this period.

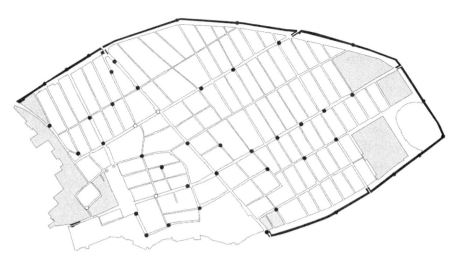

Figure 2.10 Augustan-era street network, with locations of fountains. Areas of change in gray.

The arrival of the *Aqua Augusta* around 20 BCE would have profound effects on life in the city, including its traffic, as the infrastructure for its supply and its removal would be collocated in the space of the street (fig. 2.10).[163] The introduction of these architectures (and the changes they generated) will prove to be very useful in the study of traffic,[164] but in only a handful of cases did they actually change the network of streets. For example, the construction of the *castellum aquae* at the Porta Vesuvio blocked access to the northern inner pomerial street of Region VI.[165] Soon after, the Casa delle Vestali expanded northward to the fortifications and blocked access to this street from the west.[166] The new water source also encouraged a remodeling of the Forum Baths, which expanded to the north and west, occupying the sidewalk on both via and vicolo delle Terme.

Of greater importance to traffic was the provision for drainage that accompanied the new water supply. The presence of this constant flow of hundreds of thousands of liters of water[167] provided some impetus to pave more of the streets in lava stone and to further canalize them between high curbs. The use of stepping stones also dramatically expanded in the Augustan age.[168] Slightly later in

---

[163] *Aqua Augusta*'s arrival can be bracketed confidently between 28 and 10 BCE. Keenan-Jones 2010, 240–44.

[164] Chapter 6, 174–81.

[165] Wearing on the brick pier at the northeast corner of insula VI 15 shows this earlier traffic.

[166] Jones and Robinson 2005.

[167] Keenan-Jones 2010, 255–73, esp. 262, fig. 7.3.

[168] See Chapter 4, 93–94.

this same period, in the first years of the first century CE, a comprehensive drainage system was enacted using dozens of water management mechanisms in the space of the streets. Most of these were designed to have little or no impact on the circulation of pedestrian or wheeled vehicles. In thirteen instances, however, a line of curbstones blocked the access of both wheels and water. Nine of these curbstone blockages occur on via dell'Abbondanza and via di Nocera, and six such blockages are used to completely isolate Region II from the street network, completing its co-option for entertainment purposes.[169] Finally, it is likely that insula II 5 was formed at this time from two separate blocks, but the central position of the southern entrance can be considered only circumstantial evidence of such an arrangement.

On the west side of via dell'Abbondanza at its intersection with via Stabiana, Marcus Holconius Rufus, "military tribune by popular demand, duumvir with judicial power five times, quinquennial twice, priest of Augustus Caesar, and patron of the colony," built a monumental tetrapylon.[170] Beyond providing a prominent visual marker at an important crossroad in the city, the monument also created a wide and elevated pavement in front of the Stabiana baths, within which a long drain (57 m) collected water out of via Stabiana and drew it into the Altstadt sewer. The effect of this elegant and practical monument was at once to prevent the flooding of the lower sections of the city and to sever the connection for vehicles in the street network at what was one of its most important nodes. Changes in Pompeii's final decades will only compound the effect of this closure to vehicles.

Post-earthquake(s) Period

Only the collapse of the archaic city within its fifth-century-BCE walls or its fourth-century rebirth can rival the changes to Pompeii's street network following the earthquake of post-63 CE (fig. 2.11). The destruction of the city was of sufficient magnitude to be recorded in written sources, and its reconstruction left an equally substantial mark on history.[171] As in the Augustan period, it was the forum that now witnessed the greatest transformation. The design for the new monumental Roman forum did, for the first time, entirely disconnect the heart of the city from the street network. On the east side of the forum

---

[169] Currently, vicolo del Anfiteatro is open, but a line of pockmarks on the edge of the paving stones across the full length of the intersection demonstrates that a series of curbstones once, and for a considerable period of time, blocked this street.

[170] CIL 10.830; Cooley and Cooley 2014, 185–86.

[171] Seneca *Quaest. Nat.* 6.1.1–2.

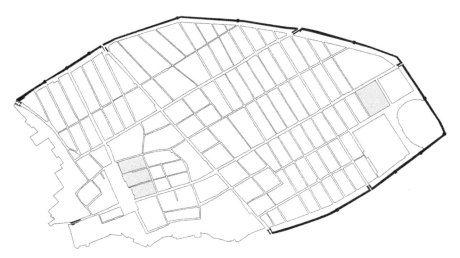

Figure 2.11 Post-63-CE street network. Areas of change in gray.

a continuous and adjusting facade was built to connect the earlier Augustan buildings—the Eumachia building and Sanctuary of Augustus in the south and rebuilt Macellum in the north—to a new and enigmatic structure called the Imperial Cult Building. This unifying construction severed both vicolo del Balcone Pensile and vicolo degli Scheletri from the forum, suddenly shifting the northeast of the Altstadt from being in proximity to the forum to being in its shadow. The construction of the Northwestern Building, including the so-called granary and forum latrine, obliquely sliced through the former vicolo del Granaio. The Northwestern Building, however, had less of an impact because the Augustan expansion of the Apollo Sanctuary had already overtaken the eastern half of vicolo del Gallo, making vicolo del Granaio a dead-end street at the sanctuary's northern boundary. At the bottom of the forum, the reconstruction of the so-called administrative buildings squeezed the vicolo del Foro from either side, while the expansion of the residential properties farther south transformed the street into a private alley.

Even those streets that did still reach the forum, such as via del Foro, via dell'Abbondanza, and via delle Scuole, were blocked off by the slope of the landscape, the placement of a fountain, or large white limestone bollards. Nonetheless, it is clear that there was a temporary route within colonnades to facilitate the final construction and adornment of the new buildings surrounding the forum. The first 10.7 meters of via degli Augustali's pavement east of via del Foro rises up to the level of the curbstones, giving vehicles access to the eastern colonnade from the north. Evidence for these carts leaving the colonnade in the south comes from a diagonal rut found on top of the curbstones beside a short paved ramp at the beginning of via delle Scuole, matched by wearing on the corner of the fountain.[172] That this construction traffic was nearing its end is shown not only by the near completion of the forum buildings[173] but also by the placement of a guard stone, itself unworn, that blocked further wear from accumulating on the fountain (fig. 1.2).

Other changes to the west side of the city would be far more disruptive. For example, the expansion and reconstruction of the western terrace houses removed the pedestrian postern at the end of via delle Terme, reducing the number of the city's western exits to two. The expansion of the Temple of Venus would further undercut access to Pompeii from the west, stepping both into via Marina to the north and the vicolo del Basilica to the east and completing the isolation of vicolo di Championnet. The growth of this sanctuary came at the expense of direct access to the forum for vehicles, forcing all wheeled traffic northward onto vicolo del Gigante then eastward on vicolo dei Soprastanti. Moreover, due to the installation of a later Augustan-era marble fountain at the west end of vicolo del Gallo and the new drainage feature midway along vicolo del Farmacista, drivers entering the Porta Marina had no choice of direction until they reached the north end of the forum. All of these changes to streets along the western edge of Pompeii only emphasized the importance of the Porta Ercolano and may help to explain its radical transformation into a tripartite gate. Wide enough to allow carts to pass one another and with pedestrians also allotted significant sidewalk space, the Porta Ercolano had become by far the largest gate of the city.[174]

In the post-earthquake(s) period the western half of Pompeii became a set of loosely connected closed systems. The entire southwest was transformed into groups of disconnected and dead-end streets. Even when access was possible for vehicles, the number of paths was reduced to no more than two. With the blockage of via dell'Abbondanza at via Stabiana, the only ways into the Altstadt from the east were by taking the via del Tempio d'Iside westward (and turning onto either the vicolo della Regina or via dei Teatri) or by taking via degli Augustali and confronting many of those eastbound vehicles that entered though the Porta Marina.

In the east, only three alterations are known to have occurred, two of little consequence and one with effects that would reverberate across the city. Near the Porta Sarno, one or perhaps two streets were lost to the agglomeration of two sets of neighboring city blocks now formed as insulae II 4 and III 7. Corner

---

[172] There is also an overriding mark on the north curb of via dell'Abbondanza, suggesting some vehicles joined the forum route to reach via delle Scuole. Gesemann (1996, 67) understood the ramp on via degli Augustali as a traffic calming device.

[173] Dobbins 2007, 173.

[174] Chapter 8, 246–47.

curbstones of both of these previous streets can still be seen along the south and north curbs of via dell'Abbondanza, and excavation within the garden of the Praedia of Julia Felix, which occupies the entire conjoined space, has found the former beaten ash street surface.[175] Based on the curbstones, it is likely that insula III 7 was once divided by a street that extended northward from vicolo del Anfiteatro.

Though still unfinished at the time of the eruption, the construction of the Central Baths would have the greatest impact on the street network for vehicles outside of the forum's closure. By taking over the space of vicolo di Tesmo to the east—as well as vicolo IX 3–IX 4 to the south—the Central Baths disconnected via di Nola from via dell'Abbondanza and interrupted an alternative route parallel to the via Stabiana. As will be demonstrated in Chapter 6, this change would force a reversal of traffic across the center and northwest of the city. Still, as important as the narrowing of vicolo di Tesmo was in Pompeii's final decades, the transformation of the street surfaces (Chapter 3) and their architectures (Chapter 4) over the preceding four centuries will provide both a reason for traffic systems' institution and the structure upon which the evidence for those systems would be inscribed (Chapter 5).

---

[175] Parslow 1998, 202–6. The wide drainage channels Parslow reports are very likely the broad, shallow ruts commonly found in battuti.

3

Surfaces of the Street

A fine-grained, salt-and-pepper grit fills the low areas of the Pompeian streets. It is washed by rainwater and blown by the wind into the ruts and small depressions along the streets. Today it gathers in especially great quantity inside several of the city gates.[176] These accumulations are a by-product of Pompeii's extinction, having neither a functioning drainage system nor inhabitants to carry away such debris. Indeed, until recently the great Altstadt sewer, leading at least 220 meters across the city, was choked closed near its origin with this grit.[177] The source of the grit, however, is common to both modern and ancient Pompeii. It is the natural erosion of the city, the millimeter-by-millimeter weathering of lava stones and wall plasters, limestones and tuffs, and the mortars that bind them. It is the death of a city by far more than a thousand cuts.

Grit has always been here. The erosion of Pompeii is a phenomenon that can be observed even on the most ancient streets known: waterborne grit was found filling a small rut worn into a fourth-century-BCE beaten ash street near the Porta Stabia. Its creation and accumulation at the same locations in both the ancient and modern city puts emphasis on the unchangeable urban realities of Pompeii. To combat this universal problem of flooding and the silting up of the bottom of the city, the Soprintendenza archeologica di Pompei commissioned a project in 2009 to redirect rainwater from its main collection point on the lower via Stabiana into the defunct aqueduct built by Domenico Fontana between 1594 and 1600.[178] Nearly two thousand years earlier, the Pompeians had instituted a far more complex city-wide drainage system that relied on the streets having being made into great box-like channels with solid stone surfaces to carry debris and wastewater outside the city. Grit, it seems, might be a kind of bellwether for the

---

[176] The material is found especially at the Porta Stabia but also at the Nola and Sarno gates, as well as in the low area at the intersection of vicolo del Gigante and vicolo dei Soprastanti.

[177] It appears, however, that when Cozzi and Sogliano (1900) investigated the sewer, it had not yet filled with waterborne debris.

[178] Rispoli and Paone 2011, 126.

health of the city, a measure of both the abrasion of its skin and the clogging of its arteries. The form of the street, therefore, might also be considered a measure of the Pompeians' *interest* in the city's health. Constructing street surfaces appropriate (or not) to the age was of course also a social phenomenon, and to extend the bodily metaphor, we cannot discount the role of vanity in producing good health. Solid streets were as much a product of political calculation as practical consideration. The subject of this chapter is thus not only the evolution of these surfaces and the architectures of the streets that accompany them but also the social forces that drove their adoption and their replacement.

Beaten Ash Surfaces

The streets of Pompeii, despite the fame of their ruts and the pavement they are worn into, were never fully paved in stone (fig. 3.1). Like the street network itself, Pompeii's street surfaces appear as a kind of patchwork of different choices in different regions. In 79 CE, paving in stone covered 78% of the excavated city. Extrapolating what is known into the uninvestigated regions, this falls to only 61%.[179] All the other streets, with only three known exceptions, have a beaten ash rather than a silex surface. Although the beaten ash surface (also called *battuto*,

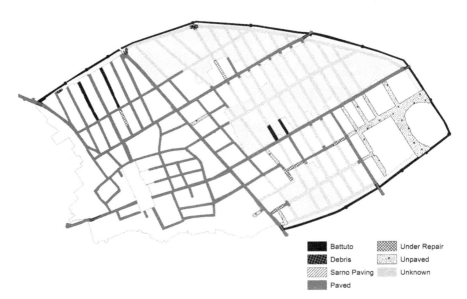

■ Battuto		▨ Under Repair	
▨ Debris		▨ Unpaved	
▨ Sarno Paving		Unknown	
■ Paved			

Figure 3.1 Street surfaces at Pompeii.

[179] Excavated area: 78% paved, 12% unpaved, 10% excluded. Total area: 61% paved, 31% unpaved, 8% excluded.

the common Italian term)[180] was the predominant if not the only style of street paving in Pompeii prior to the first century BCE, those battuti extant in 79 CE are contemporaneous with the lava stone pavements. That is, they are not obsolete artifacts of an earlier age; rather, these street surfaces were actively used, maintained, and replaced until the last days of Pompeii. The only exceptions to this final network of silex and battuti are found in the ruts worn into the exposed bedrock on vicolo del Conciapelle, the unique surface of small Sarno limestones, cruma, lava, and mortar on the vicolo di Lucrezio Frontone, and the debris streets found inside the city's northern perimeter.

The construction of beaten ash streets remained almost entirely unchanged for the nearly half a millennium between the first and final examples known at Pompeii. Continuous sequences of leveling, paving, use, repair, and finally replacement that repeats the sequence are known from excavations in the northwest (vicolo del Fauno and vicolo della Fullonica), north center (vicolo di Lucrezio Frontone), and center (vicolo IX 11–IX 12 and vicolo IX 12–IX 13) of Pompeii, while individual surfaces have been found at the Porta Stabia and Porta Vesuvio and beyond. Despite being created of ash rather than stone, the battuto is an exceptionally hard layer constructed of fine compactible materials. At Pompeii, this means the matrix is nearly always made of the gray or brownish yellow prehistoric ash deposits, though lenses of harder chipped stone (Sarno limestone and lava) are known as well.[181] The result is a smooth, sandy, and durable street surface.[182]

With the exception of the unrecognized street excavated north of via degli Augustali that likely dates to the fifth century, the earliest known street surfaces in Pompeii date to only the fourth century. Excavations on both sides of via Stabiana at the Porta Stabia have revealed several sections of what may have been an exceptionally wide street surface dating to this period. The surface, built upon a leveling fill directly over the paleosol, is described as a "mottled, hard-packed earthen surface with visible lapilli inclusions."[183] Its color is the same yellowish brown to gray of the Mercato ash below it, perhaps with a slight pinkish tint as well, indicating that this deposit was a primary ingredient in its construction.[184]

[180] I am grateful to Mark Robinson for his comments on this chapter and for reminding that these are beaten ash rather than beaten earth surfaces, a fact that improved their durability.

[181] On the geologic and prehistoric sequences at Pompeii, see Robinson 2011.

[182] Devore and Ellis 2005, 7.

[183] This surface was also found farther north; Ellis et al. 2011, 11, fig. 22.

[184] Ellis et al. 2011, 12, n. 27; 2012, 8, fig. 12. This surface was derived from the local volcanic soil and was later cut by a pappamonte structure dating it to "somewhere in the fourth century BCE." A similar "brownish-yellow" description comes from the vicolo del Fauno excavations (Sorriento 2008, 4), where the first battuto was built directly on top of the Mercato ash (Befani 2008, 3).

Above one section of this street near the Porta Stabia, within what appears to be a wheel rut, a thin layer of the waterborne grit that introduced this chapter was recovered, suggesting how the surface may have appeared when in use.[185]

Water was a perennial concern for the Pompeian road builders. While the final streets paved in silex were given a distinct camber intended to shed water toward the high curbs that border the street, battuti are found with a pronounced inward curve along their edges, pushing water away from the boundaries.[186] The function to keep water in the street, however, is equally reflected in both styles of paving. The best example of these different forms comes from via del Vesuvio (fig. 3.2).[187] Here the full sequence of the final canalized street, the bedding layers

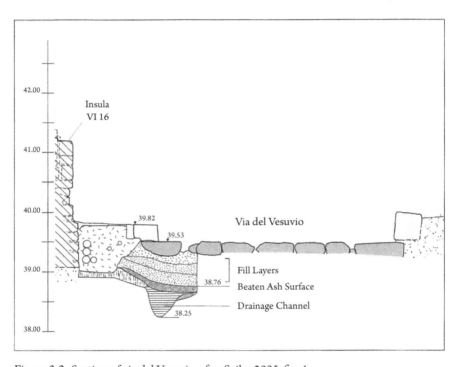

Figure 3.2 Section of via del Vesuvio, after Seiler 2005, fig. 4.

[185] Ellis et al. 2011, 11; 2012, 14, fig. 21.

[186] Examples include US 3.1–3.3 (the battuto and preparation) on vicolo di Lucrezio Frontone (Sakai and Iorio 2008, 403–4, fig. 7); US 26, 35, 41 on vicolo della Fullonica (Anniboletti et al. 2007, 6, fig. 6); US 7 on vicolo del Fauno is sloped on its western side, but the eastern edge is set by an early (ca. 150 BCE) line of curbstones (Befani 2008, 8, fig. 8); US 16 in vicolo IX 11–IX 12 (Berg 2008, 371–72, figs. 10–11).

[187] Other examples include US 26, 35, and 41 in vicolo della Fullonica (Anniboletti et al. 2007, 6, fig. 6); US 16 in vicolo IX 11–IX 12 (Berg 2008, 371–74); US 3.1 in vicolo di M. L. Frontone (Sakai and Iorio 2008, 404, fig. 7).

for it, and the slope of the beaten ash street farther below can be seen in section. The downward slope of the battuto began at least 70 centimeters west of the final curb, making the street significantly wider, but the change in elevation it produced, approximately 40 centimeters, was the same. Such a significant shift in elevation also argues against the idea that the slope is due to the erosion of the street, as the original battuto would have needed to have been exceptionally thick, the duration of its use exceptionally long, and the forms of its erosion (especially rutting) spread uncommonly evenly.

The earliest street surface yet found on via del Vesuvio, below the sloping battuto just described, however, was constructed with the opposite set of principles. Rather than keeping water within the street, a channel was cut into the natural soil beside the street into which water was directed. Though only a small section of this earliest street surface was recovered, it clearly slopes into the channel. Following the water in this channel downhill and imagining its accumulation by the time it reached the opposite end of this street returns us to the Porta Stabia and the curiously wide street (14–15 meters) suggested to have existed there in the fourth century BCE. Indeed, if these surfaces just inside the gate were part of a single pavement, they would have formed a large paved forecourt. Alternatively, due to the absence of any drainage mechanisms, such as those found below via del Vesuvio, and the obvious need for such a conduit, one might equally interpret the surfaces at the Porta Stabia as two distinct streets built on either side of what was then a seasonal stream.[188] Indeed, the natural topography here was undoubtedly shaped by just such a stream.

The need to serve the city's drainage as well as its transportation needs certainly impacted the life and the life span of these beaten ash streets. Although wheel ruts have been found in one of the earliest surfaces, the recovery of deep furrows in the battuti cut by vehicles is surprisingly infrequent, and distinct ruts are reported in only a handful of cases.[189] More general wear from carts—broad and shallow erosion on either side of a slightly higher center of the surface—is more common. The street between insulae 11 and 12 of Region IX provides the clearest example of a well-rutted battuto from Pompeii. Four long and distinct yet imperfectly linear ruts can be seen worn deeply into the street's homogenous surface, the material from which dates it to the late Republican through the Imperial period.[190] These ruts speak to the volume of traffic that once used

[188] Ellis et al. 2011, 16.

[189] Ruts are described on vicolo delle Nozze d'Argento (Nilsson 2014.), on vicolo del Fauno (US 22; Sorriento 2008, 3), and two other possible ruts (US 7, 27; Befani 2008, 4, 9); Maiuri (1929, 185, table VI) reported a curving rut pair in the oldest battuto at the Porta Vesuvio and another pair outside the northern city wall (1944, 277).

[190] Berg 2008, 371–74, figs. 9–11.

this street surface, as does its late origin and its potentially long life. By the final period, although recently resurfaced, the street had fallen out of use, with refuse (amphorae fragments and animal bones especially) covering the street without trace of rutting.[191] In other cases, deep ruts in beaten ash streets were repaired by filling the voids with compacted waste materials.[192] On vicolo delle Nozze d'Argento, the street surface below the final pavement had ruts as deep as 24 centimeters filled with soil and sand, stone, mortar, wall plaster (in the First Style), ceramics, as well as some functional items including iron nails, bronze coins, and fragments of a bone pin.[193]

Rutted or not, when battuti were no longer serviceable they were replaced. Their life span, however, could vary greatly depending on the intensity of use and the amount of water they were required to carry. As we have seen, the deeply rutted vicolo IX 11–IX 12 was in use for a hundred years or more depending on when it was first paved. Below this street surface there is only one other, which can be securely dated to the end of the third century BCE.[194] The earlier street therefore would have existed for a century or more as well. Similarly, there are surfaces found in two excavations beneath the vicolo del Fauno that appear to have existed, with repairs, for as long as 150 years.[195] On the other hand, some streets were regularly repaired and replaced. The remarkable sequence of beaten earth streets found on vicolo della Fullonica shows a long succession of twelve pavements going back to the first street surface created in the third century BCE.[196] Simply dividing these surfaces over the possible years of vicolo della Fullonica's existence gives a 31.5-year average life span. Closer examination of the sequence, however, shows a greater intensity of replacement in the third century BCE (four surfaces, 25-year average), when the grid in this area was first laid out and occupied,[197] but only three surfaces built in the final 129 years (43-year average), during which time the street had become significantly isolated in the street network.[198]

However long the life of their surfaces was, one event seems to have been common to all streets with beaten ash surfaces: by the time they were replaced

[191] Berg 2008, 363, 369.

[192] A rut on vicolo del Fauno (US 10) was intentionally filled (US 11) with debris, including some black gloss pottery and an unidentifiable bronze coin; Befani 2008, 9.

[193] Nilsson 2014.

[194] Berg 2008, 371.

[195] These are US 7 (Befani 2008, 8–9) and US 41 (Sorriento 2008, 3–4).

[196] Anniboletti et al. 2007, 5–7. In a second trench Befani (2008) found an equivalent sequence of ten battuti.

[197] Befani 2008, 6, nn. 45–46.

[198] The street was not necessarily a dead end, but the northern pomerial street was no longer connected to either the Porta Ercolano or Porta Vesuvio by the Augustan period.

by lava stone paving, they had been significantly narrowed. In fact, despite the excavation of more than a dozen streets with battuti, we still have little information about the original boundaries of these streets or, in many cases, even their fullest extent.[199] Thus, the excavation of three streets in Region VI has found that not only were the early street surfaces wider than the later curbs but those surfaces were cut by the construction of the current building facades, making at least some of the early streets wider than even the current delineation of the insula.[200] These findings are confirmed in the investigations in the north center of the city (along insulae IX 3 and IX 8) as well as at the Porta Stabia.[201] These widest and earliest streets date to the end of the fourth to the third century BCE, and it is not until the second century BCE (at the earliest) that the first curbstones are laid to create an elevated sidewalk, often in conjunction with the construction or renovation of the buildings along the frontage. For example, the first curb of Sarno limestone at the far north of vicolo del Fauno was added to the east side of the street in the second century BCE and included a small drain cut through it (fig. 3.3).[202] Farther south on vicolo del Fauno, the first curb was built at the same time, also on the east side of the street, in conjunction with the creation of a new surface. The western curb, however, was not added until the Imperial period.[203] On vicolo di Narciso the curbs were built in two phases, the later phase dating to the mid-first century BCE, which preceded the pavement in silex by only a few decades.[204] In Region VII, the first curb on via degli Augustali doesn't appear until the second half of the second century BCE.[205]

These excavations paint a fascinating picture of Pompeii's changing streetscape and broader urban development, at least as seen through the lens of the north and west of the city. At the end of the fourth century BCE, when the final urban grid is conceived and executed, relatively wide streets—at least 4 meters—divided city blocks not yet densely occupied. As the insulae were built up and filled in over the next century, street surfaces were regularly repaired and replaced. Sometime after 200 BCE, likely in the second half of the second century, the first experiments with elevated sidewalks were conducted

[199] In only one example is the edge of the road said to have been found, and this is itself a narrowing of a still older, still wider street; Ellis et al. 2012, 19.

[200] Another battuto dating to the third century BCE was found under the sidewalk of Casa del Granduca Michele (VI 5, 5), the construction of which cut vicolo della Fullonica; Pesando et al. 2006, 50; 2007, 111; Sorriento 2008, 3.

[201] IX 3, Castrén et al. (2008, 333–34) call the surface a sidewalk; IX 6; Anniboletti 2008a, 215–18; Porta Stabia, Ellis et al. 2011, 11–2, n. 27, fig. 22; Ellis et al. 2012, 8, fig. 12.

[202] Sorriento 2008, 3.

[203] Befani 2008, 8.

[204] Jones and Schoonhoven 2003, 129–130.

[205] Ribera i Lacomba et al. 2009, 95.

Figure 3.3 Beaten ash surface on vicolo del Fauno, from Befani 2008, fig. 8.

by individual property owners.[206] It is clear that issues of drainage were part of these sidewalk installations, as demonstrated by the drains cut through them, but the renovations and expansions of associated buildings also highlights their role in the aggrandizement of these new properties. From this point forward, creation, elaboration, and modification of sidewalks and curbs became part of the urban architect's toolkit to signal the social standing of a given building.[207] Whether the reason was practical or ornamental, the ad hoc installation of the first sidewalks and the raised curbs that supported them shows that their creation was not originally a project or mandate of the town government. Their effect, however, was to squeeze the space of the street between the bulging facades and the burgeoning sidewalks, creating by the late first century BCE the network of narrow and canalized streets known in 79 CE. What remained to be done to give most Pompeian streets their final form was the creation of a more durable and impermeable surface for the circulation of traffic and the flow of wastewater.

---

[206] The city was also installing curbs at this time: the Porta Stabia's sidewalk was built in the second century BCE; Ellis and Devore 2006, 12–14; Devore and Ellis 2008, 14.

[207] Hartnett 2011. The patchwork of sidewalks on vicolo del Fauno and vicolo della Fullonica shows a clear association with particular properties.

Cobbled Surfaces

Only one other variety of early street surface has been discovered at Pompeii, a kind of transitional form, which might have been an early attempt to create such a solid surface. It appears, however, to have been a short-lived adaptation inside Pompeii, as its discoveries have been largely isolated to the third century BCE and to edges of the city. The descriptions of these discoveries are remarkably similar. Recent excavations within the Porta Vesuvio have recovered a "marine pebble" surface "covered by a layer of clay,"[208] while at the Porta Stabia "granite pebbles were embedded into a thin layer of clay to form this surface."[209] Both surfaces were associated with the construction of the gates, ca. 300 BCE. Another surface, sandwiched between fourth- and second-century-BCE layers, was recovered 14 meters north of the Porta Stabia and described as a "flat, hard-packed earthen surface that was sealed by tightly arranged rounded river (cobble) stones of about 7 cm in width" (fig. 3.4).[210] Likewise, investigations below the road outside

Figure 3.4 Cobblestone street surface near Porta Stabia, from Ellis et al. 2012, fig. 12.

[208] Seiler et al. 2005, 232. Maiuri (1929, 185–86) had also found this surface at Porta Vesuvio, dating it to the mid-third century BCE.

[209] Devore and Ellis 2008, 12.

[210] Ellis et. al., 2012, 9, fig. 12.

the Porta Nocera found a "surface of river pebbles and well-beaten earth," created in the third century BCE and preserving two sets of ruts.[211] The only example of a pebble street created later than the third century BCE comes from these
same excavations as a first-century-BCE replacement of the original pebble surface using larger cobblestones. The use of small, rounded stones is exceptionally
rare in later constructions of any type at Pompeii. In fact, the only large-scale use
of those stones extant in 79 CE comes from two sidewalk pavements across via
Marina from the basilica and against the northern side of the Temple of Fortuna
Augusta. Cobbles are known from a few other contexts: a pile of washed stones
was awaiting use in the Casa di Giulio Polibio,[212] a large deposit of cobbles near
the Porta Ercolano was buried beneath the final sidewalk,[213] and another was
found in the debris pile near the so-called Capua gate.[214]

The wide distribution of cobblestones and cobblestone street surfaces
around the city—they have been found in some form near every city gate
except the easternmost—has reasonably convinced some scholars that these
are the remnants of a city-wide project to pave the entire city in late third century BCE.[215] Away from the gates, however, only one section of pebble pavement
has been found in an unpublished excavation on via del Vesuvio.[216] Although
his trench was on the opposite side of via del Vesuvio, Seiler did not report
finding evidence of such a surface 40 meters closer to the gate. Despite the
number of excavations over the past two decades, the evidence for the pebble
streets remains isolated at the gates. Therefore, it no longer seems justifiable to
reconstruct a city-wide project to pave Pompeii, or even the main streets, in
cobbles. Perhaps it is best to understand these unique road surfaces and their
limited distribution and chronology as a component of the new fortification
walls.[217] In this scenario, the (re)construction of the gates was accompanied by
the provision of a new, durable, and aesthetically pleasing surface to support
the traffic they were envisioned to carry. That these pebble streets did not continue extensively into the city might have been due simply to the boundaries of
the fortification project and to the reluctance of the city or property owners to
adopt the new paving technology.

---

[211] Nappo 1997, 95.

[212] Anderson 2011, 80.

[213] Personal communication, M. Anderson 2017.

[214] Etani 2010, 61. Robinson (2011, 24) reports "large beach pebbles" were used as an Iron Age
floor in insula of the Postumii. See also Dickmann and Pirson 2002a, 287, fig. 47.

[215] Nappo 1997, 96.

[216] Nappo (1997, 96) claims this pebble surface is approximately 30 meters south of where
Maiuri found his pebble surface, but if the address he gives is correct, it is more than 100 meters to
the south.

[217] See "On pebble streets at Fragellae," Crawford, Keppie, and Vercnocke 1985, 78, plate IVb.

Lava Stone Surfaces

Such reluctance was perfectly reasonable: in the third century BCE the beaten ash streets had worked perfectly well for generations and continued to be used for generations more. In fact, there is precious little evidence that Pompeii's famous rutted stone streets existed prior to the second half of the first century BCE.[218] Most stratigraphic examinations have found the polygonal lava pavements belong to the Augustan period or later. For example, excavations by the Pompeii Forum Project in the vicolo Storto Nuovo showed that the expansion of the Sanctuary of Apollo occurred around 10 BCE and that the basalt pavement that expansion cut through was only slightly older, if at all.[219] An equivalent date, ca. 20 BCE, has been suggested for vicolo di Narciso's pavement.[220] The bedding layers for the vicolo del Centenario[221] and for the street outside the Porta Nocera date to the Imperial era, with the later suggested even to be a post-earthquake(s) fill.[222] Finally, a section of pavement on vicolo dei Soprastanti can be dated to the reign of Claudius or later by numismatic evidence.[223]

Only the excavations below via del Vesuvio / via Stabiana show any direct evidence of having been paved in silex earlier than the Augustan era. In two places this evidence is the rare burial of an earlier lava stone surface and its replacement by a new street above it.[224] Maiuri's investigations at the Porta Vesuvio found several street levels, but two polygonal stone pavements were the last in this sequence and separated by nearly half a meter.[225] Although Maiuri offered only a generic Roman date for these surfaces, the association of the Augustan construction of the *castellum aquae* and the destruction of the western bastion of the gate with the associated paving should push the earlier pavement further back in the first if not into the second century BCE.[226] That same sequence was found again at the intersection of via Stabiana and vicolo del Menandro in excavations

---

[218] According to Livy (41.27.5), the first road at Rome was not paved until 174 BCE.

[219] Dobbins et al. 1998, 744–47.

[220] Jones and Schoonhoven 2003, 133–34; Jones and Robinson 2005, 699.

[221] The paving (or possibly repaving) in silex appears to have dramatically altered the subsurface in this sidewalk; Anniboletti et al. 2007, 6–9.

[222] Nappo 1997, 95.

[223] Tuccinardi and Ruffo 1987, 135–38.

[224] Such burial is rare. Most often the old pavement was stripped away and replaced with the fresh paving stones, set flush with the adjacent pavements. The excavation of via di Castricio ongoing at the time of the eruption attests to this practice, as do the dozens of repavings shown by the different depths of ruts on a single stretch of street at the same elevation.

[225] Maiuri 1929, 186–87.

[226] Maiuri 1929, 188; Seiler et al. 2005, 224, n. 18.

below the southern set of stepping stones.[227] At 80 centimeters below the final pavement, another substantial lava pavement was discovered, but without ruts. No evidence for the date of its creation or destruction was offered in the brief mention of the discovery.

The existence of an earlier silex surface on via Stabiana at the Porta Stabia also can be inferred from the presence of four stepping stones embedded within and now flush with the final pavement. Additionally, the water management mechanism here (a raised area of paving to push water across via Stabiana and into the western sewer through the gate) that surrounded these stepping stones can be dated by association with the drainage system it serves to the Augustan period or later.[228] Excavations below the sidewalk abutting the water mechanism further support this chronology: final alterations to both the street and the sidewalk can be placed in the late first century BCE or early first century CE by coin finds. The last sidewalk replaced an earlier surface and put out of use a stone paved ramp that connected to a street surface lower than the current via Stabiana's pavement. The creation of the earlier sidewalk, ramp, and associated architecture was dated, also by numismatic evidence, to the early to mid-first century BCE.[229] Together these facts strongly suggest the existence of an earlier street also paved in stone.

The weight of the available archaeological evidence therefore suggests that if polygonal stone paving existed at Pompeii prior to the last decades of the first century BCE, it was used only on the largest and most important streets (e.g., via Stabiana) and likely does not go back much further than the beginning of the Colonial era.[230] What is clear, however, is that in the two generations after its first application, Pompeians rushed to cover much of the city in the polygonal style of paving. By the end of the Augustan era much of the western half of the city had already been paved, while most of the streets east of via Stabiana retained their beaten ash surfaces. The exceptions—especially via dell'Abbondanza, via di Nola, via di Nocera, vicolo del Conciapelle / via della Palestra, vicolo del Menandro / via di Castricio—show that the east–west routes across the city were of particular importance to those deciding which streets were to be paved in stone. Moreover, this irregular but patterned use of silex in the eastern half of the city in 79 CE might well reflect the situation a century earlier throughout the entire city and reveal how the transformation of the west transpired. That is, in the west the paving of the largest streets and those most important east–west

---

[227] Rispoli and Paone 2011, 132–33. I thank Dottore Catello Imperatore for sharing the early results of this excavation.

[228] Poehler 2012, 115–16.

[229] Ellis et al. 2012, 16–17.

[230] The enigmatic "Road Makers Tablet" also suggests a pre-Colonial paving of at least part of via Stabiana. See Campedelli 2014, 148–9.

routes occurred first, with the smaller side streets filled in later and in a more
ad hoc fashion. In Region VI, for example, events fell exactly in this order: via
delle Terme and via della Fortuna were fitted with silex first, followed by via
Consolare, then by vicolo di Mercurio, and finally the smaller streets were paved
from the south to the north, leaving two northern segments of vicolo della
Fullonica and vicolo del Fauno still with beaten ash surfaces.

Giving an absolute date to the installation of silex is difficult not only for
the effort required to lift the massive stones and excavate under them but also
because—unlike the beaten ash surfaces—no artifacts can be found within the
surface itself.[231] We therefore have only a few surfaces dated by the construction
fills supporting them. On the other hand, the final stone pavements show something of their relative chronologies by their abutments, rutting, and repairs.[232]
For this reason, by working backwards through the paving sequence—that is,
from those streets not yet paved in stone to those currently under construction
to those recently repaired to those deeply rutted—it is possible to further trace
the evolution of and the logic behind Pompeii's final patchwork of silex streets.
For example, half of the southern section of vicolo del Fauno was in the process
of being paved and because vicolo del Labirinto, the next street to the east, had
only recently received its lava stone surface, it seems likely that vicolo del Fauno
would have been paved all the way to the fortification wall had the work not
been interrupted.[233] One reason why battuti persisted so long on these streets
is because at the far north of the city, relatively little through traffic or wastewater would be expected. Moreover, these two streets, vicolo della Fullonica and
vicolo del Fauno, also can be characterized as "back streets," as nearly all the
properties along their length open onto another street. These circumstances
reflect the lack of pressure, by need or by desire, to replace the battuti, which for
nearly four centuries had worked perfectly well.

In the east, many of the streets that retain beaten ash surfaces similarly lack
the pressures that might incentivize the investment in a more durable surface.
As one moves south and east across the city, the density of land use decreases,
as does the number of street sections that are paved in stone. In fact, the south-
eastern region (II) of the city is entirely without stone paving. Instead, every
street intersection was blocked to cart traffic (though it had once clearly flowed
through this area) and then filled in to the level of the sidewalks. The whole area
was thus given over to foot traffic. The decision was perhaps appropriate given
the presence of both the amphitheater and the Grand Palestra and because every

[231] On dating road surfaces on shoe nails typologies, see Rodríguez Morales 2014.
[232] Poehler and Crowther 2018, 583–86.
[233] Additionally, the sequence of battuti discovered on the northern section of vicolo del Fauno
makes it likely that these were the first stone surfaces on either of these streets.

private property faces a garden space onto the streets in this area. Again, the pressures to provide infrastructure for drainage and transport here were minimal, and the form of the streets reflect that absence. Only two other elevated unpaved streets are known at Pompeii: the southern pomerial street[234] and the segment immediately to the south of the Central Baths, which was narrowed by the bath's construction.[235] The Central Baths also truncated the street on its east side, vicolo di Tesmo, a street with far more importance to the circulation of traffic. Vicolo di Tesmo, however, was not buried like its southern counterpart. Instead, its lava stone surface remained in use as a conduit for wastewater, receiving runoff from north of via di Nola and carrying it as far as via dell'Abbondanza and then to the entrance to the great Altstadt sewer at the intersection with via Stabiana.

To the north and south of via di Nola, the unexcavated portions of the city prevent us from knowing fully the condition of the streets in these areas. There is evidence, however, to be found along the main thoroughfares and in the analogous situation of the excavated insulae of Region I that indicate much of the area remained without silex. That same evidence also suggests that it might have been paved soon. First, the excavated sections of every major east–west street were paved in stone, and several had already had sections repaired or replaced.[236] Those streets that continued into the unexcavated area—via dell Nozze d'Argento, via Mediana, vicolo del Conciapelle, and via della Palestra— almost certainly were paved in stone for their entire length. Deep rutting on both vicolo delle Nozze d'Argento and via Mediana suggests the importance for the circulation of traffic for both of these streets. Similarly, vicolo del Conciapelle was used frequently enough to require repaving at the time of the eruption, an event that matches the fresh pavement at the opposite end of this same street, called via della Palestra where it meets via di Nocera. Still, one cannot exclude the possibility of a beaten earth surface between the segments of lava stone pavement.[237]

Similarly, for nearly all the north–south running streets in the eastern half of the city, the presence of either silex or battuti must be inferred. One potential

---

[234] Like the northern pomerial street, this street was inaccessible to carts at its connected gates (Porta Stabia and Porta Nocera) but likely still served as a means for carts to circumnavigate the southernmost insulae.

[235] Although the general area (IX 4 and IX 6) was bombed in 1943 (García y García 2006, 153–58), the curbstones at the intersection with via Stabiana show wearing from passing carts, indicating the antiquity of the blockage.

[236] These are, from north to south, vicolo delle Nozze d'Argento, via di Nola, via Mediana, vicolo di Balbo, via dell'Abbondanza, vicolo del Menandro (recently repaved), via di Castricio (in partial repavement), and vicolo del Conciapelle (in repavement).

[237] Such is the case outside the city; Maiuri 1944, 277.

indicator of their condition is the fact that of the twenty-six street segments leading off of via di Nola and via dell'Abbondanza into the unexcavated areas, fourteen are known to have been given a polygonal, lava stone pavement at least for the first 2 to 3 meters of their length. In the great majority of cases (ten), the extent of the excavation has revealed only this much of the street. Yet there are at least three reasons to imagine that the polygonal pavement extended much farther. First, one street, vicolo dei Gladiatori, was excavated more fully to reveal a complete and well-worn silex pavement up to 65 meters from its intersection with via di Nola. Second, another street, the northern extension of vicolo del Centenario, is also heavily rutted suggesting that it too possessed a complete solid surface. Third, since all the streets leading southward from di Nola and several of the westernmost streets leading north from via dell'Abbondanza appear to begin with lava pavement, it might seem reasonable to reconstruct stone paving between at least these streets.

There is equally good reason to reject the reconstruction of an expansive use of stone pavement in the east. In the first place, at the remaining three examples of streets with short segments of stone pavement, excavation farther down these streets has shown that this pavement did not extend beyond the width of the sidewalk, stopping in each case at the edge of the insula. Moreover, in one of these examples, vicolo IX 9–IX 10, the short stone section was clearly part of the same paving event as that of via di Nola. In fact, the next three street sections to the east (though the rest of the street remains unexcavated) also bond with the pavement on via di Nola. The contemporaneity of these pavements indicates that the short southward section was not the beginning of a construction project on that smaller street but rather the end of one on the larger street it intersected. Since the lava stone pavings on the next three southern streets to the east also bond with via di Nola, the hypothesis that the pavement extended as far as via dell'Abbondanza is called into question. In at least two cases, that notion can be rejected outright. Excavations on the streets bordering the insula of the Casa dei Casti Amanti (IX 12) showed that not only were these never given a stone pavement but also the western street (between insulae 11 and 12) was abandoned in the street network by 79 CE.[238] Despite (or perhaps because of) this condition, the intersection with via dell'Abbondanza was given a unique water management mechanism (a paved ramp with drain) the width of the sidewalk.[239] Similarly, even though vicolo IX 12–IX 13 was given a short section of silex, a partial blockage to prevent cart entry was inserted at its southern end. From these observations, it is clear that the short sections of lava stone paving cannot

[238] Berg 2008; Varone 2008.
[239] Poehler 2012, 102.

be used as evidence of the existence of polygonal pavement beyond their own extents.

South of via dell'Abbondanza the streets are nearly all excavated (if not all equally exposed) and offer a potential model to understand the unexcavated streets farther north. The irregular use of silex between these insulae speaks to two overlapping trends, one general and one specific. The general trend is that the eastward expansion of the use of silex was still underway at the time of the eruption. Major streets in the east were already paved and heavily used, but only two of the lesser north–south streets in Region I had a lava stone surface in 79 CE: vicolo del Citarista and vicolo I 8–I 9. A project to repair via di Castricio also clearly extended to the south onto the unexcavated passage between insulae I 17 and I 18, yet as we have seen, the new stone surface might have been planned only to extend as far as the insula facades. Indeed, farther to the east, a section of via di Castricio was resurfaced, including an extension of paving north onto vicolo della Nave Europa and another on vicolo dei Fuggiaschi. Still, uneven as they are, these pavements and repairs show a clear eastward movement of the adoption of silex. The absence of lava stone pavements or their proxies (such as high curbs and stepping stones) from south of via di Castricio further suggests that this general eastward trend had not yet impacted the southernmost streets in Region I.[240]

Why vicolo I 8–I 9 should have been given silex ahead of others streets farther west is explained by the more specific trend: the institution of a city wide drainage system that contained wastewaters within eleven individual catchment basins and directed those waters along certain paths toward their exit from the city. One of those basins forced via di Nocera into double duty as both a main thoroughfare in the city and a primary conduit for water, each requiring a solid silex surface. The role that vicolo I 8–I 9 (and its southern extension) played in the drainage system as a primary water route also helps explain why it was paved in stone before others. At its northern intersection, a section of raised paving stones across via dell'Abbondanza redirects water onto vicolo I 8–I 9, preventing that water from continuing farther east. This redirection mechanism was one of thirteen related devices to control water on via dell'Abbondanza west of via Stabiana, nine of which were placed along the south side of the street to prevent water from flowing southward, except where designed: at vicolo I 8–I 9 and at via di Nocera.

Water-management mechanisms could also predispose a street against receiving a lava stone pavement. The blockages encircling Region II again serve as a clear example. By preventing water and wheeled traffic from flowing into

---

[240] There is evidence to suggest the intention to pave the southern extension of vicolo I 8–I 9 between I 17 and I 18 as part of the resurfacing of via di Castricio.

Region II, these curbstone blockages not only raised the level of these streets, making them an extension of the sidewalk, they also effectively stripped away the primary erosional forces that silex was meant to withstand: water and wheels. Still, the proximity of large public buildings meant that, at least on occasion, a great number of pedestrians used these routes.[241] The placement of an unusual mechanism on the north side of via dell'Abbondanza at its intersection with vicolo IX 11–IX 12, however, shows that a street could become still further isolated in the street network. Using paving stones and slabs, the mechanism gave pedestrians an unbroken passage over the intersection while allowing water to drain below onto via dell'Abbondanza. Though a ramp was created on the south side of the mechanism to permit vehicular traffic on this street, the debris above the beaten ash surface beyond it showed no evidence of cart traffic and instead suggested the space was a local dumping ground. Such a lack of concern for vicolo IX 11–IX 12 suggests that a lava stone pavement was not imminent, despite the pile of loose paving stones found among the debris.[242]

Debris Streets

In the final decades before the eruption, another kind of street surface became necessary. With the destruction following the earthquake(s), huge areas of rubble and debris needed to be cleared before rebuilding could commence.[243] This debris was at once nuisance and resource, a duality that meant it must be removed, but not far removed (fig. 3.1).[244] In the late 1920s, Maiuri excavated a great mound of spoil from the post-earthquake(s) period outside the walls between the Porta Ercolano and Porta Vesuvio.[245] The mound covered the outer pomerial road and was as high as 1.6 meters in front of the towers. The beaten ash road, paved in lava stone at both ends nearest the gates, was itself built on material that elevated it quite high above the base of the fortifications, suggesting that the

---

[241] On the other hand, the regular isolation of these streets is supported by the painted notice *cave cacator* in nearly 1-meter-high letters on both facade walls of vicolo III 4–III 5, the continuation of vicolo II 4–II 5 across via dell'Abbondanza. Jansen (2011, 171) cites CIL IV.7714–16, Della Corte (1929, 241), and Spinazzola (1917, 260–61).

[242] Varone 2008, 351–53, fig. 4.

[243] The fifth-century-BCE pomerial street at Porta Nocera was also built on debris. Chapter 2, 26.

[244] Anderson (2011) used this notion of keeping building materials near but out of the way of daily activities to test if houses were occupied during the period of reconstruction following the post-63 CE earthquake(s).

[245] Maiuri (1944, 276–81) repeats Fiorelli, who says the mound was first encountered in 1811.

area might long have been a dumping ground.[246] To the west of the Porta Nola, Chiaramonte Treré discovered similar dumps of material, also clustered around Tower VIII, with materials dating to the last decades of the city's life.[247] South of the city, Nappo posited that the same material had been used as a bedding for the road surface outside Porta Nocera.[248] Inside the city, however, it was in the space of the least used streets that great piles of debris were deposited, which turned the northern perimeter of the city and its inner pomerial route into a dumping ground. Still, Pompeians did not stop using these routes, and as they were filled in, a new street was built atop the debris. Maiuri's excavations at Porta Vesuvio also brought to light a wide (3 m) and elevated (65 cm) street east of the gate, which he described as "formed of the debris of common Roman pottery and sporadic materials of all kinds."[249] Although he said that this debris must have been an impediment to traffic, Maiuri nonetheless described the deposit as a road.

Farther west, to the north of insula VI 2, a similar discovery was made nearly eighty years later. Working to test the accuracy of the early nineteenth-century plans of this area that showed insula VI 2 surrounded by lava stone paving, including on its northern side, excavators found instead a beaten ash street of the post-Sullan period that was abandoned and covered (more deeply to the west) by refuse sometime after the Augustan era.[250] Two periods of traffic use, complete with ruts and the imprints of hooves, were discovered within these debris layers. Based on the relationship to the "lapillo sporco," these debris streets were deemed by the excavators to be early modern (eighteenth or nineteenth century). While this is certainly a reasonable interpretation, there is also reason to challenge the assumption of modernity based on the color of lapilli.[251]

At the so-called Capua gate, now conclusively established as Tower IX, a decade of excavations by the Japan Institute of Paleological Studies has revealed the existence of a superimposed series of inner pomerial streets. The earliest potential street was a beaten ash surface and ditch that preceded even the pappamonte fortifications and was buried by later fortifications. South of these later walls, a beaten ash surface mixed with lime was constructed, dating presumably to the early Imperial era, above which was 2 meters of debris.[252] In one of the nine trenches in which this debris mound was encountered, the excavators

---

[246] Maiuri 1944, 277.

[247] Chiaramonte Treré 1986, 29, table VIII. On the materials, see 57–96.

[248] Nappo 1995, 95.

[249] Maiuri 1929, 187.

[250] Garzia 2008, 1–2. Also, Fiorelli and Sorgente 1858.

[251] Sigurdsson (2007, 52) reports two types of lapilli fell during the eruption: the lower white in color and the upper gray.

[252] Etani et al. 1999, 133.

identified more than 150 different strata of heterogeneous composition.[253] Such a large number of individual depositions and their strong declination from north to south suggest a rapid and repeated dumping, apparently from people standing on top of the fortification wall.[254] It is fascinating to imagine what histories might be deposited with the stratigraphy here. Might each of these layers or groups of layers be the waste from an individual property or insula following the earthquake(s) of post-63 CE? The sequence and the seg- regation might suggest that certain types of refuse were brought here in a period of intense removal work, perhaps with each group having been assigned a period of time (a day, a week?) for dumping. Whatever the organization of clearing and dumping, individuals also seem to have used such debris piles— both inside and outside the fortification walls—for their own needs.[255] Uses could be both opportunistic, such as the jettisoning of a broken pot or remains of a meal,[256] or tender, including the burial of children and dogs. One favored pet even received a headstone.[257]

At some point after the mound had reached nearly two meters in height and required the addition of a retaining wall to prevent the inundation of the adjacent insulae, the rapid deposition of material was suspended and the great sloping mound leveled off. The level fill was then given a hard-packed surface to create a new inner pomerial street atop the debris (fig. 3.5). The entire sequence of fill and street surface was then repeated, apparently not long after, judging by the small number of interceding fill layers.[258] An investment in curbstones for such a temporary route was not warranted, but the placement of at least one guard stone along the southern limit of the street indicates the intention to guide carts away from the edge and from a long fall that would certainly destroy a vehicle and maim or kill its draft animals.[259] Such precautions seem necessary as the later street was in heavy use at the time of the eruption, as shown by the pres- ence of "innumerable ruts" running parallel to the fortification wall (fig. 3.6).[260] Intriguingly, although these ruts were found both to the east and to the west of the pomerial street's intersection with vicolo di Lucrezio Frontone, curving ruts connect only to the western series of ruts.[261] Therefore, a significant number of

[253] Etani et al. 1999, 125–30, fig. 10.

[254] Etani et al. 1998, 131.

[255] On organic remains, see Etani 1996, 63–65.

[256] Etani et al. 1998, 118, 123.

[257] Etani et al. 1998, 127; 1999, 133, fig. 13.

[258] Etani et al. 1999, 131–133, fig. 11. 2010, pl. 9. The earlier street layer is US 101, the later is US 106.

[259] Etani 2010, 55.

[260] Etani et al. 1996, 55–59, fig. 8, plates V, VII.

[261] Etani et al. 1999, 124–26, figs. 3 and 131–133, fig. 11.

Figure 3.5 Debris street at Tower IX, from Etani et al. 1996, plate V.

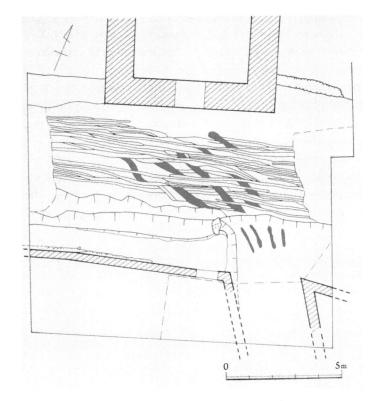

Figure 3.6 Ruts on debris street at Tower IX, after Etani 2010, fig. 14. Turning ruts in gray.

carts were either ascending the mound to make a north to west turn or were negotiating the opposite east to south turn-off of the debris street.

From these excavations into the debris along the northern perimeter of the city (at VI 2, Porta Vesuvio, and at Tower IX), we now can see that in the years before the eruption a discontinuous inner pomerial route existed atop the rubble of reconstruction in a least two phases. The creation of debris streets seems to have been a compromise among divergent pressures of reconstructing the city: of minimizing the transport costs of reconstruction and maximizing the mobility of the traffic that carried it. Therefore, on the one hand, the great debris piles were located where they would have had the least impact on circulation in the city but also where those transporting it could reach quickly and easily. On the other hand, the effort to transform a dump into a street, at least twice in one case, suggests the importance of this route for wheeled traffic. It might be argued that this was a function of the reconstruction process itself and that the street was needed only for hauling the very debris upon which it was built. But this ignores the fact that these debris streets replaced earlier beaten ash streets that respected the current alignments of the architecture. Indeed, the shape of the insulae at the pomerial route's intersection with major streets (via di Mercurio, via del Vesuvio, via di Nola, and via dell'Abbondanza) respects its presence, and the existence of previous surface demonstrates the pre-existing need for this route.

Street Surfaces as Social Capital

The devastation of the earthquake(s) and the rebuilding that followed generated many compromises in the use of urban space. The debris streets are a clear example: Pompeians tasked an otherwise minor route in the city to alternate between trash heap and service road. That decision, practical as it was, reversed more than three centuries of street-building tradition in which the practical had been in service of the personal and political desires of those who commissioned the pavements. It must be remembered that whether they were the ditch-like features of the Altstadt, the first battuto on via del Vesuvio with its side channel for runoff, or any of the early beaten ash streets, these surfaces were a substantial investment and improvement over the bare ground. In the fifth and fourth centuries BCE, those who lived along these streets benefited, and were seen by others to have benefited, from the ease of travel to and from their properties as well as the drainage that the surface offered. In this early period when not all streets were provided with such a pavement,[262] the first battuti were a credit to

---

[262] E.g., vicolo di Eumachia's earliest iteration was worn into the bedrock. See Chapter 2, 30.

those who lived along them and a distinction with those who did not. Battuti were the first prestige surfaces of the Pompeian street.

For centuries, the beaten ash street was state-of-the-art urban technology. Once the majority of the city was equipped with this surface, however, its social value as a means of distinction eroded, even though the surface itself remained the preferred pavement for another two hundred years. In the second century BCE, Pompeians chose to project their identity into the street in a new way. By pushing their houses outward and by projecting a small platform, pedestrians were forced to take heed of the house owner's importance while navigating the street. Like all fashion and good design, the creation of elevated curbs and sidewalks was copied across the city, and by the Augustan age much of the city was possessed of this new prestige surface. It is therefore likely no coincidence that, with the arrival of the aqueduct and the consequent need for a more durable street surface, lava stone pavements appear between the curbs first on the major thoroughfares but then spread rapidly throughout the more densely occupied western half of the city.

At the end of the first century BCE, silex was the premier prestige surface, and its expense could be floated only on the high tide of the Augustan economy. Indeed, prior to the first century BCE few roads outside of the great Roman highways or sacred routes were paved in stone, and the adoption of this technology into the city created allusions to no lesser institutions. Yet once again, within two generations, the allusion was losing its luster. With the widespread use of silex, status-seeking property owners had to find a new part of the street architecture by which to distinguish themselves. They found it once again on the margin,[263] taking the platform that first edged out into the street and pushing it upward, literally raising the house to prominence among its neighbors.[264] Alternatively, some Pompeians built tessellated pavements on the sidewalks in front of their homes, a decor once reserved for the floors of important rooms. The most famous of these pavements, in which the word "HAVE" was written in large red and white tesserae, fronts the Casa del Fauno. What goes overlooked in this sidewalk, however, are the large, equally spaced marble squares that frame the inscription and continue along the entire length of the façade, expressing this house owner's claim over the entire block.

Other styles abounded, as cocciopesto and pebble surfaces competed with each other, while many sidewalks had beaten ash coverings.[265] Pebble sidewalks were of particularly high status, as they exist at Pompeii only near sanctuaries. One is found on the Temple of Fortuna Augusta's northern sidewalk, and

---

[263] The use of small marble pieces in the lava stone pavement of via Marina is the only known elaboration of a silex surface at Pompeii and echoes the patterned river cobble sidewalk to the north.

[264] Hartnett 2011.

[265] Spinazzola 1953, 173, f. 213; Saliou 1999, 171–73.

another, arranged to create a repeating sequence of large diamonds bounded by squares, exists across from the Temple of Venus and abuts a broad tessellated cocciopesto surface before the Temple of Apollo. Smoothed by millions of feet, these pebble sidewalks flatten and appear to glow in the reflection of the late afternoon light. Equally impressive are the preserved sections of a wide sidewalk along via dell'Abbondanza, which pair a multicolor stone surface with the enfilade of tufo blocks to create an august yet dynamic facade for the length of a city block. These surfaces project powerful statements of great wealth, the breadth of ownership (or at least influence), and the decorative tastes of those who commissioned them. Tessellated cocciopesto, lava pesta, and pebble surfaces stand out all the more starkly among the areas of the city with sidewalks made of beaten ash. Were these later surfaces merely the cheapest available, or were they deliberate rustications, harkening back to a simpler time with simpler materials and virtues? Was the battuto a prestige surface competing with others? Even if not, the space of the sidewalk had become the predominant semipublic space for personal expression. The extent of this mode of expression at Pompeii can be seen in via Marina. Running between the basilica and the Sanctuaries of Apollo and Venus, this street had become entirely isolated from the street network in the final decades of Pompeii's existence. Embedded between the stones of the fresh, dark lava surface were large pieces of white marble, creating a tessellated street surface and signaling at once—by the gods and the city—the importance of this section of street and its new function as a strictly pedestrian thoroughfare.

At any given moment in the city's history, some Pompeians didn't or couldn't play this game of status building in the street, or at least not in all the streets that surrounded their houses and properties. Still others built prestige surfaces for economic reasons, such as the broad, paved ramps leading to inns and stables that competed for the attention of visitors at nearly every gate in the city.[266] When Mount Vesuvius erupted, much of the city was still paved with beaten ash surfaces, and some streets lacked continuous curbs and sidewalks, particularly in the east. The lag time in the adoption of the latest technology in street surfacing was at least in part an effect of social rather than technical limitations. Cost, politics, changing fashions, and grudging traditionalism kept some parts of the city generations, if not centuries, behind others in the shape of the street. Indeed, looking to a future that never happened, we can see that the earliest experiments with the next prestige space—the colonnaded sidewalk—were being built in the west while the east was still seeing its first silex. These short colonnaded sections at Pompeii, like those also found at Herculaneum, were ad hoc constructions,

[266] Poehler 2011a.

but their existence connects Pompeii to a future of second- and third-century urbanism in which status building will lift up from prestige surfaces to architectures that attach directly to the property owner. Given its narrow streets, how much like the great African, Anatolian, or Syrian cities could Pompeii ever have become? Given the rapidity of changing urban fashion and the pace of its implementation, practical concerns such as the narrowness of the street likely would not have been the only deciding factors.

4

Architecture of the Street

As the preceding histories of the street network (Chapter 2) and its surfaces (Chapter 3) have demonstrated, the physical architecture of Pompeii's final streets reflects the choices and compromises made in response to the urban terrain and seven centuries of fluctuating land use and fashions, with the predominant (but not only) trend being an increased density of inhabitation. By the end of second century BCE, much of the city was built over, and much of the rainwater that fell onto it had to be redirected into the streets instead of being absorbed by the porous volcanic soils. By the Augustan age, most streets were canalized and repurposed as storm drains, with an impermeable and durable cambered paving, high curbs to contain the runoff, and stepping stones to provide dry crossings at intersections and other desired locations. Such is the canonical shape of the Pompeian street. The purpose of this chapter is to dissect this canonical shape and examine each element—its curbstones, stepping stones, and guard stones—in a series of detailed mini-essays.

To create this form, the Pompeians used more than 26,700 metric tons of lava stone to pave the streets, another 5,800 tons of lava stone, Sarno limestone, and tuffs to create the curbs, and still 26 tons more to offer street crossings in the form of stepping stones.[267] As an investment in civic infrastructure, the scope of the

---

[267] These calculations relate to only the excavated parts of the city. The paving stone calculation is based on silex being laid over 25,245 square meters of the city streets to an average depth of 35 centimeters (8,906 m³) and with the specific gravity of basaltic stone of 3,000 kilograms per cubic meter. Curbstone calculation is based on the approximately 18,500 meters of curbs in the city, which are divided equally among lava, Sarno limestone, and tuff (specific gravity of each 1,200 kg/m³) using Saliou's (1999) estimations. Using Weiss's (2010) proportions of materials (47.3% lava, 29.4% Sarno limestone, and 23.3% tuff) together with van Roggen's (2015) dimensions, an average volume of .158 cubic meters can be derived, which gives an estimated 8,660 lava curbstones (4,100 metric tons), 5,390 Sarno limestone curbstones (1,030 metric tons), and 4,270 tuff curbstones (820 metric tons) of each material in the city. The specific gravity of Sarno limestone and tuff is approximately 1.21 kilograms per cubic meter. For the tuff, this value is taken from Bonasia and Oliveri del Castillo (1968, 415), and the value for Sarno stone is generated from my own linear (72 cm x 33 cm x 16 cm) and weight (46 kg) measurements taken in 2008.

streets' creation (and maintenance) is rivaled only by the building of the fortification walls. To create this specific final form, road builders perfected the
process of creating paving and edging materials, setting them in place, and
locking them together. This technology was not developed at Pompeii. By the
time the streets at Pompeii were first paved in stone, Romans had been laying streets in silex for more than a century and were lauded for their achieve-
ment.[268] Dionysius of Halicarnassus, writing at the end of the first century BCE,
declared that "the three most magnificent works of Rome, in which the great-
ness of her empire is best seen, are the aqueducts, the paved roads, and the
construction of the sewers."[269] Most famously, we hear such praise of expertise and benefit in Statius's description of the via Domitiana, a road close to
Pompeii in both space and time:[270]

> The first labour was to mark out trenches,
> Carve out the sides, and by deep excavation
> Remove the earth inside. Then they filled
> The empty trenches with other matter,
> And prepared a base for the raised spine,
> So the soil was firm, lest an unstable floor
> Make a shifting bed for the paving stones;
> Then laid the road with close-set blocks
> All round, wedges densely interspersed.
> O what a host of hands work together!
> These fell trees and strip the mountains,
> Those plane beams and smooth posts;
> Some bind stones, consolidate the work,
> With baked clay and tufa mixed with dirt;
> Others toil to drain waterlogged ditches,
> And divert the lesser streams elsewhere.

Leavened within this panegyric are important details of the Roman methods of
road construction, in particular the need for a firm foundation, proper drainage,
and the importance of compression among paving stones to hold the surface
together.[271]

---

[268] van Tilburg 2007, 7.

[269] Dion. Hal. *Ant. Rom.* 3.67.5.

[270] Statius, *Silv.* IV, 3, 40–55; Longobardo 2004, 277–79.

[271] Chevallier 1976, 84–93; Staccioli (2003, 105–10) translates Statius differently, believing *gom-
phi* to mean "curbstone."

Paving Stones

At Pompeii, Statius's praise of the paving process is borne out in the evidence from more than one hundred exposed street sections and especially from those still in the process of repaving at the moment of the eruption. For example, from the examination of paving materials, two general types of stone shapes can be discerned—dome-shaped and pyramid-shaped stones—both of which are irregular in the outline of their flat, top-facing sides.[272] These two paving stone forms were not the by-product of differing styles of stone masons but rather reflect the outputs of a singular process to produce paving stones. When a street pavement was to be laid, lava stone was transported to the work site as rough, boulder-like "blanks," examples of which can be found at the western end of via delle Terme (fig. 4.1). The edges of these blanks were first wedged off to create up to six dome-shaped paving stones, leaving a cubic core to be split into as many as four pyramid-shaped stones.[273] Further chiseling of the stones was required on the top to create a flat surface. This process left a pocked, chiseled surface that is most evident in areas where little or no traffic wore down

Figure 4.1 Lava stone paving "blanks" on via delle Terme.

[272] The via Appia offers numerous opportunities to see these polygonal stones; Ashby, Le Pera Buranelli, and Turchetti 2003, 95, fig. 34.1; La Regina, Insolera, and Morandi 1997, 168; Quilici and Quilici Gigli 2002, 111, figs. 6–7.

[273] Laurence (1999, 64) notes the same ovoid split of basalt stone.

Figure 4.2 Paving stones on vicolo del Farmacista.

the pavement, such as in between the guard stones of a fountain or beneath a line of curbstones. The sides of paving stones were also shaped to fit into place among those other irregular shapes already set. To make a tight, nearly seamless connection, the edges of paving stones were thus carefully cut and smoothed, which combined with the stones' sloping bottom to produce a kind of anathyrosis (fig. 4.2). Paving stones examined in their original context and in reused contexts, as well as those found in piles of materials recovered from around the city, support these observations.[274]

[274] These piles represent paving stones in temporary storage (e.g., within the rear of the Central Baths; on vicolo IX 11–IX 12), in transit (e.g., on vicolo di Tesmo at IX 6, 3; on via dell'Abbondanza

Street builders chose to create domed and pyramidal shapes of paving stones not only because of the efficient means of creating a flat, functional surface from a larger ovoid object but also because the bottom shapes served to wedge the paving stones into the filling matrix below them. Excavations below vicolo delle Nozze d'Argento have shown the fill can be relatively shallow (40 cm), though deeper fills were found under via Stabiana.[275] The fill on vicolo delle Nozze d'Argento was also characterized as a nearly sterile eroded volcanic soil, with the only finds being the flakes and fragments of lava stone left behind from shaping the pavers in place.[276] After being uniquely formed, masons laid each stone in place and then forced it downward into the fill until level. The projecting bottom of the paving stone displaced this filling matrix, ensuring that there would be no large voids within the fill and that the paving stones would be held in place by the pressure of the fill as well as by the tightness of the fit with other paving stones.[277] Flat-bottomed stones were not preferred (though not completely absent), because these can be held in place only by the pressure of their neighbors. Should that pressure be removed, only the mass of the stone could prevent it from being dislodged under the weight of passing carts. There are several examples of such failure of the subsurface in which paving stones begin to collapse into a void beneath the street or a stone becomes loose and flips vertically to become both pothole and impediment.[278] To maintain compression throughout the paving process, streets were divided into sections by low walls crossing the street.[279] It is unknown, however, if these cross walls were removed during construction or were left in place, but cut down, to keep tension. Leaving the walls in place might have been more practical because any water that might have accumulated below the pavement would have been redirected at several intervals, preventing the erosion of the bedding layers and development of large voids among the paving stones.[280]

---

at III 7, 1 and across from II 5, 2–3), or waiting to be laid (e.g., on vicolo del Conciapelle at via Stabiana).

[275] Rispoli and Paone 2011, 126.

[276] Nilsson 2014. Similarly, fragments of pappamonte stone in a foundation trench for a pappamonte wall were interpreted as being from shaping the blocks in situ; Ellis et al. 2012, 9.

[277] This process of displacement is analogous to the use of curved shims in the application of marble revetment; Ball 2002.

[278] Examples of this phenomenon can be seen in Pompeii on via dell'Abbondanza at II 2, 1 and on via del Foro. Beyond Pompeii, examples are noted on the via Appia in Terracina and on the via Traiana in Egnazia.

[279] Cross walls are found on vicolo del Conciapelle, vicolo del Fauno, and via Marina.

[280] Large voids are known below vicolo di Narciso and vicolo dei Soprastanti.

Curbstones

After paving stones, curbstones are the most numerous elements of the street structure. The curbs are mostly constructed of rectangular blocks of lava, Sarno limestone, or tuff, though other materials and construction styles are known. A city-wide survey found the use of these materials to be both highly patterned, with a single material used over long sections of a street, and about equal in their numbers overall.[281] In a more precise sampling of 33 street-length curbs, or approximately 5% of the city's total area, Claire Weiss found 1,028 curbstones made of lava, 640 in Sarno limestone, 507 in tuff, and one each in marble, limestone, and cruma.[282] Weiss's survey also found that these blocks can range in size from very small (ca. 10 centimeters) to over two meters in length, but on average are 92 centimeters.[283] Juliana van Roggen's work on guard stones in Pompeii also recorded the height of 243 curbstones, finding both significant consistency overall in curb height (61% of the curbs are between 20 and 59 cm) and areas of exceptional deviation, especially in tall curbs.[284] In function, curbstones have two primary purposes: to define the street edge and to elevate the sidewalk surface. To define the edge, parallel lines of curbstones were set slightly below the intended street surface level so that paving stones could abut these curbstones, locking the tightly fitted pavement between them. This phenomenon can be observed in streets still under construction. Instances of curbstones lying on top of paving stones therefore are usually indicative of some change to the street structure, such as an alteration of the curb.

When a street was repaved, the curbstones were regularly reused. At times, curbstones were flipped vertically to create a taller platform for the sidewalks in general, in some cases in order to elevate a particular property above its neighbors.[285] In at least one case (VI 17, 36), it can be confirmed that the curbstones were being reused by the vertical iron staining on the face of the stone, marking where the curbstone had previously met the paving stones when it was laid horizontally. In other cases, the curbstones simply remained in place and the new pavement was created against them.

For example, the unfinished project to resurface the vicolo del Conciapelle left exposed for examination several aspects of curbstone creation, use, and reuse. The curbstones, two stepping stones, and the paving stones have all been set in place at the intersection with via Stabiana, but only for the first few meters.

---

[281] Saliou 1999, 175–87, fig. 28, table 3.
[282] Weiss 2010, 367. I follow Kastenmeier et al. (2010) on the definitions of stone types.
[283] Weiss, personal communication, 2008.
[284] Van Roggen 2015, 63–64. Also, Nishida 1991.
[285] Chapter 8, 213–14.

Similarly, the eastern end of vicolo del Conciapelle, where it meets vicolo del Citarista, was also repaved for only a few meters, demonstrating that two teams were working toward each other.[286] Returning to the west, a pile of paving stones rests at the corner awaiting reuse. Rather than being relaid as pavers, however, these paving stones were instead being split in half and used as curbstones to set the southern edge. Several reworked pavers have already been placed, and one stone even shows the scoring on its bottom face in preparation for being split apart (fig. 4.3).[287] The northern curb, as it approaches the front door of Casa dell'Atrio Tetrastilio (I 2, 28), was elevated high above even the potential new street level. Its height was produced by stacking large Sarno limestone blocks on top of one another. Similarity in the size, shape, and material of the upper course of the curb indicates that these are reused curbstones, a fact further supported by presence of a drain leading out from the same house that cuts through the lower

Figure 4.3 Scored paving stone on vicolo del Conciapelle.

[286] Repaving is not always done in this way: vicolo del Fauno shows work moving only from south to north.

[287] A deeply rutted paving stone was reused on the southern curb of via delle Terme at its intersection with via Consolare.

course of curbstones, still in situ. A new drain was already in place, marking the expected height of the final paving surface.

Overflow drains are one of the most common interventions into curbstones. Nearly every property over 400 square meters had an exit for a drain cut through the base of a curbstone or at the junction between two curbstones.[288] A recent study of drain holes by Janet Dunkelbarger has found more than 850 drains in the excavated portion of the city.[289] Associating these holes with the drains and pipes found within excavated buildings reveals that the outlet along the frontage was the primary exit for wastewater.[290] Far more numerous still are the L-shaped holes cut through the top, street-facing edge of the curbstones. Weiss's study of more than a thousand examples of these holes in Regions VI and VII has demonstrated conclusively that they were used primarily for tethering animals. Arguments that these holes are artifacts of the stones' transportation process or spouts for water or were used as tie-down points for awnings covering the sidewalks do not hold up to sustained scrutiny.[291] Additionally, distribution analysis of these hitching holes shows a direct, though not simplistic correlation with areas expected to have higher levels of traffic. Thus, the widest streets had the highest number of hitching holes, and these same streets also directly connected to either the forum or to city gates. Streets with the lowest number of hitching holes support this correlation as they expected little to no traffic: vicolo del Labirinto (no holes) was blocked at one end, and vicolo del Fauno (four holes) was still under reconstruction in 79 CE. Hitching holes also correlated directly with doorways: 85% were within 10 *pedes* (Roman feet) of an entrance.[292]

Although these categories of curb alterations—raised curbstones, drains cut through curbstones, and hitching holes added (and removed)—each had a general function, the individual instances of each category could have vastly different forms. Drains in particular show a great variety of shapes, positions, and details of construction. Such variability points to some of the freedoms that individual property owners could exercise to alter the streetscape for their display, drainage, and transport needs. Research by Catherine Saliou on sidewalks, particularly on the form and materials of curbstones, has shown that the ability to choose what materials to use in the curbs and what kinds of holes to cut into them was an extension of the property owner's legal responsibility to maintain the streets. Curbs and the sidewalks they elevated, however, were not extensions of private space into the public sphere but rather public lands entrusted to the

---

[288] There are 227 properties larger than 400 square meters. Of these, 93% have an associated drain.
[289] Dunkelbarger, forthcoming.
[290] For an abridged statement of the evidence, see Poehler 2012, 99, n. 26.
[291] The water spout idea is that of Gesemann (1996, 61), who credits Lauter.
[292] Weiss 2010, 367–70.

owners of the properties that faced them; they were an extension of the street.[293] Thus, property owners could select materials and permit minor alterations, but the general form of the street was less negotiable. Saliou's research also offers a window onto the ways in which the humble curbstone reflects not only the choices of individual property owners (particularly wealthy owners) but also how civic infrastructure was maintained by partnerships of multiple property owners as well as by the city itself.

Stepping Stones

Stepping stones are the most iconic feature of Pompeii's streetscape after its ruts. The stepping stone is an elegantly simple solution to the twin problems of vehicular and pedestrian access created by the canalization of the street by tall curbstones. That is, because many streets would have regularly carried (at least) wastewater, if not trash, and because it was a significant step down into the street and another back out again, crossing points were desired to keep the pedestrian on a dry and level course. Simply extending the sidewalk was impossible because pack animals and wheeled vehicles needed a clear path and could not climb and descend a barrier at every intersection in the city. Moreover, such a pedestrian crossing would also stop the flow of wastewater, defeating the purpose of canalizing the street. The solution for the Pompeians was to set large stones in the street at a sufficient distance apart to allow people to step from one to the next in order to cross the street while simultaneously permitting traffic in the street to continue through the crossing unimpeded.

While the function of the stepping stone might be obvious to us (not least etymologically) and it might seem pedantic to describe that function in such detail, it is important to remember that at some point in Pompeii's history a need for pedestrian crossings existed and stepping stones did not. When considered in this light, the humble stepping stone becomes a solution carefully deliberated in the context of the larger street network and surface drainage system. It also becomes an amenity likely greatly appreciated by those who first used them. When considered through the lens of a future at Pompeii that did not happen, the other means to cross the street being developed by 79 CE show that the stepping stone was only one of many possible crossing mechanisms. For example, the intersection of via dell'Abbondanza and vicolo della Maschera takes the interesting and rare form of a ramp with a drain built through it that fills the intersection.[294] Pedestrians and wastewater were unimpeded and southbound

---

[293] Saliou 1999, 204. See now, Poehler and Crowther 2018, 600–604.
[294] Also, via dell'Abbondanza and vicolo IX 11–IX 12.

cart travel was facilitated by a gentle ramp, while the opposite direction was deterred by a steeper ramp of curbstones. Finally, when considered in the context of urban centers across the Roman Empire and beyond, the use of stepping stones becomes a rare and (geographically and historically) localized phenomenon. These 316 stepping stones at Pompeii are therefore best understood in the longue durée as a successful though ultimately superseded experiment in shaping the Roman urban environment.

Physically, stepping stones are consistent, though not standardized in form, dimension, and placement. Lava stone is used almost exclusively for stepping stones; only five are made of tuff or Sarno limestone (1.58%). They are also nearly all ovoid in shape, with only eleven rectangular blocks used. There is considerable overlap in these irregularities in shape and material: all the tuff and Sarno limestone blocks are rectangular, and all rest on top of the paving stones. The combination of these factors suggests that these blocks are modern additions to the streets.[295] Stepping stones also tend to be monolithic, with only twenty-two constructed of two pieces (fig. 4.4).[296] In all cases, both parts of these two-piece stepping stones show equivalent wearing, demonstrating that it was

Figure 4.4 Two-piece stepping stone on vicolo di Eumachia.

---

[295] Since 2009, two of these have subsequently been removed from the street and now rest on adjacent curbs.

[296] There are three examples of two small, abutting oval stepping stones used to create a larger crossing.

choice in the construction of the stepping stone and not an attempt to repair the stone through partial replacement. Two-piece stepping stones also are the very largest stepping stones and appear to be have been used when the width of the street would put a narrower stepping stone too far from the curb but the placement of two stones might interfere with flow of traffic.[297] Because stepping stones are some of the largest monoliths in the city, dividing these oversized objects in two seems to have been a choice constrained by difficulties in transportation and installation.[298] Indeed, one of the stepping stones found not installed in a street—and quite possibly in transit at the moment of the eruption—is one of the most massive single objects in all of Pompeii.[299]

Because most streets were narrow, just over half of the stepping stones were deployed in pairs (21%) or as a single stone (31%), and most of these (71%) were set in streets wide enough only for a single lane of traffic. These streets, though narrow, are not of identical width, a factor that influenced the width of stepping stones, the orientation of their placement, and the number of stones that would be used. For example, on one-lane streets, when a single stepping stone was used, the average street width is 2.04 meters and the average stone is 97 centimeters wide. When crossing streets wide enough for two lanes of traffic, Pompeians almost always chose to use three (or more) stepping stones. The 135 stepping stones employed in these forty-five crossings make up the largest single category of use (table 4.1). While the average street width is 3.81 meters when three stepping stones were used, the stones themselves are particularly narrow, 69 centimeters on average.[300] These comparisons suggest that there were two main categories of stepping stones: the standard narrow oval used almost everywhere in Pompeii and a variety of wider stones—fatter ovals, two-part stones, and perpendicularly placed stones—that were used to cross one-lane streets. Only the 18 stones used in pairs to cross streets wide enough for two lanes of traffic appear to fit between these categories, averaging 81 centimeters in width.

---

[297] Two-part stepping stones represent eighteen of the twenty-two largest stones.

[298] The two-part stepping stone on via degli Augustali measures 1.29 meters long, 98 centimeters wide, and 35 centimeters tall, giving an estimated volume of its oval shape of 0.35 cubic meters. This does not include the portion of the stone embedded below street level. Each half of this two-part stone would weigh at least 525 kilograms, which is equivalent to the weight of the average stepping stone, 570 kilograms (dimensions: 1.24 m, 69 cm, 29 cm). Both of these figures are greater than the maximum vehicle load set in the Theodosian code. See Chapter 5, 109, n. 349.

[299] The largest single object in Pompeii is a marble block resting on the north sidewalk of via Marina. Measuring 3.06 meters long, 99 centimeters wide, and 73 centimeters deep (2.21 m³), the block weighs at least 5,600 kilograms, or over five times the combined weight of the two-part stepping stone on via degli Augustali.

[300] The narrower width of stepping stones used in sets of three is nearly identical to the width used in pairs to cross one-lane streets as well as the four sets of four stepping stones employed to cross the widest streets in the city.

Table 4.1 **Stepping stone distribution by number and street type.**

Number of Stepping Stones	Stepping Stones on One-Lane Streets	Stepping Stones on Two Lane Streets
1	97% (98)	3% (3)
2	56% (49)	44% (38)
3	2% (3)	98% (135)
4	0% (0)	100% (16)

While these averages help to identify the broader trends in the use of stepping stones in groups or as individual objects, detailed examination of the dimensions of each stone reveals that there are no prescribed units for their length, width, or height. There were, however, important functional considerations that influenced the ultimate form of all these features that can be demonstrated in their sizes (fig. 4.5).[301] For example, 88% of stepping stones are between 15 and 39 centimeters high, appropriately matching the height of the surrounding curbs and sufficient to keep one's feet dry under normal conditions. The length of stepping stones stretches broadly between 46 centimeters and 1.76 meters, with only a slight prevalence (26%) for stepping stones between 1.15 and 1.34 meters.[302] Rather than show a clustering around a dimensional range, the length of stepping stones seems to show an important functional minimum at around 90 centimeters, which is approximately the distance needed for two people to use the stone at the same time, likely moving in opposite directions across the street.

The width of stepping stones, however, does cluster strongly (74%) between 55 and 79 centimeters, with only seven stones narrower than this range.[303] That so few stepping stones are narrower than the preferred range can be explained by the need to provide a surface wide enough to easily place one's foot. At 55 to 79 centimeters, most stepping stones' widths were two to three times the length of the average Roman's foot.[304] Beyond this preferred minimum, there is little to

---

[301] Nearly all of the dimensional measurements used here were collected by Mr. Walter van Roggen over a one-week field season in January 2014. I am very grateful to Mr. van Roggen for his efforts and intelligence in this collaboration.

[302] The shortest stones within this range are nearly all those installed perpendicular to the course of the street, turning their normal length into an exceptional width.

[303] The fifty-seven (22%) wider stones were specific responses to slightly wider streets, which used two-part stepping stones or turned the stones perpendicular to the curbs.

[304] An average Roman foot, based on calcaneus lengths from Casal Bertone, is 26.5 centimeters for men and 25.9 for women; Killgrove 2014b.

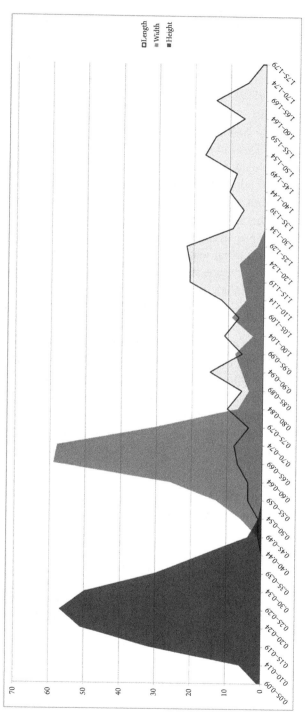

Figure 4.5 Stepping stone dimensions (in meters).

influence the width of stepping stones until their functional maximum width is reached. That functional maximum appears to be 1.27 meters, as no stepping stone is wider. This dimension is also slightly smaller than the distance between the wheels of most Roman vehicles (1.32 m, or 4.5 *pedes*; Chapter 5), which would allow carts to roll over the stepping stones unimpeded. For the smallest carts, only eleven (3.48%) stepping stones were slightly too large (up to 10 cm) to avoid being hit by them.[305]

The size of the gaps between stepping stones and the curb and between stepping stones was also of vital importance to the pedestrians who crossed the street and the drivers who would pass through such gaps. Although there are a few stepping stones that directly abut curbstones, the vast majority of these gaps (74%) are within a narrow 25-centimeter range—between 35 and 59 centimeters. It is surely no coincidence that this distance maps well onto the length of a step for Romans who lived in the Bay of Naples and at Rome (table 4.2).[306] Using the average stature of each sex, it is possible to calculate the step length for these populations, which, taken together, show an average stride length of 69 centimeters for men and 64 for women. Because the biological definition of a step is heel strike to heel strike, we must also subtract the length of the trailing foot to find the distance covered between the trailing toes to the leading heel. This distance—43 centimeters for men and 38 for women—is the average distance "stepped over" in a single comfortable Roman step. This "stepped over" distance is remarkably consonant with the average gap between stepping stones at Pompeii (45 cm), only 4% larger than the male step and 16% larger than the female step.[307]

Pompeians, of course, could have placed the stepping stones closer together or nearer the curb and made passage across the street easier for all, including children and the elderly, whose step lengths are significantly shorter.[308] Reducing

[305] The wearing patterns on these stones are intriguing. Of the eleven stones, five show no directional wearing at all. The absence of overriding marks in particular suggests carts of the smallest gauges (e.g., 4 *pedes*)—those that physically could not avoid hitting a stone—did not use these streets (via degli Augustali, vicolo della Regina, via Soprastanti) with any regularity. Since via degli Augustali is one of the most integral streets in the city, this must be a reflection of the rarity of such small-gauge carts in general.

[306] Table 4.2 is based on the work of Bisel and Bisel 2002, 455 (Herculaneum); Capasso 2001, 927 (Herculaneum); D'Amore, Carfagna, and Matarese 1964, 409 (Naples); Killgrove 2010, 95, fig. 4.13; Killgrove 2014a (Casal Bertone, Rome); Lazer 1995, 202–5; 2007, 609–10. Special thanks belong to Kristina Killgrove, who helped me translate between stature and step.

[307] The largest gaps, up to 70 centimeters, require men to stretch 63% farther, or 32% farther if they land only the front half of their foot on the next stepping stone. For women, it's an 84% stretch, or 50% landing only half a foot.

[308] According to Branting (2004, 95, table 2), the difference in stride between older men (55–75) and younger men (10–35) could be 10 centimeters, or nearly a 16% decrease. Conversely, kids are kids: Cooley and Cooley (2014) note in their dedication the delight of children in using stepping stones during a storm.

Table 4.2 **Osteological data on stature and step distances.**

Site	Author	Gender	Stature (cm)	Step (cm)
Pompeii	Lazer	Female	154.75	63.9
		Male	167.6	69.6
Herculaneum	Bisel	Female	155.2	64.1
		Male	169.1	70.2
Herculaneum	Campobasso	Female	151.7	62.7
		Male	163.8	68.0
Naples	D'Amore et al.	Female	152.6	63.0
		Male	164	68.1
Rome	Killgrove	Female	156.7	64.7
		Male	166.6	69.1

the gap, however, could have significant consequences for the vehicles passing through these spaces. Because the axles and the hubs of wheels were taller than both stepping stones and curbstones, only the approximately 5- to 10-centimeter width of the wheel itself needed to be accommodated. By this measure, the preferred distance between a stepping stone and other street features is three to five times greater than the minimum requirement. This way of formulating the problem of fitting a single wheel into a single space, however, does not accurately model the situation. It was not a single wheel passing through a gap, but two (or two sets of) wheels, inextricably connected, passing simultaneously through two gaps. When only one stepping stone was used, its placement in the middle of the street caused little difficulty. Indeed, the narrow width of such streets and the gauge of most carts made it nearly impossible for the stepping stone to impede the cart's progress. On wider streets where two or more stepping stones were needed, especially at intersections, navigating the gaps could be difficult, and in the case of vehicles with certain gauges, it was impossible not to hit a stepping stone or to grind against the curbstones.

To accommodate the needs of both pedestrian and vehicular traffic, Pompeians installed stepping stones as close to the center of the street as possible for single stones and with equidistant gaps between multiple stones (fig. 4.6).[309] Although the range of widths of single stepping stones varied enormously (closely related to the width of the street), they are all (95%) very

---

[309] On one-lane streets, discerning the centering of a stepping stone is a simple process of subtracting the distance to the curb on the left side of the stone from the same distance on the right side.

Figure 4.6 Gaps among stepping stones and curbstones.

carefully centered in the street. Only 3 of 57 single stepping stones are more than 25 centimeters from their center point in the road. Similarly, spacing between multiple stepping stones is equally consistent, which is complemented by the remarkable consistency of the widths of the stepping stones themselves. Of the 198 stepping stones found in a series of two or more, 186, or 94%, have less than 25 centimeters of difference in their spacing from their immediate neighbors, and 65% have less than 10 centimeters difference.

It is interesting to note, however, that there is a more specific spatial pattern submerged within these averaged numbers. Taking the actual size of the gaps between stepping stones rather than the number of centimeters each gap diverges from its nearest neighbors shows a consistently wider spacing between stepping stones than between stepping stones and curbstones. Thus, when two or three stepping stones are employed, the spaces between stepping stones (i.e., gap 2 or gaps 2 and 3) are on average 6.5 centimeters wider than the spaces to the curbs. Although 6.5 centimeters may not seem like a significant difference, we must remember that for two carts to pass simultaneously between two stepping stones, the gap between them must be at very least 36 centimeters wide lest the nave of one axle hit the nave of the other. The average gap between stepping stones and the curbs is 42 centimeters, which is ample space considering only one wheel and hub will pass through this gap. If the same average distance were true of the gaps between stepping stones, there would be only 8 centimeters (again, on average) for carts to avoid one another. The addition of 6.5 centimeters nearly doubles that space. These analyses demonstrate that a modest level of concern for the circulation of vehicles was enacted through a high level of precision in the placement of stepping stones.

Although in many cases it is difficult to establish conclusively the relationship between a stepping stone and the paving stones, it is clear that the vast majority are contemporaneous with the pavement. Additionally, there is no evidence that stepping stones existed prior to the introduction of silex. The positive evidence that does exist, such as exceptionally eroded stepping stones found in streets recently repaved (e.g., via delle Terme) or stepping stones being enveloped by a later pavement (e.g., via Stabiana), supports the hypothesis that these crossing mechanisms were instituted at the same time as the arrival of silex. The stepping stone at Pompeii thus was first introduced sometime in the later part of the first century BCE. These features then proliferated, at least in the western half of the city, at intersections and across large streets. Not long after, many stepping stones were supplanted by the needs of the drainage system, which in the Augustan period appears to have removed stepping stones in favor of curbstone blockages. Where paving stone ramps were built, the stepping stones were preserved and built around. In still other areas, stepping stones were removed from one location and replaced in another, which seems to have been in several cases the effect of the sidewalk projecting farther into the street.[310] In other places, they were removed entirely.

The history of the stepping stone at Pompeii is best understood as one particularly successful adaptation of street architecture to the combined needs of pedestrians and vehicles. Arriving with polygonal lava stone surfaces as early as the second half of the first century BCE, these features spread with the new pavement and not beyond. Thus, even though the eastern and southern parts of Pompeii had not yet received their first stepping stone, in the west stepping stones were being removed, enveloped, or replaced by the needs of the drainage system. Negotiation of these forms of replacement was still underway in 79 CE. From the broader historical perspective of ancient urbanism, the stepping stone was an intense but short-lived experiment. Based on the

---

[310] Ruts and repositioned stepping stones show that via degli Augustali was narrowed from the north. The removal of stepping stones at the intersection of via Consolare and via delle Terme might also have been an effect of the western curb of insula VI 4 extending to the east. A similar phenomenon occurred on vicolo delle Terme at its intersection with vicolo dei Soprastanti due to the renovated Forum Baths taking over the western side of its insula (VII 5).

few examples that survive beyond Pompeii—at Norba (10), Alba Fucens (8), Marruvium (3), Aquinum (2); Saepinum (1), and Grumentum (1)—the use of stepping stones appears to have been a phenomenon of the late Republic in Italy.[311] Of course, not all cities needed or chose to have stepping stones, but the infrastructural changes to cities in the late first and early second centuries CE help to explain their archaeological rarity. For example, the installation of under-street sewerage at Herculaneum and Ostia meant that without the expectation of large amounts of wastewater, the canalization of the street was unnecessary and the curbs could be significantly lower or removed almost entirely in these cities.

In this larger historical context, the 316 stepping stones at Pompeii are of exceptional comparative importance. First, there is the simple fact that they are the largest set of such objects from the ancient world. Beyond their numbers, however, are the complexities and interdependencies that stepping stones reveal in the production of urban form. Their wide but not universal adoption maps onto the expansion of silex pavements, illustrating the negotiation of confluent forces in late Republican Pompeii: the increase in wastewater, pedestrians, and cart traffic all vying for their space in the street. Yet even as some of the eastern streets at Pompeii were being paved and high curbs installed for the first time, creating the need for new stepping stones, experiments and adaptations with other crossing mechanisms were taking place elsewhere in the city. For example, around the forum, the solid surfaces of streets isolated or cut off entirely by the forum's reconstruction were being repurposed as drains.[312] Along the south side of via di Nola, topography allowed intersections to be repaved flush with the sidewalks, removing the need for stepping stones even as their use continued elsewhere along the same street. Finally, in a few instances the needs of the drainage and the traffic systems converged to permit the filling of an intersection entirely but with a small drain running through it to carry the outflow of wastewater. The elevated area in front of the Stabian Baths shows the largest such development.[313] Together, these adaptations point toward new drainage strategies in development and perhaps even a new sewerage system at Pompeii that might have been built by the second century CE. In the widest scope of classical urbanism, the stepping stone was a transitional artifact, one that existed concurrently with urban forms that it would supersede (beaten ash streets) and forms that would supplant it (under-street sewerage).

---

[311] I am indebted to S. Ellis for help in compiling this list. Marzabotto also has a number of features that appear to be stepping stones that I have not been able to examine.

[312] Poehler 2011b.

[313] Poehler 2012, 103.

Guard Stones

Guard stones are perhaps the most enigmatic features of the Pompeian streetscape (fig. 4.7). Set almost always at the edge of the street, these 370 objects are dispersed across the breadth of the city and employed in conjunction with both battuti and silex; there is even one on a debris street. Few scholars have made note of these objects and most have taken a descriptive rather than directly functional approach to the stones, at least in terms of nomenclature. For example, Saliou offered a few potential functions but called the stones "bornillons," a diminutive form of "borne," which was a nearly identical kind of stone found in the roads of nineteenth-century France.[314] Tsujimura offered only that they are "irregularly shaped stones of various sizes standing by the side of the curbstones."[315] In my own previous study, I called them "narrowing stones," based on the only function these emplacements could be said to have had (Poehler, 1999).[316] That is, whether it was their primary or their latent function, the effect of their presence narrowed the street by making the area beside the curb impassable where they are placed. Most

Figure 4.7 Guard stones on north curb of via di Nola.

[314] Saliou 1999, 164, n. 9.

[315] Tsujimura 1991, 60–61; Geseman 1996, 57–61.

[316] Poehler, 1999.

recently, van Roggen has closely examined these stones using a combined morphological and distributional approach.[317]

On average, a guard stone is a small piece of lava stone, set against the curb or embedded slightly within it, measuring 38 centimeters tall (dimension perpendicular to the paving stones), 33 wide (dimension parallel to the curb), and 25 deep (dimension perpendicular to the curb). A guard stone can range in size from as small as 3 centimeters high, 13 wide, and 5 deep to as large as 98 centimeters high, 48 wide, and 42 deep. Variance is greatest in height, however, with a minimum of 2 centimeters and a maximum of 1 meter. Depth is the most consistent dimension and the most important in revealing the stones' function, varying only between 5 and 57 centimeters, with 90.2% being between 10 and 39 centimeters deep. In terms of distribution, although these features are spread across the city, their strongest concentration is in the northwest, particularly in Region VI and its edges.[318] Another trend is obvious from examining the concentration in Region VI: guard stones are found with other guard stones. In fact, 86% of all guard stones are within 3 meters of another, and only fifty-four are used individually. Moreover, many guard stones (44%) are found in a sequence of three or more, spaced just a few meters apart,[319] and long series of six or more guard stones are found approaching several intersections (fig. 4.7).[320] While these series of stones tend to be found on wider, two-lane streets, guard stones in general are only slightly more likely to be found on larger streets. On the other hand, guard stones that are not part of a series are still most often (55%) found at intersections. Such clustering at intersections and in longer series approaching intersections indicates that the general purpose of the guard stone was related to wheeled traffic.

One subset of guard stones demonstrates a clear function: to protect objects of water infrastructure from being hit by carts.[321] The placement of forty-six stones at twenty-two fountains offers the best example, and the heavy wearing on them (and the consequent absence of wear on fountains) demonstrates their effectiveness. That such protection was the intention of placement and not to offer another function, such as a step up for people, is confirmed by the fact that only eight of forty-three guard stones are set in a location that would not stop carts from damaging the fountain. The opposite is also true. Of the thirteen fountains

---

[317] Much of the data for the following discussion comes from my collaboration with van Roggen (2015), for which I am grateful.

[318] Within an area of 13% of the city are 35% of all guard stones.

[319] Saliou (1999, 165) also noticed their self-associations.

[320] These series of stones are located on via di Nola, via della Fortuna, via Consolare, via di Nocera, vicolo dei Soprastanti, vicolo di Mercurio, and vicolo del Farmacista.

[321] Tsujimura (1991, 60–61) claimed the function of these stones was, at least in part, to protect fountains but in other places to protect the curbstones.

that do not have guard stones associated with them, nearly all are protected by other means: eight are recessed significantly into the curb, and three are not in the street at all. Only one fountain seems unprotected, though it appears its guard stones were removed. A similar guarding function is seen at two of the city's water towers.[322] Of the remaining twelve water towers, seven stand outside the space of the street and do not need protection, while the remaining five are at least partially recessed into the sidewalk. Finally, six large stones ring the front of the *castellum aquae*, preventing carts from even approaching the building. To judge by the particularly large size and number of the guard stones used, damage from and to vehicles was perceived as a real threat.

The dimensions of these fifty-two guard stones protecting water infrastructure in Pompeii define the specific manner in which this protection was accomplished (fig. 4.8). Because the draft animal(s) were ahead of the vehicle, there was little chance for a cart to directly impact a fountain. Without protection, the cart's wheels could scrape against the basin's side and potentially even dislodge one of the slabs forming it.[323] By adding a guard stone, vehicles were pushed away from the fountain by at least the distance that the stone intruded into the street. Thus, in large part, depth defines the guarding function of these stones. Height too is an important factor for guard stones at fountains because the wheel hub (nave)—the roughly 18-centimeter-long part of the wheel and axle that extends beyond the width of the wheel—might still reach the fountain or a person using it. When a guard stone is shorter than the axle height, approximately 50 centimeters, a cart's wheel can roll beside the stone and the hub will pass above it. When a guard stone is taller than the height of the axle, it creates a "double distancing" effect, forcing the cart driver to consider not only the location of the wheel but also the part of the axle that extends beyond it.[324] The double distancing effect was created by nearly half (47%) of the guard stones protecting objects at water infrastructure, and at least one tall stone was placed at 73% (16 of 22) of fountains in the street. It is clear that this was a conscious (if not universal) choice to protect fountains, the people using them, and perhaps the carts as well from collision.

For the remaining 318 guard stones not at water infrastructure, only 21% are of sufficient height to create this double distancing effect (fig. 4.8). Along the curbs, however, the distance that a guard stone extended into the street was

---

[322] These are at two of the busiest intersections in the city: via Stabiana at via degli Augustali and via Stabiana at via dell'Abbondanza.

[323] Nishida 1991.

[324] Likely related to their height, the guard stones in this group are relatively and proportionally wider. Guard stones protecting water infrastructure are on average 72% taller, 30% wider, and 35% deeper than the average guard stone.

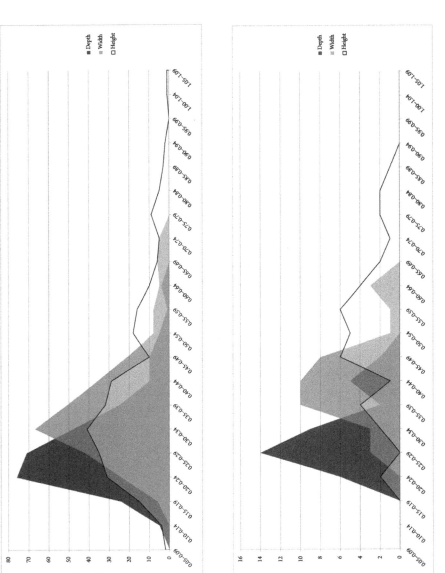

Figure 4.8 Guard-stone dimensions: all (top); at water features (bottom).

usually sufficient to protect pedestrians and other objects that might have been standing on the sidewalks. In fact, 91% of all guard stones not at water infrastructure measure between 10 and 39 centimeters in depth, which is between half and twice the minimum required to push cart's wheels away from the curb and prevent the hubs from rolling over those curbs. It is easy, if uncomfortable, to imagine the damage that a cart hub could do if it were to hit one's lower leg from behind and roll over it, crushing the ankle and breaking the bones of the leg and foot. Such an injury might be debilitating for life. Because shops, workshops, bars, and restaurants all vied for the valuable commercial real estate of intersections, we should imagine still more people here than just those passing through, increasing the likelihood of disastrous interactions between people and vehicles.

Nowhere is this association between guard stones, vehicles, and pedestrians more clear than at the intersection of via di Nola and via del Vesuvio (fig. 4.7). With its many dependent commercial properties united by an architecturally uniform facade, it seems safe to assume that the owner(s) of the casa del Torello di bronzo (V 1, 7) ordered the installation of the thirteen nearly identical guard stones along the north curb. As these shops and workshops were only meters from the one of the city's busiest intersections, the guard stones served to protect the people along its frontage. In fact, the two guard stones closest to the intersection even protected those pedestrians arriving at and leaving the area by flanking the northern stepping stone on via di Nola, which abuts the curb.

Further support for the idea of protection from vehicles comes from the association of guard stones with another form of evidence in the streets: ruts. Ruts are discussed in more detail in Chapter 5, but the positive correlation between the depth of ruts and the placement of guard stones has two important ramifications for the current discussion. First, the fact that 56% of all guard stones are found on sections of streets with deep ruts adds greater weight to the connection between carts and guards stones (table 4.3). The drop-off in the correlation, however, with lighter depths of rutting—13% of guard stones at shallow rutting, 7% at faint rutting, and 5% at no rutting—has important chronological implications as well. Ruts have often been wrongly treated as an artifact produced by a single variable, the volume of traffic, and scholars have attempted to use rut depth as a proxy for the volume of carts and, more importantly, the absence of such volume in a particular street.[325] An equally important variable, of course, is time. In this case it is not the additive effect that time has on rut depth (actually a multiplier on the number of carts) but rather the subtractive effect that repaving a street has on ruts.

---

[325] Wallace-Hadrill 1995.

Table 4.3 **Guard stone and rut depth correlation.**

Rut Depth	Number of Associated Guard Stones	Area of Streets (m²)	Percentage of Street Area	Area of Street per Guard Stone (m²)
Deep	220	10,218.02	46.25	46.45
Shallow	51	3,654.38	16.54	71.65
Faint	28	4,797.24	21.71	171.33
No Rut	19	3,422.40	15.49	180.13

For guard stones, the repaving of streets across the city shows that while paving stones were being repaired and replaced, guard stones were not. In streets where there are deep ruts, the ratio of guard stones to street area is one stone per 46.45 square meters. As the ruts become lighter, the guard stones become fewer: one stone for every 71.65 square meters of street with shallow ruts and one every 171.33 square meters associated with faint ruts. On streets not yet rutted, the association is the lowest: only one guard stone every 180.13 square meters. Why guard stones were not being replaced when the streets were repaved is not entirely clear. In some examples of streets without ruts, such as vicolo del Labirinto, vicolo del Fauno, and vicolo I 8–I 9, the pavement appears to be especially new or even unfinished, which might suggest that the guard stones simply have not been installed. In other instances of streets without ruts—for example, on via Marina and the elevated section of via dell'Abbondanza in front of the Stabian Baths—the areas have become pedestrian zones, and the absence of carts means the absence of a need for them. This explanation, however, does not address the other categories of rutting that also show a precipitous decline in guard stone use. Sections of street with faint rutting, the second largest category by area, have only 28 stones installed, compared to the 220 guard stones in deeply rutted streets, which take up just over twice as much area.

Summary

Though known at a few other sites, no other city offers the number of guard stones or as complete and contemporary a landscape in which to examine them.[326] Like stepping stones, which arrive only with the adoption of lava stone pavements and begin their obsolescence even before populating the entire city,

---

[326] These include Egnazia, Herculaneum, and Norba.

guard stones were transitional objects in the streets at Pompeii. Their presence and distribution stand as supporting evidence of the great volume of traffic that circulated in the streets and the care Pompeians took to protect themselves and their civic infrastructure, while their decline hints at the evolving streetscape and the developments underway to improve that most dynamic space of civic infrastructure. In 79 CE, the general form of Pompeii's urban streets and its particular architectures point at once to a centuries-long evolution to better manage the intensifying collocation of traffic and wastewater. At the same time they hint at a future in which water and wheels would not be contained equally by the curbs but instead be separated by the surface of the street: carts above, water below.

That surface, the familiar Roman polygonal paving, was created by cutting wedge-shaped pieces off large, irregular "blanks," forcing the pavers down into a clean soil, and then locking them together by the compression from their neighbors and stones of the curbs. Those curbs would grow taller to emphasize individual buildings or sink to a relative lower level as new pavements were built against them. Stepping stones offered dry passage across the rectangular void of the street, particularly at intersections and important locations in the middle of streets. Stepping stones were centered in the street or spaced carefully among others to offer an easy crossing for pedestrians and vehicles alike. Protecting pedestrians and other objects from those same carts, at least at certain locations, was the function of the guard stone. Though most guard stones were less than 35 centimeters tall, it was the distance they extended into the street that pushed vehicles away from the curbs and the people and fountains that stood on them. The unintended consequence of Pompeii's final street form was the creation of long vertical faces upon which the interaction of vehicles and the street's architecture could be recorded.

5

Evidence of Traffic

A *via* 'road' is indeed an *iter* 'way,' because it *teritur* 'is worn down' by *vehendo* 'carrying in wagons'; an *actus* 'driving-passage' is likewise an *iter*, because it is worn down by *agendo* 'driving of cattle.' Moreover an *ambitus* 'edge-road' is an *iter* 'way,' because it *teritur* 'is worn' by the going around: for an edge-road is a circuit; from this the interpreters of the Twelve Tables define the *ambitus* of the wall as its circuit.[327]

Ruts, worn deeply into the streets, have always evoked a sense of wonderment (figs. 3.6, 5.5, 5.7–5.8). Ruts are instantly recognizable and immediately understandable. Moreover, because they represent not only people, lots of people, but also their movement, ruts create an unconscious elision between the act of walking through the ruins and the flow of ancient traffic that coursed through the once living city. Ruts have always felt like evidence, not least to Varro, who saw the wearing caused by movement to be inseparable from the definition of the space that carries it. It is now possible to go further and examine that feeling and definition analytically and understand what ruts and other wearing patterns like them are actually evidence of. The goal of this chapter is therefore to examine the interactions between the movement of long-disappeared vehicles and the principal components of the Pompeian streetscape. Roman vehicles— both two-wheeled carts and four-wheeled wagons—were surprisingly complex objects, boasting both impressive technical innovations and ornamentation. Of importance to this study, however, are the elements of their construction and the underlying design that defined the kinds of interactions that vehicles had with the environment of the street. The most obvious and most culturally resonant interactions are the ruts, which stand as evidence for a number of aspects of life in Pompeii, including the presence, size, and volume of carts as well as some preliminary notions of how traffic circulated in the city. Ruts can also help to understand the operation of the civic administration, the responsibilities of property owners for street maintenance, and even the decision-making

---

[327] Varro. *Ling. Lat.* 5.22. I am grateful to J. Hartnett for sharing this reference with me.

processes of those groups. On the basis of extensive fieldwork as well as the work of others, ruts at Pompeii are subjected to a comprehensive study here for the first time, including a description of how they are formed and what their dimensions—width, depth, and the distance between—can tell us about wheeled traffic.

New forms of evidence inscribed on the vertical faces of street features, on the sides of curbstones, and on the edges of stepping stones are also explored to expand beyond the information from ruts alone. These new forms, the marks of carts overriding or sliding along street features, are more specific and permit the determination of the direction of travel at hundreds of locations throughout Pompeii. The discussion in this chapter is technical but appropriately so: careful analysis of both vehicles and the ruts they formed reveal the sizes of vehicles that used the streets, while the detailed descriptions of how wearing patterns on the vertical faces of street architecture illustrate how one can determine the direction those vehicles were traveling. The final section of the chapter, along with an addendum on interpreting less clear evidence and rating the certainty of that interpretation, is intended to be at once a culmination of the sustained examination of the Pompeian street in preceding chapters, the archaeological foundation for an argument establishing the traffic systems at Pompeii in the next chapter, and a kind of detachable handbook for the identification and evaluation of evidence for traffic at other archaeological sites.

Vehicles

Roman wheeled vehicles were remarkable examples of ancient technology.[328] Long misunderstood,[329] along with the relative costs of land transport,[330] Roman vehicles and harnessing systems were deemed inefficient and cited as a drag on the Roman economy. More recent research has shown the complexity of their design, the technical skill in their construction, and their importance in local and regional transport economies. Indeed, the technology of the Roman cart would not be surpassed until the eighteenth century.[331] Our present understanding is based on careful examination of the remaining evidence from art,

---

[328] Some luxurious vehicles were equipped with clocks, odometers, and swiveling chairs. Humphrey, Oleson, and Sherwood 1998, 432.

[329] The misunderstanding goes back at least to the experimental research on Roman harnesses of Richard Lefebvre des Noëttes, published in 1931. Weller (1999, "Who Was Lefebvre des Noëttes?") credits Salama (1951) and Chevallier (1976) for dispelling the myths concerning Roman harnessing. Vigneron 1968, 108–38.

[330] White 1975, 52; Laurence 1998, 126–32; 1999, 126–27; Poehler 2011a.

[331] Langdon 1986, 117; Weller 1999 ("Wagon Construction").

archaeology, and literature, which is ample but, in relation to the hundreds of thousands of carts and wagons that must have been built over the centuries, is only a tiny fraction of what once existed for us to consider.[332] The utilitarian nature of the cart meant that its representation in art would focus more often on ritual or ceremonial contexts, while its mention in literature often was only in passing or to be employed in metaphor. Absence from the archaeological record is not surprising as these vehicles were wholly recyclable objects: iron parts could be hammered into new forms,[333] wood repurposed for building or fuel, and animals set to other tasks or consumed as food. Only under rare circumstances, such as a deliberate burial or the accidental interment by a volcanic eruption, do entire vehicles survive, allowing us to examine their forms and interpret their operation.[334]

To reconstruct the kinds of vehicles that made up the traffic in Pompeii, we are therefore fortunate to have well-preserved and contemporary examples of both two-wheeled carts and four-wheeled wagons from Pompeii and Stabia. From these examples it is possible to describe the large size and remarkable construction of these vehicles as well as to learn more about the process of driving them. The most famous cart from Pompeii is the two-wheeler found by Maiuri in August 1931 at the Casa del Menandro (fig. 5.1).[335] The discovery of the Menander cart in situ offered an opportunity to study a remarkably preserved and largely still articulated ancient vehicle within its context of use. Situated at the back of the house, the stable in which the cart was found is one of the largest in the city. Fastenings found here suggested to the excavators that four animals were normally kept in the stable, though no animals were discovered. Iron, bronze, and wooden parts were recovered in association with the cart, including two iron tires 1.39 meters in diameter,[336] iron bars, bronze bells and pendants, and two bronze fittings in the shape of a thumb, one of which is affixed to the end

---

[332] If one considers only the 500-year period between 250 BCE and 250 CE, only 2,000 vehicles needed to be built per year across the entire empire to reach 1 million. Van Tilburg (2007, 47) points out that nearly every farm would need at least one vehicle.

[333] Cart parts in the process of recycling are known from the Roman fort at Newstead. Curle 1911, 288, plate LXV, nn. 2–5.

[334] For wagon burials in Italy, see Crouwel 2012, 89–90.

[335] Compared to the evidence for their circulation, relatively few carts, wagons, or their parts have been reported at Pompeii. On these remains, see Eschebach and Eschebach (1995, 117, pl. 21.2) and García y García (2006, 183) on the cast of a wheel from I 4, 28 in the old antiquarium; see Maiuri (1940, 228–29, fig. 37) on the cisium found at the Grande Palestra.

[336] This is the measurement given by Tsujimura (1991, 61). Allison (2006, 110 n. 600, plate 44.1) cites the Giornali degli Scavi for her wheel measurement of 1.39 meters; Stefani (2003, 207) reports the wheel diameter at 1.40 meters. Certainly, these discrepancies can be explained by differing points of measurement (e.g., inside to inside, outside to outside, center to center, or even inside to outside) or perhaps slight deformations of the wheel since excavation.

Figure 5.1 Cisium from Casa del Menandro after excavation, from Allison 2006, fig. 217.

of the reconstructed draught pole.[337] These finds suggested to the excavators that the Menander cart was designed primarily to carry people and identified it as a *cisium*.[338] The reconstructed vehicle reflects this interpretation.

Only loads of minimal volume—though, perhaps of exceptional weight—could have been transported by the small four-wheeled cart found in an adjacent property. The "carrettino" was discovered in the portico of the Casa del Fabbro and compared to the Menander cart, this vehicle is quite small.[339] The iron rings

---

[337] Allison (2006, 111–12, nn. 610, 625) believes that if the second thumb is from the same cart, then this reconstruction cannot be correct. On the advice of Lindsay Allason-Jones, she thinks these devices might have served better upright on the crosspiece of the draught pole to harness the animals. Alternatively, one might equally reconstruct the cart as a Y-pole type cart with two side beams rather than the single beam of a central-pole type (see Crouwel 2012, 73–78). It is also possible that the two side poles did not return to the center but instead extended as two parallel beams. This later reconstruction would allow a human to more easily pull the cart, which elides with the anatomy of the bronze fittings and also with the coincidence of the absence of draft animals from the stable. Finally, the act of tying reins to one's thumb was common enough that jurists ruled on liability when a slave's thumb was torn off (D.9.2.27.34). These bronze objects might have offered a helpful reminder and alternative.

[338] Stefani 2003, 206–9.

[339] Ciarallo and De Carolis 1999, 248–49; Allison 2006, 190, plate 88.1.

of the hubs (nave hoops)[340] are 7 centimeters in diameter, and four iron tires are only 56 centimeters in diameter, which is two-fifths that of the Menander cart's wheel. It is tempting due to the small size of this cart to associate it directly with the tools also found in the portico and interpret it as a kind of mobile tool-box, a craftsman's transportation kit needed for the dozens of kilograms of iron tools of his trade.[341] At 79 centimeters wide, however, the carrettino would not fit between most stepping stones, and with an axle height under 30 centimeters, it could not have passed over them either. For this reason, this vehicle or others like it were unlikely to be common in Pompeii's streets.

Another four-wheeled wagon was found more recently in the stable area of the villa Arianna at Stabia. Excavated in 1981 and conserved and reconstructed in 1991, this wagon provides the fullest picture of how Roman vehicles were constructed and used (figs. 5.2–5.4). Each wheel was fitted with an iron tire 1.17 meters in diameter and 3.5 centimeters wide.[342] These tires bound a multipart felloe to a large (40 cm) iron-hooped nave housing ten spokes, 28 centimeters in length.[343] The wheels were attached to solid reinforced wooden axles, the ends of which were fitted with iron flanges so that the wheels rested and rotated on a metal base.[344] The two axles supported the kind of shallow box of slat-work construction well represented in art.[345] Wooden frameworks of the undercarriage housed long iron rods that bound the box to the axles. In the front of the vehicle this iron rod also permitted the lead axle to pivot independently from the body and a complex design of the axle's connection to the draught pole allowed an even fuller range of motion.[346] Two curving wooden forks attached to the draught pole and extended toward the cart to slide within notches in the framework, just above the axle. An iron bar parallel to the axle bound the forks together a short distance in front of the axle (ca. 12.5 cm).

By this design, a bit of sway was permitted in the draught pole before force was applied to the axle causing the vehicle to change direction. Such play in the

---

[340] On issues of terminology, I follow Crouwel 2012, xiii–xv.

[341] Allison 2006, 180–91. Concerning only the identifiable iron objects, these tools include shears, a small pick, dividers, gouge, tang, a saw, tongs, four blades, four hammers, five small jugs, seven files, and eighteen chisels.

[342] There is discrepancy in the publications of this cart, listing both 1.17 meters (Miniero 1987, 192–93) and 1.15 meters (Miniero 1991–92, 224) as the diameter of the wheel. Because the later is a summary publication and the earlier the full publication, I follow the earlier here.

[343] The form and number of the spokes were recovered from a plaster cast taken during excavation; Miniero 1987, 192.

[344] Flanges, parts nn. 41 and 42, were inserted on the top and bottom of the axle: Miniero 1987, 191–92, fig. 17. On axle grease, see Chapter 7, 189–90.

[345] Miniero 1987, 207, fig. 38; Staccioli 2003, 104, fig. 85; van Tilburg 2005, 64–74.

[346] Such pivoting front axles are attested from as early as the fifth century BCE; Crouwel 2012, 92, n. 25.

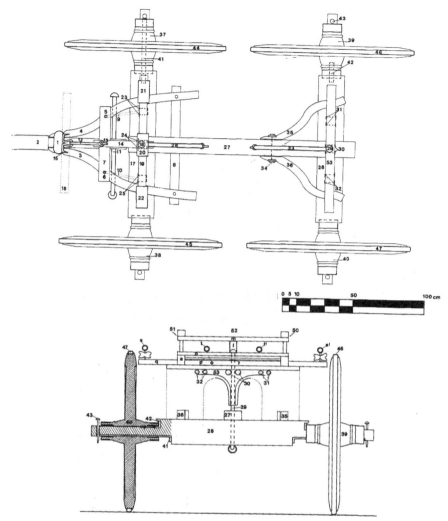

Figure 5.2 Wagon from the villa Arianna at Stabia, after Minerio 1987, figs. 7a–b, 17.

steering system—and according to the reconstruction the draught pole could move freely left or right up to 20 degrees—was of particular value because the animal(s) pulling the cart may have needed to avoid obstacles that the vehicle did not.[347] The clearest example of this is the stepping stones in Pompeii that would pass below the cart but require a single draft animal to slightly modify its course to avoid the stone. The draught pole also articulated vertically, permitting animals

[347] Note that Miniero (1987) and Rega (1991–92) differently reconstruct the front axle. Again, I accept the primary publication.

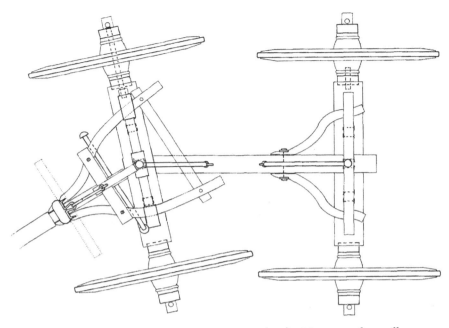

Figure 5.3 Axle pivot (12°) and draught pole sway (20°) of the wagon from villa Arianna at Stabia.

to make a step up without having to lift some of the vehicle's load to do so. A second wooden bar bound the forks again behind the axle, but it is unclear if this had an additional function in steering or simply further stabilized the forks. Once the iron bar was engaged against the axle, both wheels could turn up to the point where they came into contact with the body of the cart. Two iron plates were attached to the box here apparently to prevent the cart's wheels from damaging the body during particularly sharp turns. With the metal plates in place, the wheels could pivot approximately 12 degrees, with the draft animal(s) already 20 degrees farther into the turn (fig. 5.3). The pivoting front axle was an important technical advance for these vehicles, allowing for far greater maneuverability. Indeed, in compressed urban environments, like Republican Rome and first-century-CE Pompeii,[348] turning around many corners might have been possible only for two-wheeled carts and four-wheeled wagons with a pivoting front axle.

While the angle by which a cart's wheel impacted street features determines the behavior of that interaction, the intensity of the impact is a function of the weight of the vehicle and its load. Of course, it is not possible to know exactly what ancient vehicles weighed or what they carried (and some would have been

[348] On street widths, Chapter 6, 156; Chapter 8, 232–33.

empty), but there is good evidence to make estimates of each. The Langres wagon, which is very similar in construction to the wagon from Stabia, has been studied by multiple scholars who agree that the metal and wood used to construct the vehicle would weigh about 500 kilograms. The average *cisium* is estimated to be 250 to 300 kilograms when empty. Being a light passenger vehicle, the *cisium* would not carry much weight, perhaps another 250 kilograms consisting of a driver, two people, and their baggage.[349] Heavy four-wheeled wagons, however, could carry very substantial loads. The *Codex Theodosianus* describes the legal maximums for cart types used in the *cursus publicus*, but these legal maximums cannot be considered maximum possible loads.[350] In fact, they might be better estimates for average or even minimum loads. For example, if we apply the weight limit of the Theodosian *birota* to the *cisium* studied by Raepsaet, the average estimated load of 250 kilograms is perhaps twice what was allowed.[351] Similarly, the Langres wagon, if considered to be the *raeda*, could legally carry 1,000 Roman pounds (330 kg), yet estimates of the wine barrel depicted and its contents are estimated at about 1,000 kilograms when full, or three times the legal limit.[352] It therefore seems appropriate to imagine average total weights of the vehicle, passengers, and cargoes closer to 500 kilograms for two-wheeled vehicles and 1,000 kilograms for four-wheeled vehicles.

The most common effect of the weight of Roman vehicles was the creation of ruts in the pavements. In fact, it has been suggested that the surprisingly low load limits of the *Codex Theodosianus* were set in order to prevent damage to the road surfaces.[353] The famously deep ruts in Pompeii, however, cannot be explained by weight alone.

Ruts

The formation of ruts is determined by a number of interdependent factors, including the types and construction of vehicles traveling,[354] the weight of

---

[349] Weller 1999 ("Wagon Construction"), n. 43.

[350] Weller 1999 ("Geography and Roads") cites the *Codex Theodosianus* (8.5.8) and offers the following conversions to metric weights: *Angaria*: 1,500 Roman lbs. = 492 kg; *Raeda*: 1,000 Roman lbs. = 330 kg; *Currus*: 600 Roman lbs. = 198 kg; *Vereda*: 300 Roman lbs. = 99 kg; *Birota*: 200 Roman lbs. = 66 kg.

[351] This estimate assumes the weight of passengers was excluded.

[352] The law and the depiction, however, are not necessarily contemporary.

[353] Weller 1999 ("Geography and Roads"); most recently Russell 2014, 98, n. 18.

[354] Although surviving cart's wheels were fitted with an iron rim, other treads were possible, including iron studs and wooden or even rawhide rims. Each would wear differently on the street surface; Crouwel 2012, 30–31.

those vehicles, the volume of traffic, the duration of use, and the nature of the street environment.[355] Variables of the street environment can include the surface treatment, obstructions, the width and slope of the street as well as erosive elements, such as water, grit, and debris. Most important among all these variables are traffic volume and surface treatment. Traffic volume has a multiplying effect upon the other vehicular factors, amplifying their impact upon the street. Conversely, the street's surface treatment absorbs, resists, and deforms these effects based on the hardness of the materials used and their arrangement. The interplay of these factors means that ruts form simultaneously in two places: (1) the narrow paths where cart's wheels were most frequently positioned and (2) in the weakest areas of the pavement, the joints between individual stones, where an equal number of cart's wheels will have a disproportionate erosional impact. For the first point, the narrow paths where wheels rolled over the paving stones were determined primarily by the distance between the wheels. Although the standardization of the Roman axle width has been mythologized and claims of its preservation in modern train gauges have been debunked,[356] the data from Pompeii, reveal that there are some patterns within that variability.

To understand how such patterns might have developed, it is perhaps easiest to imagine the work of the wainwright. While there was no standard blueprint for him to follow, that does not mean that there were no conventions (or even instructions) for his craft. Moreover, because many parts of a vehicle are interdependent, it is essential that they be built to *some* standard to function properly together. Thus, opposing wheels must be the same diameter, lest the cart lean to one side; the steering mechanisms must be symmetrical lest the cart turn differently in opposite directions; the frameworks attaching the box to the axles must be of the same height lest the box slope to one side or distribute weight unevenly onto the axle, making cargo less secure. For the wainwright (and for our interpretations), the obvious solution was to choose some initial dimensional system, preferably in a known unit of measure, as the starting point for construction and create parts in proportion to that dimension.

Close examination of the Stabia wagon, starting with the axle, bears this out (fig. 5.4). The axle's reconstructed length is 1.96 meters, which is 1 1/3 *passus* (or 6 2/3 *pedes*, Roman feet; hereafter RF). The wheels—four *pedes* in diameter with hubs 1 1/3 *pedes* in length—were attached to the rounded

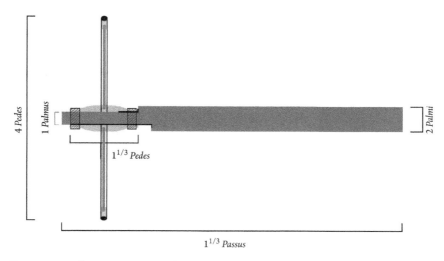

Figure 5.4 Axle reconstruction of the wagon from villa Arianna at Stabia.

end of the axle cut to one *palmus* in diameter.[357] The square section of the axle is twice this size, at two *palmi* in width and depth. The *palmus* is used again to determine the distance the hub would be recessed into the axle block. These careful calculations to form the axle also included the decision to set the wheels one *passus* (1.47 m), or 5 RF, apart. Because the box of the cart was not raised above the wheels, it could fit only between the wheels. In fact, in order to not interfere with the function of the pivoting front axle, the box width needed to be significantly narrow to allow the swing of the wheels but still wide enough to create a sufficient platform for haulage. For the Stabian wagon, this distance is approximately 75 centimeters, close to 2.5 RF. Together, these Roman measurements demonstrate the careful planning that characterized vehicle construction. Specifically, shaping the axle defined the gauge (i.e., the distance between the centers of the two wheels) of the cart at this particular dimension (5 RF) and which, consequently, defined those narrow and specific paths where wheels would most often roll over the streets. Defined gauges thus helped to create the regularity observed in the urban ruts, while the width of the street and its style of paving produce their irregularity. When one also considers the number of vehicles that must have been built with larger or smaller fixed cart gauges, it is easier to understand how the variability of rutting formed in an ancient city.

---

[357] The circumference of a four RF tire is coincidentally 12.5 RF, making the linear measurement to create the wheel easy to achieve, and as Vitruvius (10.9.1–4) explains, it can be used to create an odometer.

Specifically, the choice of gauge impacts the formation of ruts by placing many wheels on the same line, repeatedly putting stress on the pavements in a limited segment of the street. Over time, through hundreds and thousands of iterations, ruts begin to form first in the weakest points of the paving. The susceptibility of certain paving styles to rutting, however, can generate variability in the actual location of ruts. That is, while the patterns of regularity in cart construction acted to create two fixed furrows in the pavement, the particular strengths and weaknesses of different styles of paving served to prevent or facilitate such simplicity and symmetry. For example, the earliest surfaces, streets and roads formed from beaten ash, have a consistent matrix, and the weaknesses of the surface are equally dispersed across it. Ruts therefore begin to form anywhere across the surface that the wheels can roll. Over time, the fixed gauges of vehicles commonly create two wide troughs on either side of a central hump that gave a natural camber to the street.[358] Similarly, streets paved in small stones have natural weaknesses throughout their surface, permitting ruts to form anywhere the gauges of the vehicles will allow. The most iconic example of paving in small stones is a branch from the via Domitia, in the south of France, leading to the site of Ambrussum.[359] The polygonal paving style known at Pompeii and throughout Italy was widely used by the late Republican period not only for the durability of the materials (almost exclusively lava stone) but also for the strength of their arrangement.[360] The weak points in the surface, where each stone met, were few in number and only coincidentally aligned with the position of wheels.[361] Outside of Italy in the Imperial period, streets were more regularly paved, with square or rectangular blocks set perpendicular to the street.[362] Although it was a simpler means of fitting the surface together, this organization of paving materials created areas of weakness that are greater in length and more regularly aligned with axle gauges, which facilitated rut formation. An important solution was to use long rectangular blocks but to set them at a 45 degree angle to the direction of the street. In this diagonal pattern[363] the creation and installation of the pavement was more easily accomplished and

---

[358] Chapter 3, 57–58; Thomas, van der Graaff, and Wilkinson 2013, 8, fig. 13.

[359] Similar paving survives at Velia.

[360] Laurence 2008.

[361] The Romans understood this process (Procop. *Goth.* 5.14.6–11).

[362] Perpendicular paving is common in the Roman cities of North Africa (e.g., Algeria: Hippo Regius, Khamissa, and Tiddis; Tunisia: Carthage, Lepcis Magna, Maktar, Musti, Nabeul-Neapolis, Pheradi Maius, and Sbeitla) and the Near East (e.g., Antioch, Gerash, Petra). I am grateful to S. Ellis for sharing his images of Tunisian cities.

[363] E.g., Maktar, Oudna, Sbeitla, Sepphoris, and Timgad. There are also several examples where perpendicular and diagonal pavement styles are used on the same street or intersecting streets: Bulla Regia, Dougga, Djemilia, Madaure, Thysdrus, Timgad, and Thibilis.

Figure 5.5 Converging ruts at the Arch of Trajan, Timgad.

the surface presented exceptionally short areas of weakness that were difficult for cart's wheels to exploit.[364]

The narrowness of a street compounded these effects. For example, the wide streets of Timgad and the diagonal organization of its paving prevented deep individual ruts from forming. Only when compressed into the gates of the city did the volume of traffic overwhelm the durability of the pavement (fig. 5.5). Conversely, on the many narrow streets of Pompeii, paved in the polygonal style, one wheel was regularly quite close to one side of the street, leaving a rut at the curb's edge and another rut defined by the distance between the wheels. With the curb acting as a guide, these ruts tend to be narrow but distinct. On streets wide enough for cart drivers to stray from the curb, ruts most easily formed where the edges of paving stones met and aligned parallel to the curb. At first, carts' wheels produced short, discontinuous sections of rutting, with the deepest wearing in the seams between stones and shallower wear on the stones leading into and out of these furrows. On wide streets, this formation process explains why ruts seem to appear, deepen, then disappear, only to

---

[364] Instead, in the diagonal style of pavement, wheels slide laterally across the short diagonals created by the junctions in the stones, producing in some cases a kind of shallow zigzag pattern. This pattern can be seen on the *cardo maximus* at Timgad.

reappear farther down the street, sometimes offset only a few centimeters to the right or left.

The placement of street features, especially stepping stones, magnified these pressures as they forced all carts' wheels to pass though the limited spaces between them and produced their own sections of short, deep ruts. Over time, these short rutted sections became connected as carts wore down the solid stones between sections and also became widened as the edges of the ruts were eroded and parallel ruts offset by only a few centimeters were incorporated. Eventually, the entire street came to have only two, three, or four deep furrows, which became nearly impossible to avoid driving in, running over long stretches of the street. The process of rut formation was thus a feedback system, in which street width and street features first prescribed the position of vehicles and then axle gauges informed where the wheels will pass. These factors amplified the pressures upon the narrow areas of the street that were actually used, exploiting the weaknesses between the paving materials. With sufficient repetition, these areas became deeply rutted, which attracted more carts and further compressed traffic onto a specific route. The oscillation of carts of different axles gauges sliding into and climbing out of ruts already formed further widened the space of the ruts, drawing still more vehicles into those tracks.

Rut Pairs

Careful examination of well-defined pairs of ruts not only helps to illustrate this feedback system but also can be used to define the gauges of vehicles that had to be present in order to form such pairs. In 1983, Sillieres defined a simple method for measuring and analyzing rut pairs, describing them (1) by their maximum and minimum extents, as well as (2) by the center-rut to center-rut dimensions and (3) by the inner edge of one rut to the outer edge of the other (fig. 5.6).[365] Because the presence of well-defined rut pairs strongly suggests that the bulk of vehicular traffic fell into these ruts, the measure of their maximum extent defines the largest gauge of carts that regularly used this street. Conversely, the minimum extent shows the smallest gauge commonly present. Rarely does either of these measures match a known or suspected measurement for actual vehicle gauges, indicating that ruts are not primarily produced by the very largest and very smallest vehicles. Further support for this interpretation comes from the absence of the two very narrow parallel rut pairs that would form if the two predominant vehicle gauges were the largest and the smallest examples. Instead, most ruts are relatively wide, three to eight times wider than the iron tire of the

---

[365] I thank Alan Kaiser for bringing this citation to my attention.

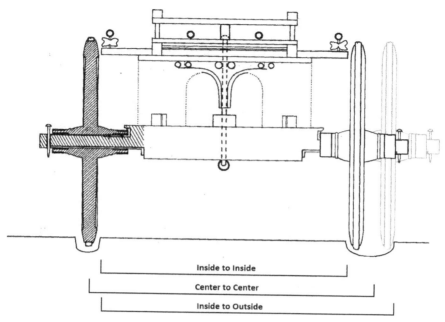

Figure 5.6 Rut measurement method.

cart that made them. Such variability demonstrates the presence of a variety of gauges as well as their lateral movement within the space of the forming rut.

Therefore, the most important dimension for evaluating the sizes of carts that formed these ruts is the measurement from the inside edge of one rut to the outside edge of another. In the rare instances where the width of each rut in a pair is identical, it is possible that all carts using those ruts were of the same size. Even then, however, the center-to-center measurement should match a known gauge as well, suggesting that the edges were equally formed only by drift across the space of the ruts and not by carts of different gauges. Most pairs of ruts are not the same width and therefore can be the product only of vehicles of varying sizes. That variation, however, was neither random nor great. Since we know that vehicles should be built to some standard—the wagon from Stabia had a gauge of 5 RF—we can expect that the variation among vehicles was the effect of these different gauges in whole and half Roman feet rather than carts being made to any size between the largest and smallest possibilities reflected in the minimum and maximum rut extents. Fortunately, Sillieres's method of measuring ruts offers a means to determine these gauges. By taking the distance from the inside of the narrower rut to the outside of the wider rut, one can determine the smallest possible gauge that could have defined those two edges. That same cart, however, could not also form the opposite edges because once one wheel reached the outside of the narrower rut, the other wheel would necessarily still be some distance from the inside of the wider rut. In combination, these inside-to-outside measurements offer two minimum dimensions to match with known (or suspected) vehicle gauges and identify the most common vehicles that made that rut pair.

The south gate into the Roman city at Ampurias offers an excellent example to illustrate this point. Sillieres's measurements show that the minimum distance between ruts was 1.20 meters, making the minimum gauge of carts slightly greater than 4 RF.[366] At the same time, carts with a gauge of 5 RF seem to have defined the widest extent of the ruts. That is, although the center-rut-to-center-rut measurement is 1.45 meters (4.91 RF), the maximum distance between the inside of one rut and the outside of another was measured at 1.46 meters (4.96 RF). Again, because wheels were fixed to the axle, this inside-to-outside distance measures the maximum sway a cart could have within the ruts and therefore defines the widest possible gauge. These measurements show that vehicles with gauges of 5 RF were particularly common at Ampurias, but those of 4 RF could not have contributed to forming these ruts. Conversely, while carts with a 5.5 RF gauge could easily have fitted within these ruts, they seem not to have contributed to the maximum distance between the inside of one rut and the outside of another, suggesting their relative rarity. Therefore, those vehicles with a gauge less than 4.5 RF or larger than 5.5 RF did not enter the south gate at Ampurias with sufficient regularity to impact the form of ruts here.

Oscan and Roman Measures

Ampurias, like Pompeii, saw the installation of a Roman colony after picking the wrong side in a conflict with Rome. Because it was allied with Rome from the late third century BCE and survived into the early Middle Ages, it is unlikely (even if possible) that native and Greek traditions and standards of measure could have influenced the gauges of vehicles entering Roman Ampurias. Between the parochialism of the Greek foot and the absence of other examples of narrow rut pairs to make comparisons, it is nearly impossible to disentangle these potential metrological systems.[367] Moreover, the measurements within the gate fit well with the Roman foot. At Pompeii, the situation is different (table 5.1). While the two systems of measure—the Roman foot and the Oscan foot—are well defined, the period between the installation of the colony and the eruption is sufficiently

---

[366] Sillieres 1983, 39–40, figs. 2–3. Sillieres has also recorded the presence and the height of cuts that presumably were produced by the hubs of carts using the gate.

[367] Broneer 1973, 63–64.

Table 5.1 **Rut pair dimensions at Ampurias and Pompeii.**

Site	Location	Width, left Rut	Width, Right Rut	Rut Width: Center to Center	Rut Width: Inner to Inner	Rut Width: Outer to Outer	Rut Width: Widest Inner to Outer	Smallest Possible Cart Gauges	Largest Possible Cart Gauges	Other Possible Cart Gauges	Source
Ampurias	South Gate	0.23	0.26	1.445	1.2	1.69	1.43	4.5 RF	5.5 RF	5.0 RF	Sillieres
Pompeii	via Consolare north of vicolo di Narciso	0.17	0.16	1.405	1.24	1.57	1.41	4.5 RF 4.5 OF	5.0 RF 5.5 OF	5.0 OF	Crowther
Pompeii	via del Lupanare at VII 12, 18	0.1	0.1	1.42	1.32	1.52	1.42	4.5 RF 5.0 OF	5.0 RF 5.5 OF	5.0 OF	Crowther
Pompeii	via del Vesuvio at V 1, 27	0.18	0.17	1.375	1.2	1.55	1.38	4.0 RF 4.5 OF	5.0 RF 5.5 OF	5.0 OF	Crowther
Pompeii	via degli Augustali east of vicolo Storto	0.27	0.19	1.37	1.14	1.6	1.41	4.0 RF 4.5 OF	5.0 RF 5.5 OF	5.0 OF	Crowther
Pompeii	via degli Augustali west of vicolo Storto	0.1	0.1	1.39	1.29	1.49	1.39	4.5 RF 5.0 OF	5.0 RF 5.5 OF		Crowther
Pompeii	via Consolare at vicolo di Mercurio	0.19	0.23	1.46	1.2	1.62	1.39	4.5 RF 4.5 OF	5.5 RF 5.5 OF	5.0 RF 5.0 OF	Poehler

(Continued)

Table 5.1 **Continued**

Site	Location	Width, left Rut	Width, Right Rut	Rut Width: Center to Center	Rut Width: Inner to Inner	Rut Width: Outer to Outer	Rut Width: Widest Inner to Outer	Smallest Possible Cart Gauges	Largest Possible Cart Gauges	Other Possible Cart Gauges	Source
Pompeii	vicolo di Mercurio at via Consolare	0.12	0.1	1.475	1.32	1.54	1.44	4.5 RF 5.0 OF	5.0 RF 5.5 OF		Poehler
Pompeii	vicolo Storto at via degli Augustali	0.09	0.09	1.36	1.29	1.47	1.38	4.5 RF 5.0 OF	5.0 RF 5.0 OF		Tsujimura, fig. 14
Pompeii	via di Nola at vicolo del Centenario	0.27	0.24	1.395	1.14	1.65	1.41	4.5 RF 4.5 OF	5.5 RF 6.0 OF	5.0 OF	Tsujimura, fig. 9
Pompeii	via dell'Abbondanza at vicolo della nave Europa	0.1	0.11	1.455	1.35	1.56	1.45	5.0 RF 5.0 OF	5.0 RF 5.5 OF		Tsujimura, fig. 13
Pompeii	via di Nola at vicolo di Tesmo	0.19	0.13	1.52	1.36	1.68	1.55	5.0 RF 5.0 OF	5.5 RF 6.0 OF	5.5 OF	Tsujimura, fig. 12

short for vehicles made to Oscan measures to have created ruts that still might be extant in the pavement. That is, it seems certain that any carts built using Oscan measurement would have continued to be prevalent, if not the predominant vehicles, in the Pompeian street for at least a generation, and many must have survived into the Imperial era.[368] Moreover, beyond the likely slow replacement of Oscan by Roman vehicles, there was also a lag time in the replacement of the pavements, and many of the ruts that survived into the Imperial age were made (in part) by carts no longer in circulation.[369]

Examination of the cart from the Casa del Menandro and several well-defined rut pairs at Pompeii reveals that carts built with Oscan units did in fact survive and might even have been still in use in the city's last moments.[370] Measurements of the Menander cart, of both its reconstructed form and the individual elements used in that reconstruction, are found in several sources. In 1990, as part of her study of ruts, Tsujimura measured the reconstructed Menander cart, and although she did not translate the metric dimensions into Oscan units, her measurements show the cart most likely to have been built to Oscan foot (hereafter OF) specifications. Thus, the box of the cart is approximately 5 OF long, 3.5 OF wide, and 1.5 OF deep.[371] More important, however, is her report of the wheel diameter and axle length, which are nearly exactly 5 OF and 6.5 OF, respectively.[372] The Oscan measure of the wheel's iron rim is supported by the dimension of two other iron parts of the Menander cart, two bars 1.5 OF in length.[373] These iron parts are of particular value because although used in the reconstructed cart, their lengths are unchanged.

Tsujimura gives the reconstructed distance between the iron rims as "a 142 cm wheel span," which calculates to an awkward 5.16 OF for the cart's gauge.[374] What Tsujimura does not do, however, is to tell us from where she measured. If this 1.42-meter dimension was not taken from the center of one wheel to the center of the other, then there are two other probable scenarios for how this measurement was achieved. Either the measurement reflects the distance from

---

[368] Survival is likely a product of the high value of these objects.

[369] Ruts on vicolo delle Nozze d'Argento were the same gauge in both the battuto and silex; Nilsson, n.d.

[370] One curious example is the dimensions of the Teatrum Tectum, which is approximately 100 Roman feet long (north–south) and 100 Oscan feet wide (east–west). Could this be a metrological symbol of concord between the colonists and the colonized?

[371] Actual dimensions of the box and their translation into ancient measures: length 1.35 meters (4.59 RF, 4.909 OF), width 1.00 meters (3.40 RF, 3.63 OF), depth 41 centimeters (1.39 RF, 1.49 OF).

[372] Tsujimura 1991, 62.

[373] The bars are 43 centimeters in length; Allison 2006, 111–12, part n. 619 (see also Supplement nos. 114–15).

[374] Tsujimura 1991, 61.

the outside of one wheel to the outside of another, or it is the opposite, from the inside of one wheel to the inside of the other. These are important considerations, because when one factors in the width of the tire, the gauge of the cart becomes either 1.38 meters (exactly 5 OF) on the inner-to-inner measurement or 1.46 meters (nearly exactly 5 RF) on the outer-to-outer measurement. With the rest of the Menander cart falling into Oscan dimensions, it seems preferable to imagine a 5-OF gauge, at least initially, for this vehicle. It is possible that the gauge could have been changed, though this would likely have necessitated the replacement of the axle or the wheels since one needed to widen rather than narrow the gauge.[375] The ancient wainwright must also have faced such ambiguity in this measurement and how to make it. Because of the closeness between five Roman and five Oscan feet (a difference of 9.5 cm) and the width of two iron tires (each 3.5 to 4 cm) the simple decision to set the wheel-to-wheel dimension on the inside of the tire or on its outside can transform the gauge of a vehicle from Oscan to Roman measure and vice versa. Although this transposition of gauge surely occurred at times, the other measurements of the Menander cart also demonstrate that vehicles made to Oscan measures also survived or continued to be made until Pompeii's final days.

Whether by the survival of the vehicles, survival of tradition, or by accident, the different gauges of carts circulating in Pompeii had important effects on the formation of ruts. On the northern segment of via Consolare, one of the oldest streets (and pavements) in the city, a clear pair of deep and wide ruts can be seen terminating at a section of newer pavement near the intersection of vicolo di Narciso (fig. 5.7). That these ruts form a pair is demonstrated by their equivalent depth and width and by the fact that there is insufficient space for a cart to fit between either rut and the edge of the street.[376] Both ruts are of moderate width, 16 and 17 centimeters, with 1.24 meters separating the inner edge of each, defining the smallest possible cart gauges to be 4.5 RF (4.5 OF). In fact, this minimum-width measurement is nearly exactly 4.5 OF.[377] Together, these dimensions create a space (1.57 m) wide enough for carts as large as 5 RF (5.5 OF). The inner-to-outer measurements (1.40 and 1.41 m) are in agreement, showing that carts using 4.5 and 5 RF and/or 5 or 5.5 OF gauges must have been the most common. Further support for the predominance of vehicles using

---

[375] That is, to narrow the gauge, one need only cut back the axle to fit the new position of the inner hub. Conversely, to widen the gauge would require the addition of material between the original cutting and the new gauge. The difficulty of creating and maintaining this retrofit might have made a new axle a preferable option.

[376] A 4 OF cart might just have fit in this space, but the regular placement of guard stones here narrows the street by ca. 20 centimeters.

[377] 1.24 meters = 4.51 OF.

Figure 5.7 Rut pair on via Consolare at VI 17, 17.

these gauges comes from the overall width of via Consolare, clearly intended as a two lane, two-direction street. At 3.33 meters wide, further constricted in some places to about 3.13 meters by a series of guard stones along the west curb, the largest gauge of carts via Consolare could simultaneously accommodate were 5 RF (5.5 OF), but the smaller 4.5 RF (5 OF) would pass with ease.[378] Finally, not only are 5.5 RF and 6 OF cart gauges too wide to make this pair of ruts, two vehicles with these gauges couldn't both use the street at the same time. Of course, these data are not evidence that vehicles of the largest sizes did not use the streets at Pompeii, only that the environment of the street would make their presence uncommon.

Narrow pairs of ruts on small, one-lane streets reinforce and refine the evidence from via Consolare. For example, the well-formed rut pair on via degli Augustali, each only 10 centimeters wide, is offset slightly from each curb in the narrow street (fig. 5.8). The center of these ruts matches well with carts made to 5 OF. The minimum and maximum extents, however, fit closely with cart gauges at 4.5 RF and 5 RF, respectively. Again, while there is ample space in the street for larger carts, no vehicles larger than 5 RF could have regularly contributed to

[378] In this calculation, the width of the naves protruding from the carts into the middle of the street must also be added. Based on excavated carts, these naves are reconstructed to be 18 centimeters each, which adds 36 centimeters to the distance needed for two carts to pass in the space of the street.

Figure 5.8 Rut pair on Augustali at VII 12, 7.

the creation of these ruts. Still another rut pair on an intersecting street, vicolo del Lupanare, repeats the findings from via degli Augustali, but its measures fall even more precisely on set gauges. Here the minimum and maximum extents are nearly exactly 4.5 RF and 5 RF, respectively, again leaving room for 5 OF vehicles between.

These measurements of clearly defined pairs of ruts (table 5.1) demonstrate that their sizes and the distances between them reflect not only a high volume of vehicles traveling within the streets but also that those vehicles were made to a narrow set of dimensional standards. On wide streets with wide ruts, such as via Consolare, the sizes of carts can be circumscribed to a relatively small group of carts with gauges between 1.24 and 1.57 meters. This group, however, includes vehicles with any set gauge between 4.5 OF and 5.5 OF as well as the odd cart not made to some standard. On narrow streets with narrow ruts, such as via degli Augustali and vicolo del Lupanare, the possible sizes of carts that could form these deep ruts can fluctuate no more than 20 centimeters, less than one Oscan or Roman foot. The narrow band of space between 1.32 and 1.47 meters incorporates the confluence of three gauges, 4.5 RF, 5 OF, and 5RF, two of which are attested in the measurements of actual carts found in Pompeii or the surrounding area. These analyses reveal that most carts using the streets were built to one of these three standards.

Directionality

The capacity of ruts to inform us about the actual circulation of vehicles was first explored by Tsujimura in her observation that curved ruts at intersections are most commonly found around the widest angles of the many rhombus-shaped insulae. Rejecting the idea that the ease of turning around an obtuse-angled corner facilitated the formation of ruts at that corner, Tsujimura instead saw these curved ruts as the direct "result of a city-wide restricted traffic system."[379] In support of this claim, Tsujimura charted the curved ruts found on via dell'Abbondanza and via Stabiana in order to illustrate the possibilities for carts turning onto and/or off of these primary thoroughfares. For the first time, her work pinned the movement of ancient vehicles to specific places in the ancient city and reduced the potential directions of travel to only two possibilities. The construction of an entire system of traffic based on this evidence, however, was undermined by her rejection of the idea that the ease of turning around a wider-angled corner facilitated the formation of curved ruts. Without this variable, Tsujimura took the absence of ruts as evidence for the absence of turning and not merely the absence of a record of that turn.

Tsujimura had pushed the analysis of traffic from rutting evidence to its logical limit, but because the system devised from these curved ruts would have been exceptionally complicated, in the end she was forced to acknowledge that exceptions were required for a realistic traffic flow.[380] Nonetheless, her work had established that careful examination of ruts could tell us about the presence and position of carts in the street as well as implying something about their numbers. Ruts alone, however, cannot tell us about the direction that a cart was traveling while creating those ruts. Fortunately, the horizontal surface of the street's paving was not the only point of interaction between vehicles and the architecture of the roadway. The vertical faces of street features—in particular, curbstones, stepping stones, and guard stones—preserve hundreds of instances where the regular and repeated action of vehicles left traces of their passage.

---

[379] Tsujimura 1991, 66.

[380] Tsujimura (1991, 67) admits that curved ruts were found turning around the acute-angled southeast corner of insula VI 14.

Unlike the evidence of traffic circulation from ruts, the wearing of carts' wheels on vertical faces commonly records a specific direction of travel. When wheels came into contact with street features, the hardness of the street feature's material and its position in the middle or on the edge of the street, as well as the weight of the vehicle, the material of its wheel's rim, and the angle of its impact, combined to produce particular patterns of wear. At a given location, most of these parameters were relatively fixed: features were made of one of three types of stone, and while carts did differ in size, they had very similar wheel construction and a high minimum weight. These factors, however, determine only the intensity of the impact, how deeply the pattern of wear would be inscribed, which influence the level of certainty that can be ascribed to any interpretation. The two most important variables for determining direction, instead, were (1) the position of the street feature and (2) the angle of interaction with the wheel; these factors determined the wear pattern's shape. Three of these shapes are sufficiently clear and consistent to tell us what ruts cannot: the direction in which ancient vehicles were traveling on almost every street in Pompeii.

Overriding Wear

The most common shape of wear was produced when a cart's wheel hit a street feature at a sufficiently high angle to force the wheel to climb its vertical face, rolling over that feature and cutting into it a rut-like mark. Termed overriding, this pattern is found especially on stepping stones throughout Pompeii. A particularly clear example at the intersection of via Stabiana and vicolo del Menandro shows how this wearing forms and how it can be recognized (fig. 5.9). Marks on the west face of the center stepping stone show that vehicles hit this stone head on, grinding down into it before reaching the flat surface at the top. Once on top, the vehicle, which we must imagine now slightly unbalanced and leaning slightly more upon one or two wheels, navigated its descent off the stepping stone but left only a general rounding of the stone's opposite side. There are two reasons why the ascent side of overriding wear is distinct while the descent side is general, making it possible to interpret direction from these marks. The first reason is the manner in which the turning wheel applies force to the stone: the forward momentum of the vehicle grinds the wheel downward as it turns during the ascent. Conversely, in falling off the other side, the same forward motion pulls the wheel away from the stone, rather than into it. These differences in the forces applied determined the differences in intensities in the different components of overriding marks.

The other determinant for the shape of overriding marks is a function of why vehicles hit stepping stones in the first place. Carts could not always avoid running into the stepping stones because the gauge fixed the placement of their

Figure 5.9 Overriding wear, stepping stone on vicolo del Menandro at via Stabiana.

wheels and the placement of the stepping stones fixed the paths between them.[381] With the addition of other carts also using the streets, the paths between the stepping stones became further circumscribed, making collisions with some stepping stones and a very specific area of those stepping stones a virtual certainty. Examination of the ruts at stepping stones bears this out: ruts converge into deep furrows between the stones and then fan out again once through the area. That is, while multiple forces compelled a cart to impact a stepping stone at a specific point, that compulsion was not always present when descending the stepping stone. The initiation of contact tended to be specific and the end of contact more general. Together with the forward motion pulling the cart over the stone, the overriding mark becomes a wearing pattern diagnostic of direction.

These factors also make identifying overriding wear relatively easy. In many cases ruts are seen approaching the wear mark, which is deeply and distinctly cut into the street feature. The often steeply curving cut is deeper on the side where the wheels approach and shallower nearer the top of the feature. In some cases, arcing striations from individual iron rims can be observed as well. These kinds of wearing are considered diagnostic, and the interpretation of direction from their pattern is reserved for times when one is 100% to 76% sure of that interpretation. The guard stone on via Consolare offers another paradigmatic example (fig. 5.10).

[381] Chapter 4, 90–93.

Figure 5.10 Diagnostic overriding wear, guard stone on via Consolare.

There are, however, many examples of overriding marks that are less clearly defined. Those marks that are indicative of direction (75%–51% certainty) do preserve the curved in-cutting from the wheel, but that shape is often less clear, especially visually. By sliding one's hand across the face of the stone, however, the location of the wear can easily be found and the slope of the wear can be felt. In some examples, the wear is simply lightly carved into the stone or cut into a stone of irregular shape. At other times only one side of the overriding mark is clear. For example, the northern stepping stone on via dell'Abbondanza at the Eumachia building has one strong edge of overriding wear, but the opposite side blends into a general erosion of the corner (fig. 5.11).

When wearing is only suggestive of direction (50%–26% certainty), the pattern is less distinct. In most cases, suggestive wearing appears (in combination with sliding wear) as a generic rounding on the corners of objects. As carts turn around corners, the iron rims of their wheels climb up and fall back down, shaving off the corner and offering a more general pattern that is broader and steeper on one side of the stone. Thus, one will be less than 50% certain of the interpretation of direction based on the presence of slightly stronger wear on one of the

Figure 5.11 Indicative overriding wear, stepping stone on via dell'Abbondanza.

faces. Despite the indistinctness of this shape, it is often still possible to determine a primary direction of travel. This can be done by examining the manner in which the lowest part of the wear—where the intersection of the street features' vertical faces are still the most distinct—cuts from one face of the stone across another. Such sliding wear is discussed in further detail below. Other examples of overriding wear that are of suggestive quality are very small or shallow and simply offer less of the pattern to evaluate and therefore less to be certain of in one's interpretation (fig. 5.12). Evidence that offers only an ambiguous (25%–1%) indication of direction is weaker still and even less distinct. The slightness of the wear on the southwest face of the easternmost stepping stone on via del Vesuvio at its intersection with via di Nola illustrates how an ambiguous overriding mark might appear.

Sliding Wear

Most overriding wear, again, is produced in the collision of a wheel and stepping stone, often at a very high angle to the object, but it is also found on curbstones, especially at corners, with the interaction occurring at much lower angles. For example, where via Stabiana meets via del Tempio d'Iside, the southwest corner is deeply overridden, with a deep cut through the softer tuff curbstones leading to the top of the lava curbstone at the corner (fig. 5.13). Measuring the angle of this wearing from parallel with the street, we see that vehicles deviating

Figure 5.12 Suggestive overriding wear, stepping stone on via Marina.

approximately 11 degrees from parallel with the street were overriding the curbstone. The western edge of the lava stone, however, also shows that many vehicles slid back down to street level, grinding off the curbstone's corner in the process. The importance of this observation is to demonstrate that interactions of wheels and street features at angles lower than 11 degrees are not sufficient for the cart to gain purchase and ride over that feature. Instead, wheels slid along the feature's face, producing two other forms of wearing that can be used to interpret the direction of an ancient cart's movement: sliding wear and cyclical wear.[382]

On stepping stones, the compounding effects of rutting and the stepping stones' own positions (as described above for overriding marks) are equally apparent for sliding wear. Thus, while vehicle gauges and the location of stepping stones can explain how very specific patterns of wear such as overriding marks can occur from high-angle impacts, in order to understand how these low-angle patterns are formed, one must consider the full experience of cart drivers as they navigated between stepping stones. In most cases, the cart's gauge and stepping-stone spacing are sufficiently matched to allow vehicles to pass unimpeded. Importantly, this also means that the cart must also guide one stepping

---

[382] Caitlin Bogdan's (2011) research and mathematical models were of great value in finding the divisions between the categories of wear and more precisely defining them. I thank her for her efforts.

Figure 5.13 Overriding wear, curbstones on via del Tempio d'Iside at via Stabiana (angle of impact superimposed).

stone directly beneath it. When pulled by two draft animals, the wheels and the animals both moved easily on the same paths between stepping stones. When there was a single draft animal, however, that animal likely moved between stepping stones rather than walking up and over one, offsetting the vehicle and its traction. The steering system of the four-wheeled wagon from Stabia had sufficient sway to allow the draft animal to make this minor adjustment without changing the direction of the cart (fig. 5.3). For two-wheeled vehicles like the cart from the Casa del Menandro and other fixed-axle vehicles, the effect was immediate. Though slight and temporary, the change in angle of the cart's wheels away from parallel to the street as the draft animal navigated between the stepping stones directed those wheels to regularly impact the corners of the stepping stones at a variety of low angles. Moreover, such impacts on those stepping stones combined with overriding wear: while some cart's wheels slid along the face of a stepping stone, others began to ascend the stone and fell back down the corners of these features. Through constant repetition of these circumscribed but still rather nonspecific interactions, stepping stones begin to take on a more diamond shape at the top (fig. 5.14).

Figure 5.14 Stepping stone worn to point, vicolo di Tesmo at via dell'Abbondanza.

Sliding along the face of a curbstone or stepping stone, cart's wheels smoothed the stone in those areas where it remained in contact, necessarily beginning at the top edge. Sliding wear is often accompanied by a mottled orange staining from sustained contact with the iron tire of a wheel. Upon impact, minute splinters of iron were embedded in street features, oxidized, and then were smeared across the face of the stone by subsequent wheels. Often running the length of a stone, such as the corner curbstone at the opposite side of via del Tempio d'Iside (fig. 5.15), sliding wear intensifies over its course, being widest and deepest at the edge facing on an intersection. The direction that carts were traveling to produce this wearing pattern can be inferred from this change in intensity: more carts collided with the stone farther along its length as those carts turned around it. More conclusive evidence for direction is found in observing the manner in which the wearing ends. That is, a direction can be determined when a street feature has wearing on one (primary) face that cuts across another (secondary) intersecting face. The secondary face may be worn or unworn, but the wearing from the primary face will clearly cut across it, leaving a boundary on the feature that marks the point that the wheels left contact with the stone. The interpretation of a direction is possible, therefore, because

Figure 5.15 Sliding wear, curbstone on via del Tempio d'Iside at via dei Teatri.

the course of the wheels' contact can be traced across the primary face of the feature to its abrupt termination at the secondary face. In the example of the curbstone on via del Tempio d'Iside, it is possible to conclusively demonstrate that carts were moving westbound along the right curb and turned northbound onto via dei Teatri.

Interpreting sliding wear is usually a straightforward endeavor. In many cases, such as the northeast corner curbstone at the intersection of vicolo di Tesmo and via Mediana one can readily see western face (side) is much more heavily worn even if the southern face (front) that intersects it is also worn (fig. 5.16). Sliding wear that is indicative of direction still has a significant disparity in the depth and size of the wearing on the primary and secondary faces. Very often the wear pattern will descend farther down the primary face along the line of its intersection with the secondary face, even reaching the level of the paving stones. Because of this downward erosion, indicative wear will have a steeper triangular shape than wear of suggestive certainty, which has a longer and shallower profile. The northeast corner curbstone where vicolo di Eumachia meets via dell'Abbondanza offers a chance to see both of these forms of certainty on a single stone (fig. 5.17). On its east face (side) a broader, stronger wear cuts across the intersection with the south face (front) of the same stone, where a shallower, more elongated triangular wearing approaches the intersection. In this example, both the definition of each wearing and the difference between them are visually distinct. Many other examples are less visually clear

Figure 5.16 Diagnostic sliding wear, curbstone on vicolo di Tesmo at via Mediana.

Figure 5.17 Indicative and suggestive sliding wear, curbstone on via dell'Abbondanza at vicolo di Eumachia.

and require sliding one's hand across the faces of the stone, feeling where the smoothness of the worn area meets the rough surface of the unworn stone. Feeling the junction where two faces intersect by placing a finger on one side of the line and a thumb on the other side can help to establish the downward extent of wear on each face and which face cuts the other. Sliding wear of ambiguous quality is fainter still, with the strength of erosion on the primary face only somewhat greater than on the secondary face. In other cases, wearing of objects of small size or irregular shape—such as the guard stone on via della Fortuna's south curb—makes interpretation uncertain. However, most sliding wear does not preserve sufficient form to make a determination of direction. These uninterpretable examples, however, can still be used to establish the presence of vehicles and to suggest something of their numbers, which is especially useful in combination with wearing patterns that are interpretable of direction.

Cyclical Wearing

Once again, those same factors that combined in overriding wear and sliding wear to produce a general erosion of stepping stones also, in rare instances, formed a very specific pattern of wear that is the clearest evidence of ancient vehicles' direction of travel. In these instances, found exclusively on curbstones, the downward turn of the wheel aligned with its forward pull to inscribe its cyclical motion onto the face of the stone. The canonical example of such cyclical wear is found at the intersection of via Consolare and vicolo di Mercurio (fig. 5.18). Examining the wear, it is not at all difficult to interpret the process that created it: as carts moved westward on vicolo di Mercurio, their wheels came in contact with the top of the stone, simultaneously moving forward and rotating downward, increasing the surface area of the stone in contact with the rim and marking out a diagnostic curve of wear. Both the size and the depth of the wear increase across the face of the stone, moving closer to the intersection with via Consolare, as more of the carts that turned to the north hit this corner curbstone. Other wear and rutting evidence at the intersection confirms the interpretation: the stepping stone has a corresponding sliding wear on its southwest corner, and deep, curving ruts are found associated with the wear on both the stepping stone and curbstone.

A closer consideration of the formation process finds that all three forms of wear, though of varying intensities, are found on the curbstone at via Consolare and vicolo di Mercurio. At the beginning of the wearing, the pattern is shallow and indistinct as fewer wheels hit this part of the stone and even those that did slide along the face, intensified their contact with the

Figure 5.18 Diagnostic cyclical wear, curbstone on vicolo di Mercurio at via Consolare.

curbstone as the wheel reached the corner. The overlapping of this sliding wear elongated the cyclical form's ideal shape, making it appear more parabolic. Near the very end and bottom of the wearing pattern, the convex downward curve begins to bend back upward into a concave shape as the point of the rim in contact with the face of the curbstone reached the bottom of its downward path and moved laterally (within a rut) to reach the end of the stone. The angle of the turn was sharper for some carts, exceeding 11 degrees. In these cases the wheel was pulled up onto the curbstone, eroding both the top and vertical faces in a manner similar to the diagonal wearing produced on stepping stones.

Cyclical wearing, because of its rarity and the specificity of its form, does not appear in the weakest categories of certainty, suggestive and ambiguous. When the interaction of cart's wheels and street features is not specific enough to create the diagnostic downward curve across the face of the stone, the pattern simply becomes more general and triangular in shape. These examples are defined as sliding wear. Instances of cyclical wear that are of indicative quality have less distinctive curves, such as the more rapid descent on the south face of the northeast corner curbstone at the intersection of via Mercurio with vicolo di Mercurio (fig. 5.19). Similarly, the more undulating curve on the west face of the curbstone on vicolo di Tesmo at via Mediana,

Figure 5.19 Indicative cyclical wear, curbstone on vicolo di Mercurio at via di Mercurio.

which also displays diagnostic sliding wear, represents cyclical wearing of indicative quality.[383]

All Wearing Patterns

These three forms of wearing—evidence of the variety of interactions between carts and the architecture of the street—have been arranged and discussed from the most general to the most specific. While overriding was a very common type of interaction and combined frequently with sliding wear, it occurred as a function of the widest range of interactions between carts and street features. Similarly, sliding wear was a very common interaction that was inscribed whenever the angle of impact was below a certain threshold. Sliding wear is also found in combination with cyclical wear, which occurred only under a very circumscribed set of circumstances. Tabulation of all the evidence (table 5.2) bears this out and brings greater clarity to the distribution of wearing evidence types across the different elements of the street architecture. Curbstones, surely for their ubiquity, recorded both the greatest number and the widest range of interactions. In fact, all examples of cyclical wear and the vast majority of sliding wear are found on curbstones. Conversely, the most

[383] This stone preserves both diagnostic sliding wear and indicative cyclical wear.

Table 5.2 **Directional evidence types by street feature.**

Street Features	Cyclical Wear	%	Sliding Wear	%	Overriding Wear	%
Curbstones	15	100%	159	80%	104	26%
Stepping Stones	0	0%	4	2%	245	123%
Guard Stones	0	0%	36	18%	46	23%
Totals	15		199		395	
Percentage of Total	2%		33%		65%	

common form of wearing, overriding wear, is found on all street features, but more than 240 examples are inscribed on stepping stones. The differences in distribution of wearing types are an effect of the different spatial distributions among elements of the street architecture. For example, because stepping stones are found in the middle of the street and aligned parallel with it, they were regularly hit head on, forcing a cart to climb the face of the stone and grind an overriding mark into it. Curbstones, on the other hand, define the limits of the street and therefore had many interactions with vehicles at exceptionally low angles. In these instances wheels slid across the long, vertical face of a curbstone, smoothing the areas where contact was regular. Rarest of all, this contact was specific enough at a small number of intersections to trace the cyclical motion of the wheel as it moved across the stone. Finally, because guard stones extended into the space of the street but not far,[384] they were overridden and slid across at equivalent rates but were neither wide nor flat enough to receive cyclical wear.

These data also reflect some basic, indeed expected, behaviors of ancient cart drivers. For now, a single example can suffice: whenever possible, cart drivers preferred to be in the middle of the street. This fact is reflected not only in the central location of rut pairs in many Pompeian streets but also by the location of overriding marks on the stepping stones of two lane streets. Of the 141 overriding marks on the sixteen streets wide enough for two lanes of traffic where they were inscribed, 84.3% are found in the gaps between stepping stones, while only 15.6% exist in the gaps between stepping stones and the curbs. Additionally, there is far less sliding wear on the outside faces of outer stepping stones. These facts support the inescapable conclusion that carts using wide, two-lane streets drove near to the curbs only when forced to do so.[385]

[384] On average 19 centimeters; Chapter 4, 96–99.
[385] Chapter 6, 152–54.

On Certainty

Included with each of the examinations of wearing types used in the determination of direction was a discussion how one might recognize weaker forms of these types and assess the confidence one might have in them. These discussions were included above because ascribing one's faith in an interpretation at the time it is established has several important effects. In the first instance, recording certainty levels helps to identify biasing factors that influence interpretation during fieldwork. Vision is the primary tool used in most fieldwork methods, but differing light conditions can alter one's determination of the color, extent, or shape of features. Because wearing on vertical street features changes the angle of a part of that feature, the intensity of light reflected from parts of its surface or the depth of shadows that might be cast can change how a wearing pattern looks and how one might interpret direction. For this reason it is best practice to incorporate a tactile component into one's interpretive regime and, if possible, to return to consider each piece of evidence multiple times. Adding a statement of certainty when recording data offers a way to evaluate not only the interpretation itself but the researcher's facility with the method. As one develops both a visual and haptic acuity in the recognition of wearing patterns, one's confidence in his interpretative abilities also increases. Having a certainty level in the database means one can begin to recognize the circumstances that led to either a different conclusion, a different faith in that conclusion, or both. This does not mean certainty levels will increase over repeated examinations. On the contrary, in many cases the researcher becomes surer that an interpretation cannot be made with certainty or that a secondary pattern is impacting the clarity of a primary pattern.

There is another reason for discussing the level of certainty one might have in the recording of evidence on street features. Documenting uncertainty not only reflects the state of the confidence of the researcher but also offers the chance to separate the dominant trends in the data from those that would otherwise be suppressed by them. Mostly, the dominant trends are revealed by those observations that are diagnostic (100% to 76% certainty) or indicative (75% to 51% certainty) of direction. Thus, wearing that is deemed diagnostic of direction is of such depth and clarity of form as to represent, on its own, a dominant pattern in the data. Having formed from hundreds to thousands of iterations of decisions by cart drivers to place a wheel on a particular path and in a particular direction, the sheer volume of shared behavior implies some form of control beyond coincidence or even implicit consensus. Moreover, wearing patterns that are diagnostic of direction rarely are contradictory of the dominant driving rules. For example, on two-lane streets only 8 of 142 overriding marks demonstrate regular driving on the left side of the street, and none are diagnostic in their certainty.

Similarly, of the seventy-four curbstones with diagnostic evidence only three (5%) conclusively contradict the dominant direction.

Those observations reveal that wearing patterns that instill less confidence in the observer—those of suggestive (50% to 26% certainty) and even ambiguous (25% to 1% certainty) quality—are still of vital importance to the determination of direction and especially to enlivening the complexities of the actual practice of driving. Though of lesser quality, these observations contribute simple numerical support to a given direction, most often the predominant direction, adding to the overall likelihood that the interpretation of an entire street's direction is correct. Additionally, these weaker wear patterns document less prevalent forms of behavior that balance or counter the dominant directions. In fact, many examples of wear that are deemed suggestive come from locations where it appears that traffic was converging from two directions, making it difficult to determine which pattern is dominant or was first. The weaker wearing pattern might signal other intentions by drivers, such as nascent official changes to the system or the existence of resistance to the prescribed paths, made by those few scofflaws who, with enough regularity, bucked the system. As Chapter 6 will show, however, contradictory evidence most often indicates that a change, a reversal, had occurred within the systems of traffic. Wear of suggestive and ambiguous qualities thus offer nuance to the data on direction and paint a more realistic picture of a natural traffic flow in ancient cities. These observations of weaker certainty balance the dominance of clearer evidence and work against an interpretation that the operation of traffic at Pompeii, though undoubtedly regulated, actually occurred in a rigid, mechanical fashion.[386]

[386] For a critique of mechanical efficiency, see Hartnett 2011.

6

The Traffic Systems of Pompeii

With the evidence for direction and how to interpret it now fully explored, an obvious question arises: how was the consistency of behavior that produced more than six hundred patterns of directional wear produced? To put it another way and to pose the title of this book as a question, were there traffic systems at Pompeii governing the circulation of vehicles? One of the first ways to approach this question is simply to reflect on the surprising consistency of behavior that these wearing patterns record: inscribed over years, each one of the thousands of iterations tells the same story of a vehicle traveling in the same direction, turning away at the same place, and sliding against or riding up over the same street features. That such exceptional coherence exists in each wearing pattern, on its own, strongly suggests a shared set of expectations for how driving would be conducted. Within a single piece of evidence is a record of each time that a Pompeian cart driver made the same choice as the drivers before him, a fact not only multiplied by the thousands of identical choices but also amplified by the absence of equivalent opposite directional wearing.

If we can read a shared intent among drivers from a single object, the next step must be to treat these objects as an assemblage and assess how well such moments of shared intent add up across the breadth of an entire city. Although this evidence and the question it is turned toward is novel, the notion that archaeologists can surmise rules and even entire systems from artifacts and architectures—settlement patterns, local or regional economies, or bathing regimes—is not. What is different, however, is that there are no direct literary sources to start from, to prove or disprove. The observations, their interpretation, and their aggregation must stand or fall almost entirely on archaeological grounds. Fortunately, the data are up to the task and reveal the presence of a city-wide system that evolved over at least a century. To describe the system, or rather systems, the totality of the data is considered through several filters that make up the structure of this chapter, including approaches that are structural (the shape of the street network), directional (the evidence for two-way and one-way streets), and chronological (the evolution of the system over time).

Consequences of the Grid: City Shapes
and Evidence Production

In 79 CE most of Pompeii was not well suited to the free circulation of traffic. As the city's wide beaten ash streets were canalized by curbstones and encroached upon by expanding buildings over the course of the second and first centuries BCE, the space for vehicular traffic was significantly reduced until only sixteen streets were wide enough for two lanes of traffic to pass. Similarly, the shape of most of Pompeii's street intersections (62%) limited rather than facilitated movement by their forms.[387]

That is, the majority of streets are offset from their extension across a four-way intersection, requiring traffic to adjust its course. Like the encroachment upon the street, offset intersections were a deliberate choice to design and adapt the city to urban desires greater than the need for a free flow of traffic. An effect of these choices, however, was the production a varied landscape of streets and intersections, the geometries of which would help both to demonstrate the need for traffic rules and to presuppose some of its most fundamental principles.

Continuous and Discontinuous Street Networks

At Pompeii, there are no fewer than nine different ways that streets formed intersections, which are defined in table 6.1, summarized in table 6.2, and visualized in fig. 6.1. Numerically, three types dominate (83% of the total): the T type (32), offset type (32), and orthogonal type (28). Geographically, offset- and orthogonal-type intersections are almost perfectly segregated into the western and eastern halves of the city. What's more, the only intersections other than orthogonal type known in the excavated eastern half of the city are found at the edges of the grid or where the presence of another structure forced the grid to be modified. Even if it were not true that offset intersections in the west were defensive in nature and intended to confound the movements of invaders, it is clear that the shape of the city created this effect on the inhabitants by restricting both their movement and vision.[388] For the ancient cart driver, the former is a constraint on his present and the later on his future. That is, the shape of any given intersection increases or reduces the number of directions the driver can travel and simultaneously alters his ability to plan his route or execute his next turn.

[387] Even if the projected shapes of unexcavated intersections are included, this discontinuity falls only to 59%.
[388] Chapter 2, 35–39.

Table 6.1 **Intersection type definitions.**

Intersection Types

Continuous Intersections	*Discontinuous Intersections*		
Orthogonal: The orthogonal type is defined as the intersection of two streets crossing at right angles to one another and where the streets opposite one another share both orientation and alignment.	**Bend:** A bend-type intersection is the conjunction of two streets to form a roughly right-angle turn.		
	Y: A Y-type intersection is formed by the confluence of three streets where the angle between the two converging/splitting streets is significantly smaller than 90 degrees.		
	T: A T-type intersection is formed by one street meeting a cross street, at a roughly perpendicular angle, without having a continuation across that intersection.		
	Offset: An offset-type intersection is represented by two streets that meet at a cross street and share the same orientation but have a shifted alignment in relation to one another. An intersection is considered to be of offset type if the insulae walls across the intersection alter the alignment of the approaching street. Sidewalks narrowing a street do not constitute an offset. Offsets types are further defined by four subtypes: 1. The northern street is east of the southern street. 2. The northern street is west of the southern street. 3. The western street is north of the eastern street. 4. The western street is south of the eastern street.	**Double Offset:** An intersection is determined to be a double offset when all four streets approaching an intersection do not share an alignment though two pairs may have similar orientations.	
		Offset T: An offset T-type intersection is a standard T-type intersection where the segments of the crossing street are not in alignment with one another.	
		Wide Offset: An intersection is said to be of wide offset-type when two streets meeting a cross street form a continuation of each other but do not lead directly into one another. In this definition, the distance between these streets on the cross street is no more than 10 meters. If the distance is greater than 10 meters, the intersections are treated as two separate T-type intersections.	

Table 6.2 **Intersection types.**

Excavated Areas			*Unexcavated Areas*
Continuous Intersections			
Orthogonal		28	16
Unique		3	
	Total	31	16
Discontinuous Intersections			
Bend		7	
Y		8	14
T		32	5
Offset		26	
	Offset T	1	
	Double Offset	1	
	Wide Offset	4	
Unique		2	1
	Total	81	20

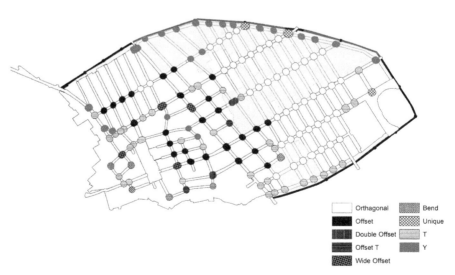

Figure 6.1 Distribution of intersection types.

At orthogonal intersections a driver can often see multiple intersections at once and has multiple options to turn at each, while at more discontinuous intersections he often cannot plan his route more than one intersection at a time and has fewer choices to execute that route.

Of course, this scenario imagines drivers without knowledge of the street grid; because most traffic was local, such a situation was certainly the exception. Nonetheless, knowledge of the street system, even a perfect understanding (surely as rare as complete ignorance) is only of limited value compared to vision. Consider the easiest way for a driver to extend his knowledge and vision: sending a runner forward to the next intersection.[389] With a runner, the driver's decision-making process is made far easier, not least because he can know what lies ahead in every direction as he approaches an intersection. Theoretically, the runner could explore the complete route through a discontinuous street system and return to direct the driver along the most efficient path. Yet while the knowledge the runner can gain about the path to his destination is potentially permanent, his ability to know about potential impediments is necessarily temporary. This is because when returning with information about the route and intersections ahead, the runner can no longer observe what is behind him. The path will not change, but the presence of other vehicles almost certainly will. Practically, therefore, the runner can effectively only aid the driver one block at a time because he can see only one block at a time. On the other hand, within a continuous grid system, the runner can see multiple blocks ahead at once and in multiple directions. He can plan both the route and its detours with far greater certainty.

These thought experiments show that neither perfect knowledge of the street system nor the use of a runner is as useful to a cart driver as having a clear a line of sight and as many choices as possible at any given intersection.[390] The point is made finer still when we imagine a cart driver who cannot avoid being impeded by another cart in his path. In this scenario, a driver without a runner approaches either an orthogonal or T intersection along a narrow street and turns to the right through an intersection to find a cart blocking the street. The impeded driver now has to decide either to wait for the other cart to move or to back up through the intersection and go a different direction. It is by no means impossible to reverse a cart, but neither is it a simple affair.[391] More importantly, in

[389] Kaiser 2011b, 96.

[390] Much ancient urban wayfaring relied on the visibility of landmarks; see Ling 1990, MacDonald 1986, 107–10; Poehler 2016, 200–202; Chapter 7, 207–08.

[391] Tsujimura (1991, 63) cites Mau (1899, 221–30) on the difficulty of reversing.

the T-shaped intersection the driver has only two available choices: to reverse straight through the intersection and turn back down the street that he originally came up or to attempt the more difficult maneuver of turning in reverse so that he could travel in the opposite direction of his original turn. At an orthogonal intersection, the same scenario gives the driver three choices after backing up through the intersection, two that do not require making a turn while reversing. These differences are especially important when other realities of cart driving are considered, the most important of which is the time such maneuvers required, time that increased the most common risk- that still another cart would approach the intersection and compound the problem by further reducing the ways out of what can now genuinely be described as a traffic jam.

Corner Shape

At the scale of the city, it is the shape of the street network and its intersections that aids or hinders the circulation of traffic. At the scale of the individual intersection, however, it is also the shape of the (mostly) four corners that impacts movement, allowing us to consider further how the urban frame structures the behaviors within it. In a completely orthogonal grid, like that in the east of Pompeii, streets meet one another perfectly aligned, with all four corners of the intersection forming right angles. In the west, the diagonal line of via Stabiana relative to the rest of the grid as well as the "herringbone" streets of the Altstadt meant that right-angled corners in this half of the city would be rare. While both the acute and obtuse angles produced in these intersections were geometrically mostly rather shallow, such corner shapes created an additional difficulty or facility for carts turning through a number of intersection forms.[392] Though born from different albeit related decisions of urban planning, intersection shape and corner shape had compounding effects on the circulation of traffic. By making certain places harder or easier to traverse and certain corners harder or easier to turn around, these two aspects of urban design—especially

---

[392] Although there is strong overlap in corner shape produced by the grid and the shape of the intersection, there is no necessary correlation between them. That is, offset intersections can be formed in a grid where all the streets run parallel and perpendicular to one another, producing only right-angled corners, while streets that cross each other at high angles can be perfectly aligned across the intersection, creating only acute- and obtuse-angled corners but no interruption in the connected streets.

when combined with street size—naturally made some locations and some turns preferable. Moreover, the repetition of shapes in the grid meant that the easier turns around lower-angled corners and the harder turns around higher-angled corners would be found in regular and predictable places throughout the city.

Acute angles predominate at the northwest and southeast corners in Pompeii, while obtuse angles are disproportionately found at the northeast and southwest corners (table 6.3). Thus, when traveling westbound, drivers would have found northward right-hand turns easier to make around the northeast corner. When traveling eastbound, the pattern is the same though inverted, making southward right-hand turns around the southwest corner easier. As has been discussed, Tsujimura went so far as to base her hypothesis for the circulation of traffic on the curved ruts that survived around these wider angled corners.[393] Of course, these shapes do not determine the behavior of drivers, but the regularity of their location tends to encourage certain driving behaviors. In practice, however, traversing the city required turning around corners with disadvantageous shapes because they were part of the most direct or only route to a destination. For this reason, Pompeians chose to make forty-two modifications to the shapes of corners at twenty-nine intersections to facilitate these turns. In these examples, the shape of the corner was altered by changing the orientation of the curbstones to encourage specific turns. All but one of these modifications occurred in the western half of the city,[394] but perhaps surprisingly they are not found only at acute corners. On average, modifications occur at acute-angled corners at slightly higher rates than at obtuse-angled corners and there is equally only a small preference for the general direction of the turn they facilitated (i.e., slightly more left- than right-hand turns). On the other hand, modifications overwhelmingly (79%) occur on streets wide enough for only one lane of traffic, whether intersecting another one-lane street (24%) or, more commonly, a two-lane street (55%). Modifications to the corners of two-lane streets were infrequent and almost always occurred at the intersection with another two-lane street.[395]

Such a preference to modify corners on narrower streets demonstrates that the impetus to change the shape of a corner was not predominantly based on the angle of that corner. If it were, we would expect more if not all

[393] Chapter 5, 123.

[394] With 36 of 71 eastern intersections exposed, only one additional modified corner is expected in the unexcavated areas.

[395] Exception is vicolo del Menandro at vicolo di Paquius Proculus.

Table 6.3 **Corner shape and modified corners.**

	Northwest Corner		Southwest Corner		Southeast Corner		Northeast Corner		Totals		
	Number of Corners	Number of Modified Corners	Number of Corners	Number of Modified Corners	Number of Corners	Number of Modified Corners	Number of Corners	Number of Modified Corners	Total Corners	Total Modified Corners	Percentage of Corners Modified by Shape
Acute	35	9	11	0	33	6	17	6	96	21	21.88%
Obtuse	24	3	34	8	19	3	40	5	117	19	16.24%
Right	34	0	36	3	35	3	37	0	142	6	4.23%
No Corner	17		29		25		16		87		
Totals	110	12	110	11	112	12	110	11	442		

acute-angled corners to be modified and fewer, if any, obtuse-angled corners to have been changed. Instead, the general restriction to narrow one-lane streets indicates that Pompeians modified many corners because of the limited space they presented to conduct a turn. Still, the limited distribution of changes to only 11% of all corners shows that, above all, it was the perceived importance to traffic of that particular intersection and not a universal desire to help cart drivers that influenced its change. For example, at six intersections both corners of the same street were modified, indicating the expectation of vehicles to debouch in both directions from a one-lane street into a two-lane street.[396] Much more common are those crucial intersections where drivers were helped to negotiate the angle of the corner, the narrowness of the streets, or the volume of other traffic using that same intersection.

The series of intersections surrounding insula IX 1 illustrates this notion of importance, as one-sixth of all modified corners are found around this one block as part of a detour to relieve the pressure on via Stabiana, especially at its intersection with via dell'Abbondanza.[397] Beginning at the intersection of vicolo di Tesmo / vicolo del Citarista with via dell'Abbondanza (fig. 6.2, A), one finds three corners were modified: the two acute corners (northwest and southeast) to facilitate turning and a less common modification at the obtuse southwest corner to disincentivize turns onto vicolo del Citarista. Conversely, strong evidence for carts turning off of the two-lane via dell'Abbondanza and northbound onto the one-lane vicolo di Tesmo is found on the northeast corner curbstone, which due to the space to turn and the obtuse angle of the corner is the only unmodified corner along this entire detour. At the next intersection to the north (fig. 6.2, B; fig. 6.11), both the northwest and southwest corners are modified to permit movement toward the intersection with via Stabiana (fig. 6.2, C), where again both corners are modified so that vehicles could disperse into this major thoroughfare in either direction. A related detour instituted around insula V 1 was meant to relieve the congestion at the largest intersection in the city, where four two-lane streets intersect: via del Vesuvio, via della Fortuna, via Stabiana, and via di Nola. Even with the detour, the northwest corner of this major crossroads was modified to ease the turning of vehicles around its acute-angled corner. The change may have been influenced also by the placement directly against the curbs of three stepping

---

[396] These are: vicoli Maschera and VIII 5–5 at via dell'Abbondanza; vicolo di Balbo at vicolo di Tesmo and at via Stabiana; vicolo di Tesmo at via di Nola, vicolo della Fullonica at via delle Terme; vicolo di Mercurio at vicolo dei Vettii.

[397] Chapter 6, 184–86.

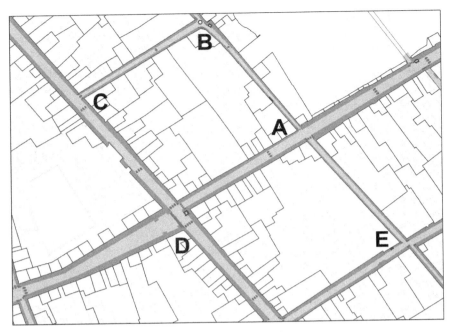

Figure 6.2 Detour 1: vicolo di Tesmo and vicolo di Balbo.

stones, which made certain turns more difficult and forced more traffic into the center of the intersection.

Examples of such dissuading architectures,[398] supporting those modifications that made some turns easier, begin to clarify how the different shapes of the city encouraged certain driving behaviors and prefigured the design of the traffic systems. In the first instance, they indicate that Pompeians not only adjusted some angles ill suited to the movements of vehicular traffic but also instituted barriers to restrict certain other turns, demonstrating an interest both to create a greater ease of travel and to constrain that movement within certain paths. At the same time, the modification of corners diagonally across an intersection on two-lane streets (as well as the locations where both corners of a one-lane street intersecting a two-lane street were modified) shows these two-lane streets to have been two-way streets. That is, if a wide street were a two-lane street with all traffic moving in the same direction, then we would expect most corner modifications to be found on only one side of an intersection. For example, if via dell'Abbondanza were

---

[398] Other examples of corners shaped to make turns more difficult include vicolo del Panettiere at via Stabiana, vicolo del Fauno at vicolo di Mercurio; vicolo del Citarista at via dell'Abbondanza.

a two-lane westbound street, then only the northwest and southwest corners should have been modified on the intersecting one-lane streets in order to ease the traffic joining the westbound flow. Instead, we find turns in opposing directions: the northwest corner of vicolo di Tesmo was modified to make right-hand south-to-west turns easier, and the southeast corner of vicolo del Citarista was changed to ease right-hand north-to-east turns.[399] While modified corners suggest two-way streets, the evidence from wearing patterns proves it conclusively.

Direct Evidence for the Systems of Traffic: Two-Way Streets

Based on the gauge of known vehicles, there are sixteen streets in Pompeii wide enough to accommodate two lanes of traffic simultaneously at some point along their lengths. To determine if a street is sufficiently wide for carts to pass unimpeded, Tsujimura developed a simple but efficient formula: add the length of the two axles, including the hubs beyond the wheels, and then subtract the length of the two outside hubs, which could roll above the curbstones.[400] When she inserted the dimensions of actual carts or rut pairs known from excavation, Tsujimura found that for the smallest carts to pass, the street must be at least 3.21 meters wide and 3.53 meters for the largest vehicles suspected.[401] Applying her formula to the actual remains of the wagon from Stabia finds a minimum width of 3.43 meters for a two-lane street. These figures are consistent with the evidence from rut pairs, which indicated the largest carts to use the streets with any regularity were between 1.32 and 1.47 meters.[402] Additionally, the widths of two-lane streets at Pompeii are well above the minimum requirements of eight Roman feet (ca. 2.36 m) for *viae* set out in the Twelve Tables. While streets of such width (3.43 m) are few in number at Pompeii, by length they are 34% of the excavated street network and naturally carried the greatest proportion of traffic in the city. Most of Pompeii's street network thus met the common expectations of most Roman urban inhabitants and the minimum needs of (at least) both cart drivers and civil authorities.

---

[399] These modifications represent two periods of the traffic system's design and demonstrate that via dell'Abbondanza was a two-way street in both periods.

[400] As a formula: (2 x wheel gauge) + (axle length − wheel gauge).

[401] Tsujimura 1991, 61–62.

[402] Chapter 5, 114–23.

Wearing patterns left by vehicles on the street architecture confirm what the evidence of corner shape has suggested: these wide streets were not only two-lane streets but also two-way streets. Moreover, this same evidence also defines one of the primary rules of traffic: Romans drove on the right side of the road. Over 420 wearing patterns were identified along these sixteen two-lane streets showing vehicles traveling on or turning off of them. Table 6.4 and fig. 6.3 illustrate the data applicable to driving on right-hand side of the street from curbstones and guard stones (stepping stones are considered separately). For each street, the number of directional wearing patterns and the certainty of each pattern was associated with a side of the street and then considered against the direction interpreted to determine which side of the street drivers were using. For example, on via di Nola, sixteen total wearing patterns were found, thirteen of which show vehicles moving either westbound along the north curb or eastbound along the south curb. These had a total certainty value of 40, which compares with a certainty value of 5 for the three wearing patterns found to suggest driving on the left-hand side of the road. The difference between these two certainty values is also expressed in table 6.4 as a percentage of the whole, in this case revealing that 88.9% of all the traffic on via di Nola moved along the right curb, while only 11.1% can be shown to have regularly impacted the left curb. The final two columns divide the total certainty values for each side of the street by the total count of patterns to find the average strength of the wearing for each side of the street. Taking via di Nola again as an example, the average strength of 3.08 reflects an average confidence in the data for right-side driving at the diagnostic (100%–76%) category, while the average strength

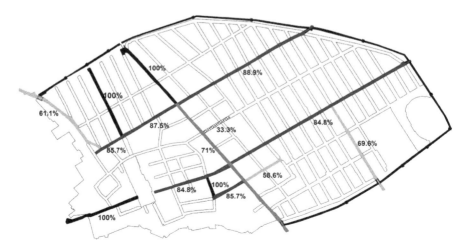

Figure 6.3 Evidence for right-side driving preference on curbstones and guard stones.

Table 6.4 Evidence for right-side driving preference on curbstones and guard stones.

Name	Right-Side Count	Right-Side Certainty Count	Right-Side Certainty Percentage	Left-Side Count	Left-Side Certainty Count	Left-Side Certainty Percentage	Right-Side Certainty Average	Left-Side Certainty Average
Via dei Teatri	1	4	100.00%				4.00	
Via del Vesuvio	1	4	100.00%				4.00	
Via Marina	4	16	100.00%				4.00	
Via di Mercurio	8	24	100.00%				3.00	
Via di Nola	13	40	88.89%	3	5	11.11%	3.08	1.67
Via della Fortuna	10	28	87.50%	3	4	12.50%	2.80	1.33
Via del Tempio d'Iside	5	18	85.71%	2	3	14.29%	3.60	1.50
Via delle Terme	4	12	85.71%	1	2	14.29%	3.00	2.00
Via dell'Abbondanza	34	89	84.76%	6	16	15.24%	2.62	2.67
Via Stabiana	9	22	70.97%	4	9	29.03%	2.44	2.25
Via di Nocera	7	16	69.57%	3	7	30.43%	2.29	2.33
Via Consolare	7	22	61.11%	5	14	38.89%	3.14	2.80
Vicolo del Menandro	5	17	58.62%	4	12	41.38%	3.40	3.00
Via Mediana	2	8	33.33%	5	16	66.67%	4.00	3.20
Via delle Scuole				1	3	100.00%		3.00
	110	320	77.86%	37	91	22.14%	3.18	2.17

of the interpretations for left-side driving is nearly one and one-half points lower, in the suggestive (50%–26%) category. As a whole, the evidence from curbstones and guard stones is unequivocal, even as it is not unanimous, as to which side of the street Romans at Pompeii drove. They drove on the right and left wear on the street architecture at a rate three times greater (110 patterns) than on the left (37 patterns).

There are, however, several streets with surprisingly high concentrations of evidence for left-side driving. Via Consolare, via di Nocera, via Stabiana, and especially via Mediana all recorded vehicles traveling against the left curb, but in each case the street became narrowed at some point, a reality that brought the left curb closer and made contact with it much more likely even while following the rule of right-hand driving.[403] In these constricted spaces, turning vehicles—like those on one-way streets turning onto two-way streets—unavoidably impacted the side of the street in the direction of their turn. Another version of this narrowing effect occurred at ramps leading off via Consolare and into stables at the Porta Ercolano. The position of the stables at VI 17, 1 and at VI 1, 1 made collisions with the left curb almost unavoidable for vehicles turning out of the former into the gate and out of the gate and into the latter. The ramps on via Mediana also have wearing from left-side driving, though these reveal another, related way this evidence was produced: wide-arching turns to the left. In these cases, such as at the intersection of via Stabiana at vicolo del Menandro, a significant volume of traffic was making long, low-angled, and easy turns across a two-way street, some of which were impacting the northeast-corner curbstones.[404] That this wearing is part of a common wide-angle turn and not a wider pattern of left-side driving is supported by the abundance of right-side drive evidence at this intersection, even on the opposite side of the same stone, and by the recognition of this pattern at other Roman cities.[405]

Because it sits in the middle rather than at the edge of the street, the stepping-stone evidence cannot be calculated in the same way as other forms of evidence. That is, while there is no ambiguity on which side of the street evidence on curbstones and guard stones belongs—indeed, these features define the street edge—the wearing on stepping stones is found in a range from near the edge to near the middle of the street. Therefore, rather than assign each wearing pattern to a stepping stone, each wearing was

[403] E.g., via Consolare at via delle Terme; via Mediana at via Stabiana; via di Nocera at via dell'Abbondanza.

[404] E.g., via delle Scuole at vicolo della Regina; via di Nocera at via della Palestra; both ramps on via Mediana.

[405] Chapter 8, 230–1.

instead associated with one of the gaps between stepping stones. On streets wide enough for two lanes of traffic, nearly every crossing required a set of three stepping stones, though two sets of four and eight sets of two were also used.[406] In nearly all cases, therefore, there were four gaps to consider: Gap 1, between the left curb (either west or south) and the first stepping stone; Gap 2, between the first and second stepping stones; Gap 3, between the second and third stepping stones; and Gap 4, between the third stepping stone and the right (either east or north). Figure 4.6 labels these gaps in a set of three stepping stones. In only a small number of cases were stepping stones overridden head on, leaving a wear pattern that could not be assigned to a gap. These are listed as Gap 1/2 and Gap 2/3 in fig. 6.4. In order to assess the preference for right-side driving, the number of wearing patterns on stepping stones were divided by the direction that each indicated. Thus, each street was listed twice, once for either its westbound or northbound direction, the other for its eastbound or southbound direction. Finally, the directional evidence and the certainty of its interpretation were tabulated for each gap and for each direction.

The results of this analysis support two important interpretations. First, the preference of driving on the right is again demonstrated, though the volume of evidence is less than is found among curbstones and guard stones. For

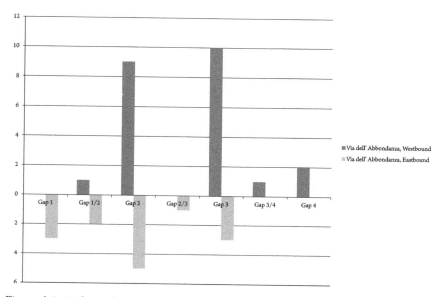

Figure 6.4 Evidence for right-side driving preference on stepping stones.

---

[406] For consistency, only sets of three and four stepping stones are used in the following analyses.

example, while 85.7% of the evidence (by certainty) recorded in both Gap 1 and Gap 4 was created by drivers hugging the right curb, nearer the middle of the street, represented by Gaps 2 and 3, the data show near complete equanimity. The latter pattern represents the second important trend in the evidence: namely, that Pompeian cart drivers preferred the center of the street. While this result is not surprising, the degree of that preference is: fully 84.4% of all directional evidence on stepping stones was recorded in Gaps 2, 2/3, and 3. This means that whenever possible, carts rolled over the center stepping stone. Also supporting this interpretation are the differential depths of ruts at sets of stepping stones, which are deeper in the center lane and, when present in the outside lanes, tend to be found close to the curbs. The strength of the evidence for driving in the center of the street, since it demonstrates travel in both directions on the street, helps to explain not only why the evidence for the use of the outside lanes was less prevalent but also why the use of those lanes was necessary. Indeed, the presence of oncoming traffic may have much to do with why vehicles hit and overrode the stepping stones in the first place. Imagine two carts approaching a set of stepping stones from opposite directions, each using the center lane. As the analysis above on wearing in gaps has shown, each cart would adjust to the right-hand side of the road to avoid the oncoming vehicle. Depending on the size of vehicles, however, only one cart was required to shift to an outside lane, while the other might need only to slide farther to the right within Gaps 2 and 3, which were, on average, larger spaces.[407]

Such a preference for both directions of traffic to use the middle of the street also offers clues about how deep ruts relate to driving behaviors. As described in Chapter 5, ruts are the product of the weaknesses of paving styles, the sizes of carts, the erosional environment of the street, the duration of use, and the volume of traffic. While the first two variables (the paving style and vehicle size) help to explain the position of ruts in the street, the last two (duration and volume) multiply to explain the intensity of rutting. The preferential use of the center lane by all traffic and its deflection to an outside lane due to a sufficient volume of oncoming vehicles indicates that traffic volume was more important at Pompeii than duration in the formation of ruts.[408] Such a claim can be made based on the fact that the deflection of carts to an outside lane requires that the volume of traffic was sufficient to force vehicles away from the center. We must imagine that ceding the center to another vehicle was a common enough occurrence for the wearing patterns in the outside

---

[407] Chapter 4, 90–93.
[408] cf. Kaiser 2011b, 73 n. 33.

gaps of the stepping stones to form and also for the exceptionally strong evidence at the very edge of the street—on the curbstones and guard stones—to be inscribed.[409] If duration were the primary factor in rut formation, then we would expect to find center-driving evidence almost exclusively. Still, the fact that 84.4% of all directional wearing on stepping stones occurs in the center of the street demonstrates that the volume of vehicles be sufficiently low such that traffic not be rigidly bifurcated onto the two outside lanes alone. Of course, carts were occasionally parked along the curb, which forced vehicles using that outside lane to temporarily join the center lane, but it is difficult to imagine the frequency of this event was sufficient to be the cause of this center-driving phenomenon. Indeed, too many parked carts would make the strength of wear on the curbs harder to explain.

From the preceding analyses of directional patterns worn into the architecture of the street it is abundantly clear that Romans at Pompeii had several streets wide enough for two lanes of traffic, which they had divided into two-way streets based on the rule of driving on the right. From the same analyses, it is equally clear that neither the volume of traffic nor the adherence to this rule was sufficiently great to keep ancient drivers from using the center of these two-way streets whenever possible. The volume of traffic was sufficient, however, to be the primary factor in the creation of deep ruts and in the subsequent need for repair and replacement of the pavements. At the same time, the volume of traffic seems to have been a reason for the stringent application of the rule of right-hand driving—though this was likely already a long-standing tradition—as well as a de facto form of enforcement.[410] That is, the amount of oncoming traffic repeatedly pushed approaching vehicles into compliance with the rule in order to avoid collision. Yet the data also show that this rule was not applied in a mechanical fashion, with center-lane driving being the norm and left-side driving occurring exceptionally rarely (1.3% by certainty in Gaps 1 and 4) in the middle of the street and only in particular circumstances when turning. The evidence found on the many streets intersecting these two-way routes reveals that Pompeians went beyond the rule of right-side driving, developing rules and applying restrictions on the many narrow one-lane streets.

---

[409] Many silex surfaces had not existed long enough for duration to be a determining factor.

[410] Romans preferred the right side in nearly all ways; Wagener 1912; Poehler 2003; Ellis 2011, 166–69. On de facto enforcement mechanisms, see Chapter 7, 202, 204–5.

Direct Evidence for the Systems of Traffic: One-Way Streets

At Pompeii, nearly all the streets are limited by width to a single lane of traffic. How one quantifies that fact changes the degree of its perceived impact. One-lane streets are 84% of the named streets, 69% of the block-length street segments, and 66% of the total excavated street length and an estimated 77% of the total street network. However one calculates the percentage of narrow streets, for the ancient cart driver, the experience was the same: one enters Pompeii on a two-way street and almost any turn off of it leads into the confined space and reduced directionality of a one-lane street. Leaving the primary thoroughfare was thus either a conscious choice by an informed driver to take the most direct route to his destination or it was a gamble by the visiting driver that a side street would continue for more than a few blocks without interruption or detour. Yet the congestion that even a single cart could create on these narrow streets would plague the stranger and the experienced driver alike: someone had to back down the street and reverse through a turn at the nearest intersection or just wait.

Compared to the broad avenues of later Roman cities, the large number of one-lane streets was certainly a detriment to the circulation of traffic once a certain volume was reached. Similarly, when compared to the wide beaten ash streets of third century BCE Pompeii, the city in 79 CE was far less amenable to wheeled traffic, with several dead-end streets and even streets that were disconnected from the street network entirely.[411] The rarity of these kinds of routes is important because they lead to significant blockages and delays throughout the street network. On dead-end streets, entering and exiting traffic must use the same intersection, which forces a cart driver to wait on—and likely block—an intersecting street if the dead end is already occupied. The same is true for disconnected streets, such as the vicolo del Gallo, which would require a cart driver to stop and block vicolo del Gigante in order to unload his cargo and port it further up the disconnected street.[412]

By the late first century BCE, the evidence from two-way streets shows the volume of traffic using the streets had increased significantly, and while keeping the streets open was a necessary means to keep traffic moving in the city, it was no longer a sufficient one. Although we do not know the exact trigger, it seems most likely that the volume of traffic and the constricted environment combined to create such congestion that action had to be taken. The evidence from wearing patterns on one-lane streets reveals that the solution was to limit the use of these narrow streets to a single direction. Tables 6.5 and 6.6 summarize

---

[411] Poehler 2011b, 160, table 10.1.
[412] Newsome 2009, 128–32.

Table 6.5 **Evidence of one-way traffic on north–south streets.**

Name	Northbound Count	Northbound Certainty Count	Northbound Certainty Percentage	Northbound Average Certainty	Southbound Count	Southbound Certainty Count	Southbound Certainty Percentage	Southbound Average Certainty
vicolo del Labirinto	10	24	100.00%	2.40				
vicolo di Narciso	4	13	100.00%	3.25				
vicolo del Gigante	3	10	100.00%	3.33				
vicolo III.2–III.3	2	4	100.00%	2.00				
vicolo VIII.5–5	1	3	100.00%	3.00				
vicolo del Centenario (north)	1	2	100.00%	2.00				
vicolo III.1–III.2	1	2	100.00%	2.00				
vicolo IX.11–IX.12	1	3	100.00%	3.00				
vicolo III.4–III.5	1	3	100.00%	3.00				
vicolo del Anfiteatro	1	2	100.00%	2.00				
vicolo III.7–7 (projected)	1	2	100.00%	2.00				
vicolo di Cecilio Giocondo	6	14	87.50%	2.33	1	2	12.50%	2.00
vicolo di Modesto	10	27	84.38%	2.70	2	5	15.63%	2.50

(*Continued*)

Table 6.5 Continued

Name	Northbound Count	Northbound Certainty Count	Northbound Certainty Percentage	Northbound Average Certainty	Southbound Count	Southbound Certainty Count	Southbound Certainty Percentage	Southbound Average Certainty
vicolo Storto	5	11	78.57%	2.20	1	3	21.43%	3.00
vicolo III.5–III.6	1	3	75.00%	3.00	1	1	25.00%	1.00
vicolo del Farmacista	3	10	71.43%	3.33	1	4	28.57%	4.00
vicolo del Centenario	2	7	63.64%	3.50	1	4	36.36%	4.00
vicolo IX.7–IX.11	4	9	60.00%	2.25	2	6	40.00%	3.00
vicolo III.7–City Wall	1	3	60.00%	3.00	1	2	40.00%	2.00
vicolo della Maschera	4	9	56.25%	2.25	3	7	43.75%	2.33
vicolo della Regina (north)	3	8	53.33%	2.67	2	7	46.67%	3.50
vicolo dei Vettii (north)	10	30	53.13%	2.62	13	34	46.88%	3.00
vicolo di Giulia Felice	1	2	50.00%	2.00	1	2	50.00%	2.00
vicolo III.6–III.7	1	1	50.00%	1.00	1	1	50.00%	1.00
vicolo dei 12 Dei	4	9	47.37%	2.25	4	10	52.63%	2.50
vicolo del Lupanare	7	17	45.95%	2.43	9	20	54.05%	2.22
vicolo del Citarista	5	16	44.44%	3.20	6	20	55.56%	3.33

vicolo della Nave Europa	2	44.44%	2.00	4	2	5	55.56%	2.50
vicolo di Paquius Proculus (south)	2	42.86%	3.00	6	3	8	57.14%	2.67
vicolo dei Gladiatori	1	42.86%	3.00	3	1	4	57.14%	4.00
vicolo IX.10–IX.14	1	42.86%	3.00	3	2	4	57.14%	3.125
vicolo di Eumachia	4	42.11%	2.00	8	5	11	57.89%	2.20
vicolo di ML Frontone (south)	1	40.00%	2.00	2	1	3	60.00%	3.00
vicolo di Octavius Quartio	1	40.00%	2.00	2	1	3	60.00%	3.00
vicolo IX.12–IX.13	1	40.00%	2.00	2	1	3	60.00%	3.00
vicolo dei Gladiatori (south)	1	40.00%	2.00	2	1	3	60.00%	3.00
vicolo di Tesmo	11	33.62%	3.55	39	26	77	66.38%	2.96
vicolo di Lucrezio Frontone	1	33.33%	2.00	2	1	4	66.67%	4.00
vicolo I.8–I.9	2	28.57%	2.00	4	4	10	71.43%	2.50
vicolo dei Fuggiaschi	1	25.00%	1.00	1	2	3	75.00%	1.50
vicolo dell'Efebo	1	25.00%	1.00	1	1	3	75.00%	0.00

(Continued)

Table 6.5 **Continued**

Name	Northbound Count	Northbound Certainty Count	Northbound Certainty Percentage	Northbound Average Certainty	Southbound Count	Southbound Certainty Count	Southbound Certainty Percentage	Southbound Average Certainty
vicolo I.9–I.11	1	2	20.00%	2.00	3	8	80.00%	2.67
vicolo della Fullonica	1	1	12.50%	1.00	2	7	87.50%	3.50
vicolo delle Terme	1	3	10.71%	3.00	8	25	89.29%	3.125
vicolo del Fauno					4	12	100.00%	3.00
vicolo IX.13–III.1					2	2	100.00%	1.00
vicolo IX.14–III.8					1	2	100.00%	2.00
vicolo III.10–III.11					1	3	100.00%	3.00
vicolo IV.2–IV.3					1	2	100.00%	2.00
vicolo IV.1–IV.2					1	4	100.00%	4.00
vicolo III.11–III.12					1	4	100.00%	4.00

Table 6.6 **Evidence of one-way traffic on east–west streets.**

Name	Westbound Count	Westbound Certainty Count	Westbound Certainty Percentage	Westbound Average Certainty	Eastbound Count	Eastbound Certainty Count	Eastbound Certainty Percentage	Eastbound Average Certainty
vicolo del Conciapelle	1	3	100.00%	3.00				
vicolo del Balcone Pensile	4	14	87.50%	3.50	1	2	12.50%	2.00
vicolo di Balbo	6	19	63.33%	3.17	3	11	36.67%	3.67
vicolo di Mercurio	32	92	61.70%	2.88	20	57	38.30%	2.85
vicolo delle Nozze d'Argento	4	11	61.11%	2.75	4	7	38.89%	1.75
vicolo degli Scheletri	5	8	42.11%	1.60	6	11	57.89%	1.83
vicolo delle Parete Rossa	2	4	40.00%	2.00	3	6	60.00%	2.00
via della Regina	6	21	38.89%	3.50	13	33	61.11%	2.54
via della Palestra	2	3	30.00%	1.50	2	7	70.00%	3.50
via di Castricio	4	9	16.67%	2.25	19	45	83.33%	2.37
vicolo del Panettiere	1	1	11.11%	1.00	3	8	88.89%	2.67
via degli Augustali	2	3	8.57%	1.50	17	32	91.43%	1.88
vicolo IX.3–IX.4					4	12	100.00%	3.00
vicolo I.2–I.3					2	4	100.00%	2.00
vicolo dei Soprastanti					1	4	100.00%	4.00
vicolo del Gallo					1	4	100.00%	4.00

all the directional data from one-lane streets that run either north–south or west–east. To assess the direction of each street, all the data were divided into two parts, those indicating northbound or southbound travel and those indicating westbound or eastbound travel. The total number of wearing patterns attested for each direction as well as the total clarity (certainty) of those interpretations is given in the first two columns of each direction. Following these is the percentage of all certainty values on a street that a direction represents. For example, the total certainty value for the westbound direction of traffic on vicolo di Mercurio is 92, which is combined with the certainty values for eastbound traffic (57) to make up 61.7% of all the directional evidence on that street. For each direction the average certainty of the interpretations on that street is given as a way to assess the overall strength of the evidence supporting a particular direction and in the cases where more than one direction is attested, to support a comparison between them.

At first glance, these data might seem to be an underwhelming reflection of systematic driving behavior. Indeed, the evidence shows that on more than 40% of the streets two directions are attested with nearly equal certainty. On the other hand, over one-third of all the streets do indicate only a single direction, a percentage that rises to 57% when we include streets with the great majority of their evidence (i.e., above 70%) reflecting a particular direction. These data are appropriately mixed, however, because they are not merely a snapshot of 79 CE but instead reflect the evolution of Pompeii's traffic systems and the realities of driving behaviors that occurred within them. As was mentioned earlier in the assessment of ruts, some parts of the street architecture are particularly old and preserve patterns of use long since superseded. Some of the wearing, however, also reflects the systematic circulation of traffic and its reorganization in the post-earthquake(s) period. Region VI, in the northwest of the city, serves as an excellent case study.[413] Beginning at the region's western edge, the data show that vicolo di Narciso was a northbound street (100%), as was vicolo di Modesto (84.4%). The next street, vicolo della Fullonica, was southbound (87.5%), and its intersection at via delle Terme was even modified to facilitate south-to-west turns. East of via di Mercurio, a two-lane street that divides the region in half, the evidence shows vicolo del Fauno definitively as a southbound street (100%) and that vicolo del Labirinto (100%) unequivocally carried northbound traffic. Conversely, the easternmost one-lane street, vicolo dei Vettii, and the main east–west thoroughfare, vicolo di Mercurio, show the presence of traffic in two directions in nearly equal proportions.

---

[413] Poehler 2006.

Excusing the last two streets momentarily, the patterns of wearing in Region VI demonstrate the unmistakable presence of directional control—or at very least consensus—exercised over nearly the entire region (fig. 6.5). Moreover, the alternation of direction between southbound and northbound traffic on adjacent streets shows that such control was not enacted at the level of the individual street but at least at the regional level. The equivocal evidence on vicolo dei Vettii and vicolo di Mercurio, however, would seem to undermine that notion of control. A judicious examination of vicolo di Mercurio reveals the opposite: the overlapping directions are not oppositional but sequential, with westbound traffic replacing eastbound traffic at a specific point in the history of the city. In at least two places wearing evidence demonstrates this reversal of direction. The first is on a stepping stone at via del Vesuvio, where an overriding mark cuts into previous eastbound sliding wear. The second occurs at the northwest corner of vicolo di Mercurio and via di Mercurio. Here, wear on the corner curbstone's south face establishes a significant flow of eastbound traffic. While the later placement of a guard stone at the end of that curbstone prevents the creation of further eastbound wear, it also records strong evidence of vehicles turning south to west onto vicolo di Mercurio.

On vicolo dei Vettii the distribution of directional evidence is particularly complex but similarly suggests that a reversal occurred, exchanging northbound for southbound traffic. Although both northbound and southbound traffic were identified in the twenty-three patterns of wear found, eight of the nine patterns documenting northbound traffic were discovered north of vicolo di Mercurio. Conversely, the evidence for southbound traffic was spread evenly across vicolo dei Vettii. These data can be separated chronologically by two changes to the street that occurred in the final period before the eruption. First, the southern end of vicolo dei Vettii at its intersection with via della Fortuna was narrowed by more than a meter and preserved southbound evidence exclusively. Second, the owners of the Casa dei Vettii installed a set of three stepping stones at their entrance way, covering existing ruts and interrupting the previous pattern of traffic.[414] Finally, because northbound traffic[415] continued after the reversal of vicolo di Mercurio to westbound, there was less time for the evidence for southbound to be inscribed. For this reason, the overall shallowness of the southbound evidence indicates

---

[414] The redecoration of this house in Fourth Style painting should also be paired with the changes to the exterior.

[415] Southbound: 14 patterns, average certainty 2.36. Northbound, 9 patterns, average certainty 2.88.

that vicolo dei Vettii had been switched to southbound only in Pompeii's final years.[416]

The Evolution of the Traffic Systems

These data from one-way and two-way streets leave little doubt that Pompeii was equipped with a set of simple but effective rules to manage the increasing flow of traffic of the early Imperial era as it circulated through the city's late Republican-era landscape. Like the volume of traffic, the rules of the road also changed over time. Certainly, there was a time when there were no organizing principles for driving a cart in the ancient world, but it is hard to believe that the concept of keeping to one side of the road to avoid oncoming traffic was not a very early convention. For the Romans, right-side driving would be the cornerstone of any urban traffic system they devised. This is the case at Pompeii, where right-side driving is attested unequivocally in the oldest and in the youngest patterns worn into the streetscape. Although undoubtedly a later invention than right-side driving, one-way streets are also in evidence at Pompeii by the end of first century BCE. Much of that same evidence also shows that over the last century of the city's existence, the system of traffic continued to change and to evolve.

Because the age of most wearing patterns can be established only relatively as one pattern overlaps or occludes another, precisely dating changes to the system is difficult. In fact, since directional evidence is formed only on the vertical faces of street architecture, the lag in the creation of sidewalks across the city makes the origin of the traffic system hard to establish and makes defining its extent spatially harder still. What's more, some sidewalks and their curbstones were replaced, particularly at intersections, excising the earliest evidence from our data set. Still, some large-scale changes to the city—the arrival of the aqueduct and its accompanying architectures (e.g., fountains and water towers) and infrastructures (e.g., piping and mechanisms of the drainage system)—locked in place a portion of the early evidence and prevented additional wear patterns from accruing. It is the relationship of the evidence for directionality to the mechanisms of water supply and removal that allows us to both witness changes in the organization of traffic and establish that the most significant of those changes occurred in the Augustan era. At the same time, we can also see that there was both a

---

[416] It is possible to read at least the data north of vicolo di Mercurio as contemporaneous, but the width of the street at 2.95 meters cannot abide even carts with a 4.5 RF gauge moving in two directions.

simpler pre-existing organization of traffic as well as a suite of significant changes that occurred in the post-earthquake(s) period. In the following discussion, these traffic patterns are named, in chronological order, the diverging system; the alternating system, fountains period; the alternating system, drainage period; and the post-earthquake(s) detours. The direction of each street and reason for the determination of that direction is listed in table 6.7 and illustrated in figs. 6.5–6.9, for each of these periods.

The Late Republican and Augustan Eras
The Diverging System of Traffic

To the degree that we can rely on certain elements of the water systems to belong to the Augustan period (and there are some reasons for caution),[417] the first systematic organization of traffic can be dated to at least the third quarter of the first century BCE. This first traffic system is recognized in the eastern half of Pompeii, along via dell'Abbondanza especially, and appears to be a simple diverging or bifurcating system in which the predominant directions were southbound for streets intersecting from the south and northbound for streets intersecting from the north (fig. 6.5). As we will see in the discussion of the diverging system's replacement by an alternating system of one-way streets, there is strong and specific evidence to place such a system chronologically before the arrival of the water supply system at Pompeii. There is also more general but equally strong evidence that illustrates the operation of this first traffic system. For example, along via dell'Abbondanza, nine of the twelve streets intersecting from the north show evidence for northbound traffic, and eight of the thirteen streets intersecting from the south have evidence for southbound traffic. A similar tally is found on the south side of via di Nola, where eight of ten streets preserve wearing from southbound vehicles. North of via di Nola, however, the pattern breaks down precisely at the point excavation extends only to the facades: west of vicolo dei Gladiatori three of four streets show northbound traffic, while no northbound traffic could be identified on any of the five streets farther east. More importantly, in every instance in which the earliest direction on a street can be definitively established, those directions stand in support of an initial diverging system of traffic.

For cart drivers, the diverging system provided a simple set of options that perfectly served the needs of those using this primary thoroughfare. Thus, if one

---

[417] Ohlig (2001, 76–79) has argued for an earlier aqueduct, though without a city-wide distribution. On typological grounds, Dybkjaer Larsen (1982, 63) suggests that water towers are Claudian or later.

Table 6.7 **All directional evidence, by period.**

Street Name	Diverging System	Certainty	Alternating System, Fountains	Certainty	Alternating System, Drainage	Certainty	Detours Period	Certainty
Region I								
via della Palaestra	EB	5a	EB	5a	EB	5a	WB	5a
via di Castricio	EB	4a	WB	4a	WB	4a	WB	4a
vicolo del Citarista	SB	5b	SB	5b	SB	5b	NB	5b
vicolo del Fuggiaschi	SB	1	SB	1	SB	1	SB	1
vicolo dell'Efebo	SB	2	SB	2	NB	2	NB	2
vicolo della Conciapelle	EB	0	EB	0	EB	0	WB	3b
vicolo della Nave Europa	SB	3b	NB	3b	NB	3b	NB	3b
vicolo di I.16-I.17	SB	3b	SB	3b	SB	3b	SB	3b
vicolo di Paquius Proculus (North)	SB	4a	A	4a	B	4a	B	4a
vicolo di Paquius Proculus (South)	SB	5a	NB	5a	NB	5a	NB	5a
vicolo I.1-I.5	U	NA	U	NA	U	NA	U	NA
vicolo I.2,19-I.3,10	WB	0	EB	3b	EB	3b	EB	3b
vicolo I.8-I.9	SB	2	NB	2	SB	3a	SB	2
vicolo I.9-I.11	SB	4a	SB	4a	A	4a	A	4a

Region II							
vicolo del Anfiteatro	NB	3a	NB	3a	B	4a	B	4a
vicolo della Venere	SB	0	SB	0	B	4a	B	4a
vicolo di Juilia Felix	SB	4a	NB	4a	B	4a	B	4a
vicolo di Octavius Quartio	SB	2	NB	2	B	4a	B	4a
vicolo II.5-II.5	NB	0	E	NA	E	NA	E	NA
Region III							
vicolo III.10-III.11	SB	3b	NB	0	NB	0	NB	0
vicolo III.11-III.12	SB	3a	SB	3a	SB	3a	SB	3a
vicolo III.1-III.2	NB	3b	SB	0	SB	0	NB	3b
vicolo III.2-III.3	NB	3b	NB	3b	NB	3b	B	4a
vicolo III.4-III.5	NB	3b	NB	3b	NB	3b	NB	3b
vicolo III.5-III.6	NB	4a	SB	4a	SB	4a	SB	4a
vicolo III.6-III.7	NB	1	NB	1	NB	1	NB	1
vicolo III.7-7	NB	3b	SB	0	B	4a	B	4a
vicolo III.7-City Wall	NB	2	SB	2	SB	2	B	4a
vicolo III.8-III.9	SB	0	NB	0	NB	0	NB	0
vicolo III.9-III.10	SB	0	SB	0	SB	0	SB	0

(Continued)

Table 6.7 **Continued**

Street Name	Diverging System	Certainty	Alternating System, Fountains	Certainty	Alternating System, Drainage	Certainty	Detours Period	Certainty
Region IV								
vicolo di IV 3 - IV 4	NB	0	NB	0	NB	0	B	4a
vicolo di IV 4 - IV 5	NB	0	SB	0	SB	0	B	4a
vicolo IV 3-5, City Wall	NB	0	SB	0	SB	0	SB	0
vicolo IV.1-IV.2	NB	0	NB	0	NB	0	NB	0
vicolo IV.2-IV.3	NB	0	SB	3a	SB	3a	SB	3a
Region V								
vicolo di Cecilio Giocondo	SB	2	SB	2	SB	2	NB	3a
vicolo del Centenario (North)	NB	3b	NB	3b	NB	3b	NB	3b
vicolo del Gladiatori	NB	1	NB	1	NB	1	NB	1
vicolo delle nozze d'Argento	EB	3a	EB	3a	EB	3a	WB	5a
vicolo di Lucrezio Frontone	NB	2	SB	2	SB	2	SB	2
vicolo di Lucrezio Frontone (South)	SB	2	NB	2	NB	2	NB	2
vicolo V 5 - IV 1	NB	0	SB	0	SB	0	SB	0

vicolo dei Vettii	NB	2	NB	2	NB	2	SB	3b
vicolo del Fauno	SB	3b	SB	3b	SB	3b	SB	3b
vicolo del Labirinto	NB	3b	NB	3b	NB	3b	A	4a
vicolo della Fullonica	NB	2	NB	2	SB	3a	SB	3a
vicolo di Mercurio	EB	3a	EB	3a	EB	3a	WB	5a
vicolo di Modesto	SB	2	SB	2	NB	3a	NB	3a
vicolo di Narciso	NB	3b	NB	3b	NB	3b	NB	3b
vicolo del Farmacista	NB	4b	NB	4b	SB	4b	A	NA
Region VII								
via degli Augustali	EB	3b	EB	3b	EB	3b	EB	3b
via del Lupanare	SB	3a	SB	3a	NB	4a	NB	4a
vicolo degli Scheletri	WB	3a	EB	3a	EB	3a	EB	3a
Vicolo del Balcone Pensile	EB	3a	WB	4a	WB	4a	WB	4a
vicolo del Gallo	EB	3b	EB	3b	A	4a	A	4a
vicolo del Gigante	NB	3b	NB	3b	NB	3b	NB	3b
vicolo del Granaio	U	NA	U	NA	U	NA	B	4a
vicolo della Maschera	NB	3a	SB	4a	SB	4a	SB	4a
vicolo del Panettiere	EB	2	WB	2	WB	2	WB	2
vicolo delle parete rossa	WB	5b	WB	5b	EB	5b	EB	5b

(Continued)

Table 6.7 **Continued**

Street Name	Diverging System	Certainty	Alternating System, Fountains	Certainty	Alternating System, Drainage	Certainty	Detours Period	Certainty
vicolo delle Terme	SB	1	SB	1	SB	1	SB	1
vicolo di Eumachia	NB	3a	NB	4a	SB	5a	SB	5a
vicolo di Soprastanti	EB	3b	EB	3b	EB	3b	EB	3b
vicolo di Storto Nuovo (South)	SB	0	SB	0	E	NA	E	NA
vicolo Storto	NB	2	NB	2	SB	2	SB	2
vicolo Storto Nuovo (North)	SB	0	SB	0	A	4a	A	4a
Region VIII								
vicolo dei 12 Dei	SB	5b	SB	5b	NB	5b	NB	5b
vicolo del Basilica	A	4a	A	4a	A	4a	B	4a
vicolo del Chapionett	A	4a	A	4a	A	4a	B	4a
vicolo del Foro	U	0	U	0	E	0	E	0
vicolo della Regina	EB	5b	EB	5b	WB	5b	WB	5b
vicolo della Regina (North)	NB	5b	NB	5b	SB	5b	SB	5b
vicolo della Regina (West)	A	3c	A	3c	A	3c	A	3c
vicolo VIII.5-5	NB	3b	NB	3b	NB	3b	A	4a

Region IX

vicolo IX.10-IX.14	SB	4a	NB	4a	NB	4a	NB	4a
vicolo del Centenario	SB	5a	SB	5a	SB	5a	NB	5a
vicolo del Gladiatori (South)	SB	3b	SB	3b	SB	3b	SB	3b
vicolo di Balbo	EB	5a	EB	5a	EB	5a	WB	5a
vicolo di Tesmo	SB	5a	SB	5a	SB	5a	NB	5a
vicolo di Tesmo (North)	NB	5a	SB	5a	SB	5a	NB	4a
vicolo di Tesmo (Very North)	NB	5a	SB	5a	SB	3a	E	4a
vicolo IX.11-IX.12	NB	3a	NB	3a	NB	3a	B	3a
vicolo IX.12-IX.13	NB	2	SB	2	NB	2	B	4a
vicolo IX.13-III.1	NB	0	NB	0	NB	0	SB	3b
vicolo IX.14-III.8	SB	3b	SB	3b	SB	3b	SB	3b
vicolo IX.3,6-IX.4,5	EB	3b	EB	3b	EB	3b	EB	3b
vicolo IX.7-IX.11	NB	4a	SB	4a	SB	4a	SB	4a

NB: Northbound; SB: Southbound; WB: Westbound; EB: Eastbound. A: Alternating; B: Blocked; E: Excluded; NA: Not applicable; U: Unknown

5a: New direction cuts older on same stone. 5b: New direction on a stone that blocks older.

4a: Older direction blocked by object, new on opposite corner 4b: Older direction associated deep ruts, new with fainter.

3a: Multiple directions present, sorted by relation to pattern 3b: Only one direction, fits pattern 3c: Multiple directions, alternating street

2: Multiple directions present, no relations to pattern.

1: Direction present, cannot fit pattern. Excluded.

0: No directions present

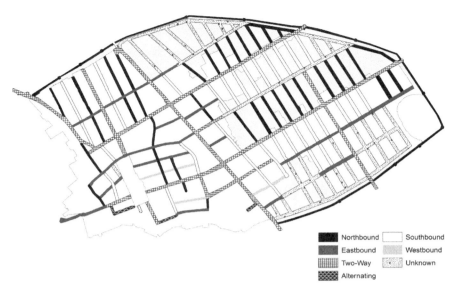

Figure 6.5 The diverging system.

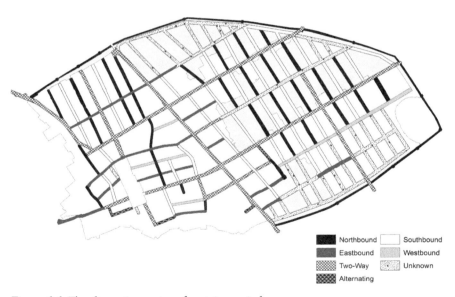

Figure 6.6 The alternating system, fountains period.

needed to turn northward, most streets to the north were limited to this direction, while those who wished to turn south found nearly every street in that direction to be southbound. In fact, it is only the last streets of the eastern grid that oppose the rest of their series: the last street before the Porta Sarno south of via dell'Abbondanza is northbound, and the last street in the north before the grid meets via Stabiana is southbound. The pattern was repeated along via di Nola, at

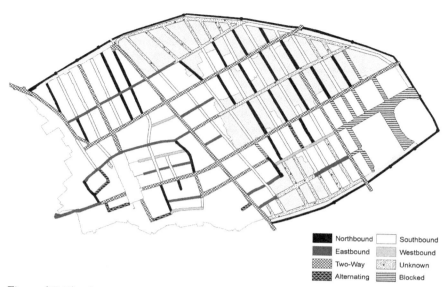

Figure 6.7 The alternating system, drainage period.

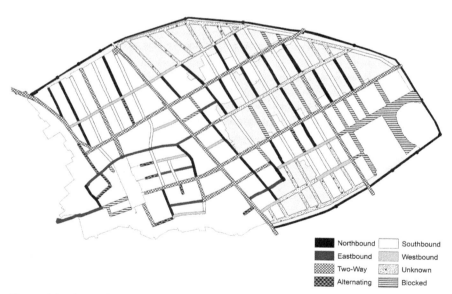

Figure 6.8 The traffic system of Pompeii, 79 CE.

least in the west. Such an organization had consequences: when drivers wanted to return to the main thoroughfare, their options were limited. For example, after turning south off via dell'Abbondanza, many drivers were forced to turn eastward onto via di Castricio and travel to at least via di Nocera, a two-way street that offered a northbound lane. Such an organization also had significant benefits: via dell'Abbondanza and via di Nola served as great diffusers of traffic, permitting

Figure 6.9 Fountain on via dell'Abbondanza blocking wearing at vicolo IX 7– IX 11.

vehicles to access the areas of the city on either side with streets that nearly all flowed directly into those areas. The most important advantage of the diverging system was that exceptionally little knowledge of that system was required by the cart driver. All he needed to know was that southward streets were southbound, that northward streets were northbound, and that turning around would require finding one of the few streets, often a two-way street, that went the opposite way.

The Alternating System: Fountain Period (ca. 20 BCE)

Though elegant, the diverging system also placed the burden of almost an entire region's traffic on only one or two secondary east–west streets, which given a sufficient volume of vehicles, would create substantial bottlenecks and undermine the value of the organization of one-way streets. The introduction of the water supply system (ca. 20 BCE) added additional challenges, as several streets were encroached upon by fountains and water towers. It was for these reasons that the diverging system was subsequently replaced by a series of alternating streets like that of Region VI (fig. 6.6). The evidence for this assertion of both control and chronology comes from half a dozen examples on the main thoroughfares, where previously inscribed patterns of directionally specific wearing have been interrupted by the insertion of water-related architectures.[418] In particular, the placement of several fountains near intersections preserved (and blocked further growth of) wear patterns that preceded their introduction. The intersection of via dell'Abbondanza and vicolo di Paquius Proculus offers a paradigmatic example. On the south side of the intersection, vicolo di Paquius Proculus and its previous southbound traffic were blocked by the introduction of a water tower, which narrowed the street to 1.40 meters and allowed only the smallest carts to pass. On the north side at vicolo IX 7–IX 11, the last curbstone at the northeast corner is diagnostically worn from west-to-north turns but is also

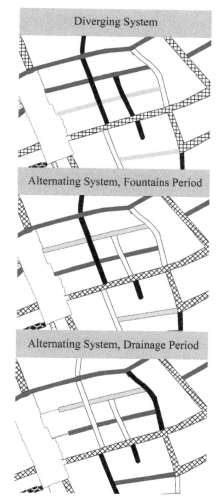

Figure 6.10 Altstadt traffic.

[418] In seven places across the city, fountains or water towers block or occlude a street, causing a change in direction on those streets.

abutted by the fountain, the insertion of which would no longer allow northward turning carts to impact the curbstone (fig. 6.9). On the northwest corner, the opposite is true: the lava curbstone is worn diagnostically from south-to-west-turning traffic. It is thus nearly certain that the fountain's placement coincides with the street's reversal of direction to southbound. That these features date to the Augustan period is further suggested by the build-up on the water tower of sinter, which indicates a long duration of use before a significant (seismic) disruption of the supply system.[419]

One block to the south, where vicolo di Paquius Proculus meets vicolo del Menandro, the scenario not only plays out again but also complements the pattern of directions of the diverging system and their reversal into an alternating system in the fountains period. At the southwest corner another fountain blocks the wear from the previous east-to-south turns and is itself unmarred by the passage of vehicles. In fact, the only guard stone protecting the fountain is placed against the east side, anticipating the north-to-west turns onto vicolo del Menandro that are documented by wearing along the east face of the curbstones at this intersection. These facts reinforce the interpretation that the water tower blocked the entrance to vicolo di Paquius Proculus at via dell'Abbondanza and marked the end of southbound traffic on this street in favor of later northbound and north-to-west-turning traffic.

Concurrent with (and almost required by) this change on vicolo di Paquius Proculus is a reversal of via di Castricio from eastbound to westbound. Such a change can be identified and dated to the alternating system, fountains period, by a number of factors. First, all the evidence for turns off of via di Castricio to the south are from eastbound vehicles, while the only evidence for northbound turns occurs when westbound traffic is using this street. The evidence for one of these west-to-north turns—at the northeast corner of via di Castricio and via di Nocera—is particularly important because it clearly precedes the introduction of the blockages introduced by the surface drainage system in the following period. These blockages are found at every intersection leading into Region II, sealing off this entire section of the city from wheeled traffic and providing a terminus ante quem for the evidence of westbound traffic on via di Castricio. The evidence from two additional streets in Region II lends further support to the existence of a diverging system and its replacement by an alternating system with the arrival of the piped water system. The first of these is vicolo di Giulia Felice, where, at its intersection with via dell'Abbondanza, a fountain sits just west of the final curbstone and blocks the wearing from previous east-to-south-turning traffic. On the opposite curbstone, across vicolo di Giulia Felice, wearing from north-to-east-turning vehicles is also present but is interrupted by the rough blockage that crosses the intersection. The other street, vicolo di Octavius Quartio, has a similar pattern of both southbound and northbound traffic at its intersection with via dell'Abbondanza prior to its closure by its own drainage mechanism. Both of these streets therefore demonstrate

---

[419] Keenan-Jones, Hellstrom, and Drysdale 2011, 141–44.

that before the isolation of Region II there were two streets using two sets of directions, and in the case of vicolo di Giulia Felice it is possible to show northbound traffic replacing southbound when the fountains arrived in the city.

These changes represent not only two sequential sets of directions but indeed two overlapping systems of traffic. Implementing this new system, however, was not a complicated task. Indeed, with the reversal of only vicolo di Octavius Quartio and vicolo di Giulia Felice to northbound, every street in Region II now reversed the direction of its neighbors, including the street that once divided the insula II 4. What's more, these changes fit perfectly with the presence and with the chronology of the first alternating system in the Fountain period elsewhere in the city. For example, as in Region II, only two streets in Region I—vicolo I 8–I 9 and vicolo della Nave Europa—needed to become northbound streets to effect the transition to an alternating system there. On the north side of via dell'Abbondanza, in Regions III and IX, the changes to the diverging system were again minimized, as only five (of thirteen) streets between via Stabiana and the eastern fortification wall were flipped to carry southbound traffic.

The evidentiary anchors of these directions and their chronology once again come from the placement of fountains and blockages along via dell'Abbondanza. The fountain on the north side of via dell'Abbondanza at vicolo di Paquius Proculus[420] and its blockage of previous northbound wearing has already been discussed. Its reversal to a southbound street as part of a city-wide system of alternating directions is supported by another emplacement that equally demonstrates the cessation of northbound traffic and its replacement by southbound directions along via dell'Abbondanza. This second example comes from vicolo III 5–III 6 where the installation of a large Sarno limestone guard stone, itself unworn by turning vehicles, interrupts the path of earlier west-to-north turns. In these instances, evidence for southbound traffic is found to either predate the occlusion of the street, which most likely occurred contemporaneously with the other water structures, or to appear in association with the clear end of northbound traffic.

Along via di Nola identical evidence of reversals comes from several streets, including vicolo IX 10–IX 14, where curving ruts and a worn curbstone show that east-to-south-turning traffic was interrupted by a fountain and water tower. These architectures were positioned, however, not to impede the subsequent northbound traffic that left diagnostic evidence of its north-to-east turns. Four blocks to the east, another fountain was placed on the east side of the intersection of via di Nola and vicolo III 10–III 11. Once again, a guard stone blocks the wearing from previous turns southward onto vicolo III 10–III, while still more stones protect the fountain from the expectation of northbound carts turning around the fountain to the east.[421]

These two locations on via di Nola, like those on via dell'Abbondanza, clearly demonstrate the reversal of traffic from a southbound direction within the earliest

[420] The street to the north is named vicolo IX 7–IX 11.
[421] It is unfortunate, however, that no wearing patterns could be identified to conclusively establish northbound traffic.

diverging system of traffic to a northbound flow upon the arrival of the fountains and the alternating system that accompanied it. Unfortunately, evidence for the equivalent changes on two other streets intersecting via di Nola has been erased by the replacement of much of the street architecture. On the other hand, the newness of the stones on vicolo IX 14–III 8 shows that the evidence for north-bound traffic found here comes from a later time in the city's life. On the north side of via di Nola, the evidence is less secure. Due to the presence of soil cover-ing the intersections and vegetation covering the curbs (especially lichens), only two streets demonstrate wearing from more than one direction. Nonetheless, beginning at the western edge of Region V, an alternating pattern of traffic does appear with the first four streets. The absence of evidence farther east, along with replacement and repair, may also be due to the smallness of the easternmost insu-lae and the consequent lack of importance of the surrounding streets in the over-all network of traffic. That is, there might simply have been very few vehicles ever needing to use these streets, and the evidence of their passing was therefore rarely inscribed. Still, the streets known to have been reversed to northbound along the south of via di Nola complement one another's position within a series of alter-nating streets, as do others, and the pattern itself complements those seen con-temporaneously along both sides of via dell'Abbondanza.

As has been described, Region VI participated in the alternating system of traffic during the fountains period, and although it saw some reversals in Pompeii's final years, there is very little evidence that the diverging system once existed here. Interestingly, there is evidence that even prior to the arrival of the Serino aqueduct and its related architectures of water supply, at least the eastern areas of Altstadt, if not Region VI as well, was already organized by an alternating system (fig. 6.10). When the fountain and water tower were placed along vicolo del Balcone Pensile at its intersections with vicolo di Eumachia and vicolo della Maschera, respectively, both streets carried northbound traf-fic, and both features prevented the continued use of vicolo del Balcone Pensile as an eastbound street. In fact, the fountain blocked the previous north-to-east turn in a manner now familiar, with its only guard stone positioned at the foun-tain's northwest corner, a placement that anticipates no vehicles approaching from the south.

Southbound vehicles on the next street to the east, vicolo del Lupanare, how-ever, left significant evidence for westbound turns around the very sharp corner with vicolo del Balcone Pensile. Additionally, because the water tower narrowed vicolo del Balcone Pensile street at vicolo di Eumachia, there was no choice but for vicolo della Maschera to reverse direction and carry southbound traffic, as there would otherwise be no exit for any traffic that reached the intersection of vicolo della Maschera and vicolo del Balcone Pensile. These directions and their rever-sals show that even before the arrival of the Serino aqueduct, a one-way system of streets existed within the Altstadt with northbound (vicolo di Eumachia) and southbound (vicolo del Lupanare) routes along the boundaries and a central route (vicolo della Maschera) that reversed direction along with the east–west routes (vicolo del Balcone Pensile and vicolo degli Scheletri). This evidence now suggests it is entirely possible that while the eastern orthogonal grid of Pompeii was using the diverging system of directions, these relatively few streets of the Altstadt became the model and the proving ground for the alternating system's utility, feasibility, and eventual wider adoption across the rest of Pompeii in the late first century BCE.

Alternating System, Drainage Period

The Altstadt as a locus of urban experimentation would not be unprecedented. Indeed, I have argued above for the novelty of the logic embedded in its earliest network of streets and have argued elsewhere that the Altstadt may also have served as the origin of the city-wide drainage system.[422] It was the arrival of this system and associated additions to the water supply system that next changed the traffic system within the Altstadt as well as the easternmost sections of the city (fig. 6.7). The creation of a single blockage at the intersection of via degli Augustali and vicolo del Lupanare, which covered and preserved the evidence of previous east-to-south turns, was sufficient to reverse this later street to northbound and spur another street, vicolo di Eumachia, to flip to become southbound. On the west side of the intersection where vicolo di Eumachia meets via dell'Abbondanza the well-known white limestone Fountain of Abundance was installed, which interrupted the sliding wear left by east-to-north-turning vehicles.[423] Additional evidence for northbound traffic on vicolo di Eumachia is found on the opposite, northeastern curbstone, which is itself cut over by still stronger wearing from later south-to-east-turning traffic.[424] These directions are further supported by turns found onto and off of their cross streets—northbound from vicolo del Lupanare onto westbound vicolo del Balcone Pensile and southbound off vicolo di Eumachia onto eastbound vicolo degli Scheletri—the latter of which had already reversed in the previous period.

Between the blockages at vicolo di Eumachia and vicolo del Lupanare and the overlapping and reversing wearing patterns associated with each, the relative sequence of directions in the Altstadt is especially clear. In this case, however,

---

[422] Chapter 2, 28–31; Poehler 2012.

[423] The wear on the northwest corner curbstone is surprisingly heavy, but it must be remembered that prior to this period the forum area was still accessible to wheeled vehicles and that several streets, including vicolo degli Scheletri, vicolo del Balcone Pensile, and perhaps vicolo del Gallo remained directly connected to the forum.

[424] Chapter 5, 131–33.

there is also important evidence for the absolute chronology of these changes. The Fountain of Abundance, one of only four such white limestone or marble basins in the city, is situated in direct association with the southern entrance to the Building of Eumachia. Built by the priestess Eumachia in the first decade CE, likely in imitation of the Porticus Liviae at Rome,[425] the building is also fitted with great quantities of white marble, including the internal colonnade, portions of its stylobate, internal and external revetments, an intricately sculpted door frame opening onto the forum, and the great white limestone colonnade that carried the building's monumental inscription. In fact, it is the monumentalization of the forum with this colonnade that finally excluded all wheeled traffic from the urban center and which required the installation of three large white limestone bollards at the western end of via dell'Abbondanza.[426] The placement of the white limestone Fountain of Abundance, with its iconographic and material connections, therefore fits perfectly into these late Augustan urban developments at Pompeii.

The expansion of the Sanctuary of Apollo on the forum's western edge shows a similar pattern and chronology. Dated by excavation to about 10 BCE, and by inscription to c. 3/2 BCE, the Temple of Apollo's enlarged precinct eliminated both the eastern portion of vicolo del Gallo and southern half of the vicolo Storto Nuovo and also narrowed what remained of their intersection to the point of being nearly unusable. In fact, the only remaining corner and even shape of insula VII 15 itself had to be modified to make any passage possible over the next twenty years.[427] It was these changes that allowed or perhaps required the later placement of another white fountain at the western end of vicolo del Gallo, blocking a formerly significant volume of traffic that had made north-to-eastbound turns onto this street.[428] With the closure of the forum and this new fountain in place, all traffic that entered Pompeii through the Porta Marina was forced to circumnavigate the forum in a great arc to reach the eastern areas of the Altstadt: from via Marina to vicolo del Gigante to via degli Soprastanti to via degli Augustali to vicolo di Eumachia and finally onto via dell'Abbondanza. Because of the blockage on vicolo del Lupanare, the reversal of vicolo di Eumachia to southbound was a key part of this detour. Finally, when we recognize another white limestone fountain at the intersection of via degli Augustali and vicolo di Eumachia,[429] it is possible to see these rare but contemporaneous fountains marking the edges of a great detour required by several late Augustan architectural and infrastructural building

---

[425] Richardson 1978, 191–202.

[426] The presence of overriding marks from vehicles show that, on occasion, vehicles continued into the forum area despite the blockage.

[427] Dobbins et al. 1998, 744–47.

[428] On this fountain, see Newsome 2009, 126–28, 134–35.

[429] Note that the fountain's placement blocks previously formed ruts and made east-to-north turns almost impossible.

programs. Moreover, these developments around the forum and in the city's surface drainage system not only offer a date for the introduction of the second alternating system in the Altstadt but also explain why such changes were necessary.

In the south of the Altstadt, below via dell'Abbondanza, an equivalent and complementary set of changes unfolded in the alternating system, drainage period.
By at least the time of the water supply system's arrival, traffic in Region VIII was
based largely on a counterclockwise path circulating insula VIII 6. Strong wearing
on the corner where vicolo della Regina meets its northward bend shows east-to-
north turns, while west-to-south turns are in evidence diagonally across the insula
at the intersection of vicolo delle Pareti Rosse and vicolo dei 12 Dei. At this latter
intersection a water tower was installed against the north side of vicolo delle Pareti
Rosse in expectation and accommodation of such west-to-south turns. Likewise,
the fountain on vicolo della Regina at its awkward junction with vicolo dei 12 Dei
is deeply recessed into the southern curb to facilitate the eastbound traffic as well
as those southbound vehicles turning off of vicolo dei 12 Dei.

There is especially clear evidence that this circulation was reversed in the following period. The deep wear cut into the northward bend of vicolo della Regina
is covered over and blocked by a guard stone that preserves the overriding mark
of south-to-west-turning vehicles. Moving across insula VIII 6 diagonally once
again, examination of the intersection of vicolo dei 12 Dei and vicolo delle Pareti
Rosse shows that a new curbstone was placed at the southeast corner that both
covers the earlier west-to-south turns and carries the evidence of the new pattern
of northbound and eastbound traffic. Finally, it is unknown if these changes were
related in some way to the removal of vicolo VIII 5–5's southern half, a street
that showed a nascent northbound direction before its closure.

Farther east, in Regions I and II, the installation of the drainage system and its
related monumental architectures had profound effects on the circulation of traffic. Along the south side of via dell'Abbondanza (east of via Stabiana), fully ten of
its thirteen (77%) intersections were modified by the water management mechanisms and of these seven blocked both water and vehicles. Undoubtedly related
to the construction of the Grand Palestra and its removal of six city blocks, as
well as their need for regular supply, these curbstone blockages sealed off all of
Region II from wheeled traffic. In Region I the blockage of vicolo del Paquius
Proculus only formalized the closure of a street that had already been excluded
from the traffic system. The blockage at vicolo I 9–I 11, however, removed a
previously southbound street, leaving only northbound streets in the middle of
the region. The alternating pattern was reinstated, however, by reversing only
one street, vicolo I 8–I 9, to become southbound once again. Because blocking
the bottom of a street only pools water behind that blockage, there are no full
curbstone blockages along the north side of via dell'Abbondanza. Instead, a rare
drainage feature—a stone ramp with an opening for wastewater was constructed
across vicolo IX 11–IX 12, similar to a feature built at vicolo della Maschera.

Within the alternating system, the line of vicolo di Tesmo / vicolo del Citarista, a major southbound route, seems mostly to survive the Augustan reversals. As a secondary route running nearly the width of the city, these streets were especially important as means to relieve some of the traffic volume from via Stabiana. Certain sections, however, were more important than others: these formed portions of minor detours that were crucial to both the operation of the traffic system and to our understanding of it (fig. 6.2; also, see fig. 7.1). By the Augustan era these detours were instituted, or had evolved, to allow drivers to avoid the congestion of the largest intersections in the city—both along via Stabiana— where four two-lane streets exchanged their flows of vehicles. All along the vicolo di Tesmo there is abundant evidence for the passage of southbound carts, and (as described above) at its intersection with via dell'Abbondanza, the modification of the northeastern corner indicates that many carts were once expected to (and did) turn westward. The advantage in this earliest route may have been to avoid the traffic on via Stabiana and, after having turned westward onto via dell'Abbondanza, being able to cross straight through, rather than turn through, that congested intersection.

In approximately the year 1 CE, the tetrapylon of the Holconii was built across via dell'Abbondanza and blocked all wheeled traffic coming from the intersection with via Stabiana (fig. 6.2, D).[430] This construction added to an intersection already crowded by a water tower and fountain that had been built at the southeast corner a few decades before. These changes not only removed the most direct route west toward the forum and Altstadt but also further narrowed an already congested intersection, making alternative routes all the more attractive. The evidence for this rerouting is found in diagnostic wearing that shows some vehicles on vicolo di Tesmo continued southward across via dell'Abbondanza onto vicolo del Citarista (fig. 6.2E) before turning westward toward via Stabiana and further toward the Altstadt area. Moreover, we can see traffic coming from the north on via Stabiana and avoiding the intersection with via dell'Abbondanza by turning eastward onto vicolo di Balbo to join the vicolo di Tesmo detour. The expected traffic flow on vicolo di Balbo was disproportionately large: not only is there wearing that demonstrates east-to-south turns but also the corner curb and even the insula itself are angled to accommodate such a turn (fig. 6.11).[431]

There is also evidence from the north of Pompeii that during the Augustan era cart drivers had another detour available to avoid the congestion at the intersection of vie Vesuvio, Nola, Stabiana, and Fortuna. At this time vicolo di

---

[430] Chapter 2, 49.

[431] Additionally, there is evidence of eastbound traffic on the stepping stone on vicolo di Balbo at via Stabiana.

Figure 6.11 Intersection of vicolo di Tesmo at vicolo di Balbo.

Mercurio and vicolo di Nozze d'Argento were part of an important, if secondary, eastbound route across the north of the city. One block east of via del Vesuvio a significant proportion of this eastbound traffic turned south onto vicolo di Cecilio Giocondo, which, like vicolo di Tesmo at Abbondanza, meets via di Nola with its western curb angled slightly to ease south-to-west turns. Again, the purpose of turning back toward the major intersection again might have been to move directly across rather than turn through it. The northeast corner of vicolo di Cecilio Giocondo shows carts turning to the east onto via di Nola, and many of those same vehicles that needed to travel farther south—or especially into the Altstadt—did so by turning southward onto vicolo di Tesmo, toward its detour of via Stabiana and onto via dell'Abbondanza.

Post-earthquake(s) Detours

In the post-earthquake(s) period these detours would remain essential adjustments in the overall traffic system—especially as two additional streets were removed from the street network—though the directions they carried were

Figure 6.12 Northwest corner of vicolo di Citarista at vicolo del Menandro.

reversed.[432] The evidence for this change in direction is as unambiguous as for the original detours. At the northwest corner of the intersection of vicolo del Citarista and vicolo del Menandro a large guard stone was placed against the final curbstone's east face, preventing all further wearing on this stone (fig. 6.12). While the guard stone was worn generally, the southern side of the corner curbstone shows diagnostic wearing from vehicles overriding this stone as they turned northward onto vicolo del Citarista.[433] The north end of vicolo del Citarista also yields evidence for northbound traffic: the southeast corner with via dell'Abbondanza was angled to permit north-to-east turns, and the small guard

---

[432] These streets are vicolo IX 11–IX 12 and vicolo III 2–III 3. Both were partially blocked and, judging by the condition of the former (Berg 2008; Varone 2008), abandoned. The exclusion of these two streets appears to have been the impetus to reverse the directions on the streets between them.

[433] The height of this guard stone (71 cm) would also have prevented many east-to-north-turning vehicles from overriding this same corner curbstone (21 cm high), indicating that these marks are from vehicles with wheels larger than 4 RF in diameter, that there was a lag between the reversal of vicolo del Citarista to northbound and the guard stone's placement, or both.

stone at the southwest corner, which made east-to-south turns harder, was also diagnostically overridden by northbound carts. Diagonally across the intersection with via dell'Abbondanza, the northwest corner at vicolo di Tesmo was deeply eroded by the outside wheel of carts sliding along its face, while the inside wheel cut and overrode the stepping stone once farther through the turn. What's more, this wearing joins with that from previous southbound traffic to carve the western side of the stepping stone into a point (fig. 5.14), a stark indication of two directions of travel converging at a single place but, in this case, at different points in time.

The wearing patterns left by northbound carts are present along the entire length of vicolo di Tesmo, but the most important among these is the north-to-west turn inscribed at the southwest corner of the intersection with vicolo di Balbo. The very same adjusted corner curbstone that showed earlier east-to-south-turning carts also preserves equally clear evidence of its reversal, as does the opposite end of vicolo di Balbo, where carts completed the detour from via dell'Abbondanza by making a west-to-north turn onto via Stabiana.[434] That the reversal to northbound of the rest of vicolo di Tesmo was not instantaneous or perhaps was not accomplished at the same time as the detour is suggested by a large guard stone in the middle of the intersection of vicolo di Tesmo and vicolo di Balbo. Standing in the center of a pair of ruts produced by previous southbound traffic, the stone's placement was very careful measured: it allows just enough space for northbound carts to pass on the east side of the street (cf. figs. 6.2 B; 6.11). Surprisingly, there is also sufficient room for southbound vehicles to pass on the west side of the guard stone, space that is afforded by the angle of the northwest corner. The effect of the angled corner and the blocking stone, however, was to force any southbound vehicle to turn westward onto vicolo di Balbo. It is easy to imagine that flipping a street's direction would not occur overnight and that there might be good reason why some number of vehicles would continue to use vicolo di Tesmo for southbound travel. On the other hand, the precise placement of the guard stone within the older ruts indicates that a change had been made, and the space permitting northbound carts to continue equally suggests that (along with all the rest of the northbound wearing) the entire street would be reversed. Still, the angle of the northwest corner, the southbound wearing there, and the space allotted by the guard stone's placement all demonstrate that the southbound traffic on vicolo di Tesmo was expected to join the westward flow of vicolo di Balbo, which can only be done once that later street's direction had been reversed to westbound as part of the detour's inversion.

That the complicated evidence at this intersection is clear on direction but less clear on chronology accurately reflects the compromises and messy realities

---

[434] West-to-south turns are also in evidence at the southeast corner of vicolo di Balbo and via Stabiana.

of ancient urban life. In many ways, the complexity preserved at vicolo di Tesmo and vicolo di Balbo is a benefit to our understanding of the reality of traffic flows as it illustrates the realistic lag between the institution of a rule, its dissemination to the drivers, and the application of it in practice. At the same time, the complexity here also usefully reflects the interlocking nature of the evidence and its interpretation, as undergirded by the logic of how the physical act of driving must have occurred. That is, once the guard stone was placed in the middle of this intersection, like the fountains and guard stones at other intersections, vehicles were physically impeded from a path. While it would not be impossible in some cases to circumvent such an obstacle, the interpretation of that blockage's success is bolstered by the absence of evidence of such regular attempts and the presence of evidence for a reversal of direction. In these cases, we witness not only cause and effect but also planning and intent, as the needs of one infrastructural system (traffic) are negotiated within the context of another (water).

What's more, as the interpretation of one intersection is added to that of another and still another, we see how the evidence for traffic becomes interlocking in support of larger interpretations but not interdependent. That is, specific forms of evidence, such as blockages or turns in particular directions, can be shown to work in service of a region-wide pattern. For example, the blockages inside the Altstadt east of the forum demonstrate reversals on vicolo di Eumachia and vicolo del Lupanare that are themselves complemented by changes in the directions of turns onto and off the streets that intersect them. With all these observations fitting tightly together, it is clear that Pompeians reversed directions on several streets in the same period and did so in response not only to the physical impediments of other infrastructures but also to the needs of drivers who would use those streets.

Such an interpretation, however, is not dependent upon all the data supporting it being extant or even complementary. That is, even without the evidence for turns or for directions prior to blockage, the remaining information would not therefore become reflective of a different overall pattern in the area. In fact, there is a slight wearing from north-to-west-turning carts at the southwest corner where vicolo della Maschera meets vicolo del Balcone Pensile that cannot be accounted for within the current regional interpretation. It appears, reminiscent of the complexity at vicolo di Tesmo and vicolo di Balbo, that some carts continued to travel northward even after vicolo del Balcone Pensile had become a westbound street, forcing vicolo della Maschera to carry southbound vehicles. Once again, what might seem a rogue form of evidence actually offers nuance to behaviors that were more complex than the evidence for the dominant pattern can reveal but does not disqualify that larger interpretation. A lag between the introduction of westbound traffic and the creation of the water tower on vicolo del Balcone Pensile could explain this evidence. Thus, even as the northbound traffic on vicolo della Maschera or the southbound traffic on vicolo di Tesmo ran counter to what would become the dominant direction, they each turned westward, participating in a reversal that is key to circulation at the regional level.

Finally, when considered together at the scale of the entire city, the totality of the evidence reveals not only a natural increase in the amount of information available to describe the circulation of traffic in each period but also a growing level of confidence in what that evidence tells us. These trends are revealed in fig. 6.13, which graphs the certainty levels of directional interpretations from table 6.7 for each of the four periods in the traffic system's evolution. One trend is that streets without directional information (0) became fewer over time, indicating that more and more of the city was participating in the traffic systems or at the very least more of the evidence for traffic was being recorded and preserved. At the same time, the abundance of evidence available in each period shows strong agreement between individual instances of direction and larger patterns of movement (3) within the system of each period. Preservation of previous patterns has much to do with another trend illustrated by this graph: the notable increase in the number of instances of convincing chronological evidence for each direction and its reversal (4, 5). In part, these trends are to be expected, as one must have evidence of an earlier pattern to have evidence that another

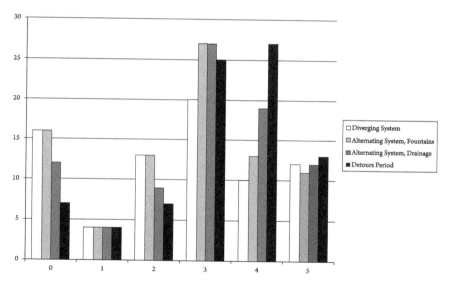

Figure 6.13 Certainty of street direction by period. **0**: No directions present; **1**: Direction present, cannot fit pattern. Excluded; **2**: Multiple directions present, no relations to pattern; **3**: 3a. Multiple directions present, sorted by relation to pattern, 3b. Only one direction, fits pattern, 3c. Multiple directions, alternating street; **4**: 4a. Older direction blocked by object, new on opposite corner; 4b. Older direction associated with deep ruts, new with fainter; **5**: 5a. New direction cuts older on same stone, 5b. New direction on a stone that blocks older.

superseded it. But such an expectation harbors an important assumption—that the traffic system would continue to exist and to change over time. Looking to the removal of stepping stones and changes to the water systems, it is clear that such continuity cannot be assumed even in large-scale, city-wide infrastructural systems. Abandonment of the system was always a possibility. At their broadest scope, these trends in the data—the increase in the amount of evidence and its clarity—document a municipal investment and continual reinvestment in the organization of traffic over the last century of Pompeii's existence.

Summary

In many ways the intersection of the vicolo di Balbo and vicolo di Tesmo is a microcosm of the many overlapping urbanistic and infrastructural decisions that presupposed the forms of both Pompeii's final system of traffic (fig. 6.8) and the evidence that would reveal it. The shape of the intersection, for example, reflects the decision made around 300 BCE to create a discontinuous, hierarchical network of streets in the western half of the city. The shape of the intersection also made certain turns more difficult (e.g., turning south to west around the southeast corner of insula XI 2), and so later Pompeians adjusted the angle of the curbs to facilitate this traffic pattern. As this space became the fulcrum of a detour away from a congested intersection of two-ways streets, even the wide-angled corner had to be bent to accommodate the volume of traffic that turned first to the right, then to the left around it. The narrowness of both vicolo di Balbo and vicolo di Tesmo had much to do with these changes, giving too little room to make turns and requiring that they—like most of the city—be restricted to a single direction. As a detour, these streets played a crucial role adjusting traffic to Pompeii's compressed street network. Beyond this intersection, that same network served as the basis for the traffic system's design, initially as a simple diverging system that made turns off a main street (e.g., via dell'Abbondanza) simple but returning to that main street difficult and, later, as an alternating system (e.g., Region VI) that solved this problem by making every other street flow in a different direction.

The archaeological evidence from Pompeii has proven to be remarkable in many ways, not least in its clarity and its abundance. Indeed, it is the strongest evidence for how traffic circulated anywhere in the Roman world, permitting the preceding chapter to be written about its organization and its evolution. What remains to be understood—and what stands beyond the limits of this archaeological evidence alone—is how such a complex system might have been created and maintained. The following chapters therefore explore how Pompeii's traffic system could have been administered (Chapter 7) and how that system fitted into the larger world of Roman urbanism (Chapter 8).

7

World of the *Mulio*

As Sabinus looked around the stable, he couldn't decide if it was too small or too full. The dirt floor of the main room was interrupted by the brick piers supporting a second story where he and the stable boys slept. Unplastered, like the rest of the walls, the piers divided the stable yard into three parts. The larger two areas, nearer the exit, were occupied by a pair of road-weary vehicles—a two-wheeled *cisium* and a four-wheeled *plostrum*—while the third served as a corridor with doorways to the manger and to the toilet. A small rain-fed basin provided drinking water for the animals in the corner.[435] The swishing tails of the mules drinking there seemed to occupy more than their share of the space, and the dog that ran through their legs and around the vehicles appeared to claim the entire stable by movement alone.[436] *They certainly owned most of the smells*, Sabinus complained to himself. At least his toilet had a window above it and a cesspit that drained below the sidewalk outside the house.[437]

All along the walls objects hung on nails—short chains, iron hooks, bronze bells,[438] leather straps, loops of rope and bundles of twine, and even a pair of rarely used saddles[439]—while building materials and loose bales of hay bulged out of the small rooms beside the latrine.[440] Between the doors to these rooms, a line of jars sat on the floor, all stoppered and some sealed.[441] These contained the rendered animal fat that Sabinus used to grease the vehicles' axles and the aged urine he used in salves to cover the cuts his mules seemed to always be getting on their legs.[442] Hidden among these larger vessels was a jar of Gallic honey, one of a few prizes pilfered by the stable boys when there were

---

[435] Ling 1997, 118–23.

[436] The only animal found in the stable was a dog (Allison 2006, 112, n. 627). On animals, see also Poehler 2011a, 207, n. 36.

[437] Cesspits are known from under several sidewalks: Ling 1997, 108; Dobbins et al. 1998, 746–47; Jones and Robinson 2005, 695, n. 6; Anniboletti 2007, 6–9; Hobson 2009, 63–69.

[438] Ling (1997, 114) found nail holes in room 20. On objects from the stable, Allison 2006, 110–12 ns. 603 (plate 44.2), 605, 606–8, 611, 615–16, 620.

[439] See forum paintings, fragment 2; Olivito 2013, 37–40, figs. 20–21.

[440] On building materials, see Allison 2006, 114, n. 632; for hay, though at Oplontis, see van der Graaff et al. 2016, 11–12.

[441] Allison (2006, 113, n. 631) reports three amphorae were cut and refilled with something other than lime.

[442] On the use of lard as a lubricant, see Harris 1974; for urine as a veterinary medicine, see Flohr and Wilson (2011, 149–50).

mistakes in the inventory lists.[443] It's safe there; nobody ever counts the jars of piss and fat. In the corner, near the exit, sat a great stack of empty amphorae and a pile of lime.[444] The amphorae were so many that they covered a small horseshoe-shaped stove Sabinus used to render the fat, onto the side of which Sabinus had attached a comic mask for good luck and a laugh.[445] Although the lime had sloughed out into the floor, it was the jumble of amphorae that annoyed Sabinus most.[446] *There are plenty of other rooms to store these rather than my stable*, Sabinus thought, as he scraped the rust from the iron rims of his wagon, collecting the orange flakes in his hand.[447] His real complaint was how the amphorae had been allowed to build up: *there are more than two trips to make, even with the* plostrum!*[448]

The preceding fictional narrative is set in the stable of the Casa del Menandro. Undoubtedly, there was a *mulio*, a mule/cart driver (or several), who lived here, but we know nothing about him. Such a lack of information in this case will prove to be an advantage. I have chosen to employ Sabinus as my narrative vehicle to explore how traffic at Pompeii operated and how as a system it was maintained. My hope is that a rich image of life in the Pompeian street might enliven some of the deep archaeological detail prevalent in this book. I give particular attention to the things Sabinus would have seen and encountered; some of them have been discussed already, but many other aspects of the *mulio*'s world have yet to be explored. Sabinus is thus my conceit to attach a profusion of detail excluded from previous discussions. He is also a means to explore the more speculative aspects of traffic management while simultaneously signaling the hypothetical nature of such exploration.

The idea of having a fictional character live out one's archaeological or historical arguments is not new. Indeed, the inspiration came both from Diane Favro's father and son walking in Augustan Rome and Steven Mithen's John Lubbock touring the Neolithic world.[449] Nor will this be the first fictionalized academic

---

[443] The jar was actually found in corridor P; Allison 2006, 109, n. 588.

[444] Found were 43 amphorae, of two or three types. Stefani 2003, 210–12; Allison 2006, 113–14, no. 631.

[445] Unprovenanced mask fragments were cataloged by Allison (2006, 261, n. 33).

[446] Lime: Allison 2006, 114, n. 632; amphorae: Allison 2006, 113–14, n. 631, with discussion on 320–21; Stefani 2003, 210–13.

[447] Pliny *NH* 34.45–6; Harris 1974, 33.

[448] If the two-wheeled *cisium* was used, its load would have to be carefully balanced. See Sandor's (2013, 693–700) review of Crouwel 2012, including an amusing image (fig. 2) of what happens when too much weight is at the back.

[449] Favro 1996; Mithen 2003.

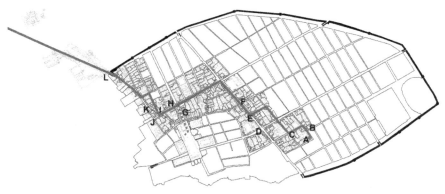

Figure 7.1 Route of Sabinus across Pompeii.

narrative set in Pompeii.[450] To explain why an appeal to fiction might be necessary when writing an archaeological history, I find Mithen's justifications particularly apt:

> I make use of John Lubbock to ensure that this history is about people's lives rather than just the objects that archaeologists find. My own eyes cannot escape the present. I am unable to see beyond the discarded stone tools and food debris, the ruins of empty houses and the fireplaces that are cold to the touch. Although excavations provide doors to other cultures, such doors can be forced ajar and never passed through. I can, however, use my imagination to squeeze John Lubbock through the gaps so that he can see what is denied to my own eyes and become what the travel writer Paul Theroux has described as a "stranger in a strange land."[451]

Sabinus is my stranger, and Pompeii, seemingly so familiar, is my strange land.

In the three acts that follow, Sabinus encounters many aspects of Pompeii's 79 CE streetscape, including other drivers, their driving habits and cargoes, and the feel of the street, as well as several ways to learn the rules of Pompeii's final traffic system. Figure 7.1 maps Sabinus's route through Pompeii, with each letter indicating his location throughout the text. Following each excursus is a treatment of the evidence for what he sees, which extends into a series of discussions about how the traffic system might have been administered. The first of these discussions demonstrates the municipal control over the

---

[450] Hopkins 2000, 10–45. I thank Jason Moralee for bringing this book to my attention.
[451] Mithen 2003, 6.

traffic system and its operation. The second argument explores how, in the absence of direct enforcement mechanisms, such municipal power could have been exercised to produce the consistency of behavior shown in the directional wearing patterns. Essentially, the task of managing the traffic system is one of information transfer, and underlying that management are the mechanisms by which such communication could have been accomplished. Sabinus will thus experience three scenarios that serve as overlapping hypotheses for how drivers at Pompeii might have learned and implemented the information necessary to drive within the traffic systems' regulations. These are (1) by means of the social networks that connect local drivers to civil authorities, (2) through the observation of the environment and other drivers, and (3) via direct contact with information proxies, such as inscriptions, maps, or hired guides.

Excursus 1: The Stable

As Sabinus contemplated the daylong journey to his master's country estate,[452] the sound of sandaled feet in the corridor announced that the journey would be starting immediately. A man in a dark tunic[453] entered the stable and wrinkled his nose at the smell. He was Quintus Poppaeus Eros,[454] the master's freedman who, despite his self-importance, still lived in the house, claiming to be overseeing its reconstruction.[455] It was for this reason that the master, and thus everyone else, jokingly called him Cerylus. Despite how comical he sounded when attempting an imperious tone, Cerylus couldn't help but condescend in giving Sabinus his orders.

"Take this pile of jars out to the villa today and be sure to use the correct streets and their correct directions this time. As you know, master, that is, *your* master, was once aedile,[456] and we cannot have his own slave breaking the rules he helped to maintain and improve! If you need reminding of the routes, consult the directory in the forum, if you can read it.[457] If not, see the public slave in the archives. He will educate you . . . again."

---

[452] Ling 1997, 105; Poehler 2011a, 207–8.

[453] A piece of blackened cloth was found with the skeletons in corridor P1; Allison 2006, 107, n. 567.

[454] Q. Poppaeus Eros is known from bronze seal found inside the Casa del Menandro; Ling 1997, 142.

[455] Anderson 2011, 84–85.

[456] CIL 10.827; Castrén 1975, 209; Ling 1997, 143.

[457] Digressus 3, below.

As usual, Sabinus couldn't help taking the bait. "I've been driving for twenty years in this city! I knew all the routes and all the detours before the earthquake and I know them now."

Cerylus enjoyed watching Sabinus's face flush from his insults and thought he might try to make the red color go farther down his neck. "Well, be careful then, that old *plaustrum* is nearly an heirloom now.[458] Some of the parts were forged before Pompeii was Roman.[459] It's almost as decrepit as you are. Break that wagon and master might not bother to replace *it*, but he would certainly replace *you*!"

Cerylus waited for his words to kindle an explosion.

"I've driven every kind of vehicle in my days, from the *pilentum* to the *carrago*. The Gallic *Benna*, the Persian *Angaria*![460] Never have I broken so much as a draught pole!" Sabinus retorted.

Cerylus smiled. "See that you preserve your spotless record then, or you might find yourself more than bespeckled in your new work emptying the *praefurnium* and the cesspits."[461]

A shit pun from a shit libertus, thought Sabinus, as he smirked in silence to end the exchange. As Cerylus whistled his way back up the corridor and into the peristyle, Sabinus turned the *plostrum* to face out the stable door and began stacking the amphorae on it between layers of hay. With careful packing he hoped it just might take only two trips.

Digressus 1

Drivers

Cart drivers in antiquity were mostly of servile or freed status and known for their ill tempers, loud and rough language, and the accidents they caused.[462] Famously, the constant shouting and cursing of drivers is one of the nuisances of the night common to Rome in Juvenal's third satire, possibly a reflection of the Lex Iulia Municipalis's ban on daytime traffic.[463] One dispute was of such intensity it resulted in a boy being crushed.[464] Petronius's Trimalchio had trained a

---

[458] On the ancient debates over pronunciation of this wagon's name, see Suet. *Ves.* 22.

[459] Chapter 5, 119–20.

[460] There are at least two dozen known vehicle names, but little is known of their actual descriptions. According to Chevallier (1976, 178–79) those mentioned are 1. *pilentum*: a lady's light carriage; 2. carrago: military baggage vehicle; 3. *Benna*: four-wheeler with wicker box; 4. *Angaria*: used for haulage in the *cursus publicus*.

[461] On *stercorarii*, see Koloski-Ostrow 2015, 89.

[462] Adams 2001, 156

[463] Juv. 3. 232–38.

[464] D.9.2.52.2.

slave to shriek louder than a muleteer or a street hawker.[465] Many ancient authors also had a low opinion of *muliones* as being slow,[466] dirty,[467] and detestable.[468] Prostitutes were often called *mula*, and thus by association the mule driver was made to carry the most pejorative characteristics of his animal—servility and sexual sterility—both passively in the language and actively in insults to male slaves, comparing them to eunuchs and whores.[469] In legal cases drivers are seen to destroy their cargo[470] or injure their mules[471] (or themselves[472]), run people down while overtaking,[473] and crush others with their unbalanced loads.[474] In each example the driver is a slave. On the other hand, jurists assume that mule driving is a form of skilled labor and find them (or their masters) at fault when the *mulio* is both competent and careless.[475]

Despite its stigma, the profession of mule driving could be a lucrative one. The two most famous people associated with the *muliones* were P. Venditimus Bassus and the emperor Vespasian, neither of whom could entirely escape the negative connotations of that association. For the future emperor, mule driving was a very profitable business opportunity he was unable to refuse, having at that time (i.e., 60s CE) no other, or at least no better, option. According to Suetonius, men of higher birth still derided him as *mulio* despite or because Vespasian had risen into the ranks of senators and consuls.[476] P. Venditimus Bassus also saw his star ascend. Beginning as a transport contractor for the army, he distinguished himself first in Caesar's civil wars and later led successful campaigns against the Parthians under Anthony.[477] Since the sixteenth century Venditimus Bassus has been associated with the fictional character Sabinus the Muleteer from the Vergilian *Catalepton*'s tenth poem.[478] Whether this connection is true or not is inconsequential—it is Sabinus's story that is important. In the poem, Sabinus begins as a slave named Quinctio, who changes his name to Sabinus upon gaining some higher status, likely his manumission. In his rise, Sabinus overcomes his rivals Trypho and Cerylus and earns an ivory chair befitting his status as a

---

[465] Petron. *Sat.* 68.

[466] Mart. *Ep.* 9.57; CIL IV 5092.

[467] Sen. *Ep.* XLVII.

[468] Cic. *Fam.* 10.18.3; Juv. 8. 146–48; Hor. *Epist.* 1.18.

[469] Kronenberg 2015, 193–94.

[470] D.19.2.25.7

[471] D.19.2.30.2; D.19.2.60.7.

[472] D.9.2.27.34; Martin 1990, 308–9.

[473] D.19.2.13.

[474] Juv. III, 249–67.

[475] Martin 1990.

[476] Suet. *Vesp.* 4.

[477] Plut. *Vit. Ant.* 33.4

[478] Syme 1958, 73.

magistrate. That he began as a lowly enslaved muleteer makes his rise remarkable but also ripe for parody. Recently, Shaw has argued that the poem is Flavian in date and should be read as a sneering satire of lower-class social mobility, bolstered by Kronenberg's observation of the many sexual connotations that can also be read in the poem.[479] Additionally, Shaw connects both the names Sabinus and Cerylus to the emperor Vespasian, the former as a family appellation and the latter as the name of one of his wealthy freedmen.[480]

It is this Sabinus the Muleteer for whom our Pompeian cart driver is named. We can imagine not only that a cart driver of the Flavian era might be (and might even want to be) called this, but there is also reason to imagine that a house owner who has a prominent image of Menander on his walls, "the first to write comedy," might be amused to call his mule driver Sabinus and his hubristic but languishing freedman Cerylus.[481] Both the novelty and the naughtiness of the poem might entertain a wealthy and literary Pompeian (and possibly Roman)[482] elite. If he also knew, as Suetonius reports, of the emperor Vespasian's quotation of Menander to rebuke his own very rich freedman named Cerylus,[483] our owner of the Casa del Menandro might be all the more tempted to use these names. How could he resist casting his driver and his freedman in a farce played out daily and in his own house while at the same time, by naming his freedman Cerylus and his driver Sabinus (after himself and the emperor), subtly remind each man of his place and elevate himself to the place of the emperor?

The Driver and Society

When it comes to understanding how drivers like Sabinus actually navigated throughout Pompeii, we are aided by the relatively small size of the city. That is, as a network, the streets of Pompeii are not terribly complex, and memorizing the flow of traffic through it would not be particularly difficult. Consider, for context, the modern taxi exam for London. Called "the Knowledge," the test requires familiarity with approximately 25,000 streets and takes, on average, thirty-four months to pass.[484] By contrast, with 79 (modern) named streets, the *mulio* at Pompeii would need to know only one half of 1% as much as his modern counterpart. Additionally, given the comparatively limited governmental apparatus of a late Republican / early Imperial city, the civil authorities were

[479] Shaw 2007; Kronenberg 2015.

[480] Shaw 2007, 137.

[481] CIL IV 7350b.

[482] On the ownership of the Casa del Menandro, see Ling 1997, 142–44.

[483] Suet. *Ves.* 23.

[484] Rosen 2014.

practically disadvantaged to directly implement mandates with such a wide and intrusive scope. These basic factors point toward the drivers themselves being the locus of administrative control for traffic. On the other hand, the consistency of the evidence for traffic, its coherence as a system, and that system's ability to respond comprehensively to small-scale problems (detours) as well as institute city-wide changes (reversals of direction) indicate that individuals, even as cooperatives, had neither the authority nor ability to establish and then alter a system that would impact the behavior of so many people in the context of public space.

Our best evidence, therefore, indicates that the municipal government was the origin and executive force of Pompeii's traffic systems, while drivers enacted the day-to-day circulation of vehicles. And yet that evidence still lacks the connective tissue linking the rule makers and the rule followers.[485] How, then, did the city communicate the rules of its system to those who would operate within it? It is common from our modern perspective to ask, "but how were the rules enforced?" Approaching the problem as one of information transfer rather than enforcement opens up a wider range of possibilities for consideration. By changing the interrogative form from "how" to "who" allows us not only to look for physical, visual mechanisms (Excursus 2) but also to consider the role of Pompeii's social network in transferring information verbally (Excursus 1, 3) about the traffic system.

At first glance, the "who" in this question could hardly be farther apart on the social scale. The magistrates who created and executed the traffic regulations and the drivers who followed those regulations would seem to have little to connect them other than the system itself. On the other hand, those few houses with ramps and stables at Pompeii are also some of the largest properties in the city, demonstrating a direct connection between the elites and drivers. Indeed, it is not difficult to imagine that the magistrates of the city might own one or more of these drivers, making information transfer a simple command. With four annually elected magistrates, two of whom (the aediles) were directly responsible for the maintenance of the streets, it would not take long before most if not all (residential) Pompeian stable owners were responsible for maintaining the traffic system. Beyond his own home, of course, it was rarely if ever the magistrate himself who communicated this or any other information. Along with a scribe, four public slaves, a haruspex, and a flute player, the aedile's retinue described in the Lex Coloniae Genetivae included a crier who would have made public pronouncements and possibly personal deliveries of information.[486]

---

[485] Critiques of this research have pointed out this concern; Beard 2008, 69; Hartnett 2011, 137–41; Kaiser 2011b, 73, n. 33; Newsome 2011, 5, 12.
[486] LXII ll. 11–20; Crawford 1996, 422.

The social network of the magistrates also served as a conduit through which traffic regulation could flow to many other cart drivers as well. From his peers to his business associates and clients to his freed and servile dependents, each magistrate stood within a ready-made hierarchically structured network. Among these contacts, high-status clients, *apparitores*, and freedmen would have been especially important in his network as bidirectional nodes within "a finely stratified sequence of status between the *eques* and slave."[487] At Pompeii, at least two groups of individuals, the *Augustales* and the members of *collegia*, were good candidates to be such nodes for both their regular contact with the many drivers and a personal interest in seeing them follow the rules. Filling the role of the *eques* in cities outside of Rome were the *Augustales*,[488] a semi-religious, semi-administrative order ostensibly devoted to cult practices but whose place between the decurions and the plebs served as an unofficial "second ordo."[489] Equally, these ambitious and wealthy freedmen fit economically between the commercial class and the landowning elite. "Just as there were extensive links between the 'two orders,' as the *ordo* appointed the *Augustales*, . . . so there were also links between the *Augustales* and the complex network of institutions and offices that characterized the *collegia* of Italian towns."[490] In fact, an *Augustalis* might even have served as the president of a *collegium*.[491]

Augustales are not well documented at Pompeii, but two of the twelve known stand out as representative as of the linkages between municipal government and professional associations.[492] A. Vettius Caprasius Felix was the adopted adult son of A. Vettius Firmus, who like Firmus stood for aedile *viis aedibus sacris publicisque procurandis* with the recommendation of his neighbors.[493] Later, Caprasius would stand for *duumvir* with the Neronian elite Paquius Proculus, but there is no evidence that Firmus sought higher office.[494] When Firmus died, the obligations of his wealthy freedmen (the famous owners of the eponymous house, VI 15, 1.27), A. Vettius Restitutus and A. Vettius Conviva, *Augustalis*, fell to Vettius Caprasius. In addition to the support of these men, those who would use the public ways on a daily basis, the porters (*saccarii*), similarly asked for Vettius Caprasius's election to aedile.[495] The *saccarii* were clearly drawn to connection

[487] Purcell 1983, 127.

[488] Ross Taylor 1914, 231.

[489] Patterson 2006, 245.

[490] Patterson 2006, 260.

[491] Patterson 2006, 262.

[492] The nature of *collegia* is still debated. While Liu (2008) doubts the nature of these associations generally, excepting building trades, Wilson (2001, 291) asks if they were not the source of economic structures, then who was?

[493] CIL IV 3687; Franklin 2001, 181–85.

[494] CIL IV 222; CIL IV 935h.

[495] CIL IV 497.

M·CASELLIUM · AED·D·R·P·FAC
FIDELIS·FBRLI   A·VETTIUM · AED
SACCARI ROG

Figure 7.2 Plaques and inscriptions of the *Saccarii* and *Fabrili*.

with the *Augustales* and to those in charge of streets and crossroads: they also backed M. Cerrinius Vatia, freeborn son of M. Cerrinius Restitutus, an *Augustalis* and *magister pagi et compiti*.[496] The porter's inscription for Vettius Caprasius was painted facing the northeast entrance to the forum and paired with a plaque depicting two men carrying a large amphora on a pole (fig. 7.2). This plaque and dipinto combination was mirrored, including the unique format of the inscription, at the forum's northwest entrance. The builders' plaque depicted a mule,[497] head down and straining against its load, below which they asked for M. Casellium also to be elected aedile.[498] While it is possible these two associations were supporting rival candidates,[499] their mutual economic interests and the identical (and unusual) style of the inscription combine to suggest the *saccarii* and the *fabrilii* joined forces in support of these candidates. *Augustales* are known to have been associated to the building trades as well as paving streets in their own name,[500] but it seems we must also see them directly connected to the transport industry.

The *saccarii* were not the only group related to transport, and Vettius Caprasius was not the only member of the Pompeian political and economic elite with such strong connections to those industries. Just inside the Porta Ercolano (Excursus 3), the mule drivers endorsed their candidates for *duumvir*

---

[496] CIL IV 274; CIL X 994; CIL IV 60; Franklin 2001, 189–90.

[497] The animal on this plaque has been previously identified as a goat. Depictions of mules, especially those pulling a load, are better comparanda. See Fulford 1998, 98; van Tilburg 2005, 15, 67; Cinerary Urn BM n. GR 1925.6–10 (Sculpture D 87).

[498] CIL IV 540.

[499] The call for Cerrinius Vatia is not dated.

[500] Ostrow 1985, 69–70, 82; Laird 2015, 248–72.

and for aedile: C. Julius Polybius, descendant of an Imperial freedman, and C. Cuspius Pansa, member of a long-standing elite family, whose father held the *praefectus iure dicundo ex decreto decurionum lege Petronia*, overseeing the post-earthquake(s) reconstruction.[501] The wood haulers also canvassed for their man at the Porta Nola; he was the same M. Casellium that the *saccarii* endorsed.[502] Such professional associations at Pompeii were numerous[503] and apparently influential,[504] as can be seen by their political connections. Indeed, C. Julius Polybius was directly connected not only to the millers and the bakers (as well as the *muliones*), but also to the makers of barrels, in which large-volume materials were transported. Certainly, it is easy to imagine how the negotiations to bring the bakers, coopers, millers, and muleteers into political cooperation might have had significant economic implications.

The preceding example also shows one pathway through which information about the traffic systems might have flowed: from magistrates to *Augustales* and patrons of *collegia* and to their members, who were all interconnected in a fluid, if asymmetrical, social network. Drivers were also connected to magistrates through more direct "vertical" relationships. Although these were complementary systems in practice, the annual reconstitution of elected officials meant that these intermediating institutions were a more stable mechanism for information transfer. Moreover, these social and economic relationships with intermediary groups also provided motivations for drivers to follow the traffic rules and to spread them "horizontally" across his own social network: to support one's patron, one's guild, or one's own self-interest not to be stuck constantly in traffic. The consistency of the behavior that produced Pompeii's directional-wearing patterns thus does not stem simply from the enforcement of regulations. Instead, that behavior derives also from a series of overlapping social incentives, which in their communication carried the knowledge of the traffic system from aedile to *mulio*.

Excursus 2: The Detour

Mules always complain the loudest leaving the stable (fig. 7.1, A), even though the harnesses are always lowest against their chests.[505] By order of the emperor, Sabinus wasn't technically allowed to drive the wagon,

---

[501] CIL IV 97; Franklin 2001, 148–49, 172.

[502] CIL IV 485. M. Casellium Marcellum was endorsed three more times at the gate: CIL IV 490–91, 493.

[503] Mouritsen (1988, 66) recognized 34 collective recommendations of candidates in electoral *programmata* using 23 occupational terms.

[504] Tacitus (*Ann.* 14.17) notes that these associations were blamed for the riot in 59 CE and subsequently banned.

[505] Chapter 5, 103.

so one of the stable boys, holding an extra set of reins, led the way.[506]
Sabinus kept control over the vehicle, of course, but the boy had his
uses, especially since he could see farther ahead. Lurching and creak-
ing, Sabinus drove the old *plostrum* out through the double doors of
the stable with the same smirk he gave Cerylus and turned left without so much as a glance right for other traffic.[507] With the pavement
ripped up for repairs on the adjacent street, drivers had to find other
routes, and no one had been on his street for a week (fig. 7.1, B). But
Sabinus knew the street builders from hauling boulders[508] on a previous job, and they always let him through. *At least the intersections are all
resurfaced on the main street or there would be no way to go eastward in
the southern half of the city*, Sabinus thought.[509] More importantly, the
chance to disobey Cerylus and travel north through an officially closed
street without consequence brought immediate satisfaction.

His own route to the *Porta Saliniensis* (fig. 7.1, L; fig. 7.5) would be
full of twists and detours, but these redirections were more permanent.
As he turned left again, Sabinus was glad for the broad and smooth
pavements that his master had paid for in front of his house, which did
not continue to the right—as did Sabinus and his *plostrum*—all the
way up the next street (fig. 7.1, C).[510] The mules dipped their heads
and snorted at the additional effort required to pull their load up the
incline. At the end of the street Sabinus slowed the mules and crept
them out into the busy intersection, despite the boy's calls that the way
was clear. Indeed, no one was coming from the left and Sabinus could
see even beyond the next intersection to the gleaming white arm of
Marcus Holconius Rufus's statue (fig. 7.1, D).[511] Though pleased to
have no eastbound traffic to manage, its absence still surprised Sabinus;
by this time of the morning that next intersection was one of the busiest in the city. In fact, the usual congestion there was why he was crossing over the main street and slipping between two other carts that were
also detouring away from it.

After a block and a quick left turn Sabinus reached the end of the detour
(fig. 7.1, E) and saw a line of southbound vehicles with their drivers
standing in the street, cursing a group of men who stood blocking that
normally busy intersection (fig. 7.1, D). Four huge men held a steam-
ing stone vessel cradled by long poles and struggled to pour its glow-
ing contents onto the street. *How impatient these waiting drivers are*,
thought Sabinus, as he turned northward to the right. They would have
to wait only another few minutes for the iron slag to set and the men
would move aside; it can take weeks to relay new silex. Still, he knew
those waiting for their deliveries would be no more understanding:

[506] Suet. *Claud.* 25.2.
[507] The angle of the curb at the stable's entrance and the presence of a lava stone led Ling (1997,
108) to believe turns were both to and from the south.
[508] Chapter 4, 79–81.
[509] Chapter 1, fig. 1.3.
[510] Ruts on vicolo del Menandro north of IX 10 are shallower than elsewhere around the insula.
Tsujimura 1991, 64. fig. 5.
[511] Chapter 2, 49.

Figure 7.3 Intersection of via Stabiana at via degli Augustali.

one wagon carried a great leather wineskin, squeezing out around the ropes that bound it to the box.[512] Another was full of ripe produce from the fields,[513] while still another was heaped with building debris, destined for the dumps at the edge of the city.[514]

Only five *passus* from his turn onto via Pompeiana and already Sabinus was struggling to navigate the deep ruts those huge men were repairing. Each time one of the wheels slipped down into the deep cut between two paving stones, another wheel would rise up out of a different rut and onto the flat surface in the middle of another paving stone, leaving the wagon leaning to one side and sometimes even twisting through the frame. The ride was slow and jolting, leaving Sabinus ample time to wonder if the old-timers were right: the old ash streets were better. Sure, they wore out faster, but that meant only they were replaced faster, too.[515] Parts of this dilapidated[516] silex street must be more than eighty years old!

"Damn this spot, too," Sabinus muttered to himself as he reached the next intersection (fig. 7.1, F; fig. 7.3). "Does every single person have

[512] Baldassare 1990, vol. IV, 1009, 1019, figs. 6, 23.

[513] Mart. *Ep.* 3.47.

[514] Chapter 3, 69–73; Dicus 2014.

[515] Chapter 3, 57–58.

[516] Campedelli (2014, 21) discusses dilapidation as a legal term.

to come to the corner of via Pompeiana and via Mefiu?"[517] Pedestrians all seemed to converge here, some darting across the stepping stones and between the vehicles, others loitering at the archway and the fountain. One old woman and her bucket were forced to cower between the fountain's guard stones as the driver of a *cisium* and his passenger pushed through the crowd. Up and down the street, a few carts were parked to unload their cargo, forcing other vehicles into oncoming traffic in the middle of the street. Meanwhile, shop owners were moving their tables and wares onto the sidewalk, forcing some pedestrians into the road.[518] Worst of all, another cart was stopped at the intersection, and its driver, unattended by a runner, looked with confusion down each street.

Seeing Sabinus approaching, the driver called out: "Which way to the forum?"

"West," replied Sabinus impatiently. He could tell the man was not from Pompeii, not only by his accent, but also simply because Sabinus knew almost every driver in the city, who he worked for, and if he always followed the one-way system or not.

"Yes, I know, but this street beside the fountain only seems to allow vehicles from the left," the man responded. "I followed another driver through the detour back there, same one you used, but lost him in this crowd."

"Follow me if you like," offered Sabinus, "but it's simple going from here. Do you see that white fountain up ahead? Turn left there. Then go past the old house of the Satrii—you can't miss it, biggest place in town.[519] A temple will be on your left. That's the Fortuna Augusta temple. Turn left there and hitch up along the colonnade. You can park in 'my spot': look for *Sabinum* (fig. 7.1, G).[520] The forum's straight ahead from there, but it's closed to *plostra*. While you're in the square, memorize the itineraries posted under the equestrian statues. You won't be lost next time."

Digressus 2

Municipal Control of Street Paving

As they are today, events of paving and repaving were undoubtedly one of the greatest impediments to ancient drivers, interrupting the usual routes and flow of traffic. For the archaeologist, however, they are also some of the very best

---

[517] A GIS network analysis of the streets and doorways of Pompeii indicates the intersection of via Stabiana (Pompeiana) and via degli Augustali / via Mediana (Mefiu) would be the busiest place in the city. Poehler 2016, 186–90.

[518] Hartnett 2011, 137–41.

[519] The Casa del Fauno has been thought to be a play on the name of the owners.

[520] CIL IV 514.

evidence for determining who had administrative control over the streetscape and how that control was enacted. That individual property owners were legally responsible for the maintenance of the streets those properties border is well known from municipal charters, as is the legal process by which the magistrate announced and enforced the need for repair.[521] In the more than one hundred seventy events of paving and repaving at Pompeii, one can see the higher-order municipal control over the process—defining the sections of streets to be replaced, who was responsible for those sections, and what the general form of the street would be. In fact, in neither Tsujimura's map of differential rut depths (fig. 1.3) nor in our ongoing research on paving are there unequivocal examples of pavements that align with the frontage of individual buildings that indicate initiative by the frontager.[522] What's more, the form and material of silex never varies in front of any of the hundreds of buildings at Pompeii. The absence of such evidence for private initiatives of paving or repair at individual properties indicates that it was the aedile who first called upon the frontagers of a street to fulfill their civic responsibilities.[523]

On two-lane streets, the general paving pattern shows long stretches of more deeply rutted pavement separated by small sections of repair, often within intersections. The clearest example is via dell'Abbondanza, which saw approximately half of its intersections repaved, with most repairs having equally shallow ruts, suggesting these repairs were completed at approximately the same time. Via di Nola is the same, with five of twelve intersections resurfaced. This does not include one section of repair four blocks long that extended southward a few meters on the streets intersecting from the south. Importantly, on only one occasion was a segment of deeply rutted street between these restored intersections also resurfaced. Why should only the junctions (and then only some of them) be repaired on these most important thoroughfares in Pompeii? Why not entire blocks, as on many smaller streets? Perhaps it is because intersections wore out more quickly or because the aediles were responsible for repaving of the city's major intersections since technically no building owner actually faces into its space.[524] But equally, we see the magistrate's control in the prevention of repair on sections of the main routes that were clearly in need.

The central section of via Stabiana and the easternmost portion of the via della Fortuna have the most dilapidated pavements in Pompeii, yet not even

---

[521] See Chapter 1, 17–18; Campedelli 2014, 32.

[522] Poehler and Crowther 2018, 603.

[523] At Fregellae there may be evidence of property-by-property repair; Crawford, Keppie, and Vernocke 1985, 78, plate IVb.

[524] The Lex Iulia Municipalis (ll. 29–31) makes pavements before public buildings the aediles' responsibility.

their intersections were resurfaced. The reason for the delayed replacement can be explained only by the volume of traffic needing to use those streets. Indeed, these four blocks of via Stabiana were used by more traffic than any other equivalent section of the city, and disrupting that area would have had significant ramifications for traffic flow everywhere else. A recent survey, however, has revealed that these streets had been repaired just before the eruption not by relaying the surface in stone but rather by the surprising and still only partially understood practice of pouring a slurry of molten iron slag onto and below these deeply rutted surfaces. These iron streets are the subject of their own publication, but for our purposes the more than 430 examples of solid pieces, stains, splatters, and large poured repairs clearly demonstrate both that this remarkable process occurred and at a city-wide scale that can only reasonably be attributed to the municipal government.[525] In sum, the practices of paving and repaving streets shows the extent of municipal control over the process: on narrow streets, magistrates ordered repairs more often by block than by property, whereas on wider streets they equally chose what would be repaved (i.e., intersections) and what would not be repaved (e.g., via Stabiana) and applied novel emergency procedures to compensate for these decisions.

Driving in Theory

From this extended discussion of repaving practices, it is clear that the municipal authority at Pompeii controlled the higher-order issues, including when repaving would occur, the format of the street, and the specific manner and materials in which the street's surfaces would be paved. Other problems were left to private citizens to figure out: where stepping stones would go in the middle of the street, what kinds of materials would be used in the curbs, and how the sidewalks would be covered.[526] At base, the city government established the theory of the street's architectural form and left much of the practice of actually creating that form up to individuals. It is likely the same philosophy underpinned the administration of the traffic system as well. Pompeii set the rules, and largely on their own, the drivers followed them.

One way driving practice might have worked, in theory, is simply through the physical and psychological effects the system had on drivers within the space of the streets. The experience of space itself produces physical restrictions, informal instruction, and a mental map of a place and its social practices.[527] For the

---

[525] Poehler, van Roggen, and Crowther 2019.
[526] On material choice in curbstones, see Saliou 1999.
[527] Gottdiener 1993, 131.

municipal administration of traffic, space could be used and modified to facilitate or to bar certain pathways across the city. Modified corners to ease certain turns and the use of curbstone blockages rather than ramps as water-management mechanisms are just two examples. For the untrained cart driver, the space of the city therefore could provide information by implication and by example, as certain choices were made simpler or impossible and as he followed along in the flow of choices made by others.[528]

As Sabinus witnessed, perhaps the easiest ways to learn Pompeii's basic traffic rules would have been to observe the system in action. By following another driver's actions, a lost driver in Pompeii learned of an important detour (fig. 7.1, C, E), and by seeing the impossibility of turning in a particular direction (fig. 7.1, F), that driver came to understand both the physical (narrowness of the street) and behavioral (rule of eastbound traffic only) limitations of that part of the network. Space in this sense is even more powerful than information, and its dictates are often undeniable. Our fictional lost driver is physically blocked from breaking the traffic rules, even as he is tempted to do so, by the behavior of those following the rules. It is easy to underestimate the combined power of observation and the constraints of space, but most visitors to Pompeii without a guide likely navigated first by relying on such observational information and then by asking for directions; the act of mentally extending the abstraction of space one has not yet experienced. Of course, these theoretical benefits of the system for those ignorant of it could work only if that system were already established and most people were actually following the rules.

Reading the Rules

Once again, we are left with questions about the mechanisms that connected the system in theory to the actual circulation of vehicles in practice. How, on the traffic system's first day, were its rules communicated? How were major changes to the system such as detours and reversals implemented? How, in the absence of street signs or perhaps even in some cases recognized names, could the constant stream of new drivers in the city be informed of the rules of the road. In Digressus 1, the question of information transfer was examined through the lens of the network through which it could have flowed. The absence of any known physical means of communication pushed the network hypothesis to the forefront, but there are good reasons to think that the traffic regulations also would have been materialized and posted in a public location.

---

[528] Lefebvre 1991, 23.

Insight into what such objects might actually look like is bolstered by recent research on Roman maps and itineraries. Across the empire, Romans had a number of different textual means, both literary and epigraphic, to describe their perceptions of space. Despite the variety of these texts, there are some important commonalities in the conventions they employ. These include

- a regular, list-like format of origin, destination, and distance;
- sequential treatment of destinations along a route;
- frequent shifts in viewpoint as new routes are described;
- connections made to locations beyond the local network;
- an abstracted, depersonalized geographical expression.[529]

The Antonine Itineraries, the *tabellaria* of Autun and Tongeren, the Itinerarium Burdigalense, and the text of the Polla monument each fit generally into this model. Only one text, a Claudian-era inscription from the Lycian city of Patara, somewhat deviates from these general practices by taking a more nodal approach, describing all destinations and distances from each town in the list before moving on to one of those towns and repeating the format for that town:

> Tiberius Claudius Caesar
> Augustus Germanicus, son of Drusus
> emperor of the habitable world, made
> roads throughout the whole of Lycia
> through the services of Quintus
> Veranius his legatus propraetor; of
> these (roads) the measurement is written
> below:
> From Patara to Xanthos, 56 stades
> From Xanthos to Sidyma, 104 stades
> From Sidyma to Kalabantia, 24 stades
> From Xanthos to Pinara, [.] 6 stades
> From Xanthos to Tlos, 152 stades
> From Xanthos to Neisa, 176 stades
> From Neisa to Choma, 192 stades
> etc.[530]

---

[529] These points paraphrase Salway's (2007, 209) conclusions.
[530] Salway 2007, 195.

Eventually returning to Patara, the itinerary creates a circuitous, roughly clockwise route around Lycia and at the same time generates linkages throughout the entire road network such that a reader could use the text in a discontinuous way (i.e., not only following the route).

To apply these disparate and generalized Roman expectations to a possible textual expression of Pompeii's traffic system requires both imagination and circumspection. While Roman itineraries offer a format and a formula to follow, they do not offer any geographical or directional indications. In the context of interurban travel, information about whether another city was east or west was likely unnecessary, as it was common knowledge. Distance was much more useful information for planning a trip. In Pompeii or any city with organized traffic, the opposite would be true. Intraurban distances are exceptionally short, but the possibilities of direction could be many and irregular. Though not from itineraries, directional information systems are known from the Roman world. Cadastral plans, such as those from Orange, use a Cartesian-like system to indicate the position within a surveyed landscape together with numbers to indicate the intersecting roads. In one example, a section of land is identified as being "right of the 6th *decumanus*" (*DD, dextra decumanum*) as one moves westward along it and "before the 5th *cardo*" (*CK, citra kardinem*).[531]

Yet cadastral systems describe plots rather than routes. To apply the logic embedded in information systems such as cadastral plans or itineraries, we must imagine that the direction of a street, or more likely the direction of a permitted turn, would replace position of the plot or the distance to destination as the operative datum. On a street like via di Nola, the direction of the allowed turns at each intersecting street might be represented by a letter, such as D for *dexter*, S for *sinistra*, or ~ for "no turn allowed." Where absence of evidence for street names would seem to undermine the itinerary model, the sequential nature of the gridded street network, like the cadastral systems, makes the sequence of information implicit even without street names. All one needs to know is at which gate his route begins. For example, our putative inscription might list the *angiportūs*[532] that intersect via di Nola (possibly called via Campaniensis)[533] from the north and south with an abbreviation and a number. For example, upon entering the Porta Nola on via Campaniensis, the first streets would be represented as *AIS · D* and *AIA · S* to read *angiportum primum septentrionem, ad dextram* and *angiportum*

---

[531] Piganiol 1962, 45–47, 107. Frontinus uses a similar notion to describe the source of the *Aqua Appia*; Laurence 1999, 83. For *citra* as a directional at Pompeii, see CIL IV 3864.

[532] I've chosen *angiportus* because this word, used in opposition to *via* (Kaiser 2011b, 26–34), referred commonly to unnamed streets (van Tilburg 2007, 8) and could indicate a dead end (Campedelli 2014, 10).

[533] Laurence 1994, 38–39.

primum ab austro, ad sinistram. In a diverging system, the next street would simply be *AIIS · D* and *AIIA · S*. Repeating this formula requires only that a driver remember the number of streets intersecting on one side of via di Nola and the direction of only one street he might want to take. The addition of named streets, such as via Pompeiana, would pose no problem, as they could simply fit into the sequence. In this example, the two intersecting streets are two-way streets, which might be listed simply without directional information: via Campaniensis—via Pompeiana, __. The entire route from Porta Nola to Porta Ercolano and the directional information of each intersecting street could be listed in this way, including making connections to other routes of the itinerary. For example, at the intersection of via Campaniensis and via Pompeiana, as in the Patara inscription, the Pompeian itinerary might shift to extend first northward two blocks to reach the Porta Vesuvio and then return southward describing two intersections to connect to via Mediana (*Mefiu*) before returning to the eastward march along via Campaniensis. These textual excursions would take up only a few lines but make a clear connection to the other routes of the itinerary. Moreover, these few named streets would also offer important reference points both when using this imagined itinerary and when asking directions from other drivers.

To describe Pompeii's relatively small street network would require only seven routes to be described across the city. To imagine the physical object on which those seven routes might have been presented, we are fortunate to have the so-called forum paintings from the Praedia of Julia Felix (fig. 7.4). Discovered in 1755, the eighteen fragments of this fresco depict scenes of daily life within the shade of a portico: people make and sell bronze vessels, shoes, and cloth, children receive lessons (and punishments), scribes take dictation, and men consult documents. In fragment 14 a long, narrow panel is affixed to the front of three equestrian statue bases. If these frescoes are a genuine representation of the forum at Pompeii, then there can be only two places this scene can depict: in the middle of the forum, facing the bases on the western side, or at the Macellum, facing the bases abutting the colonnade. The elongated panel is shown as white in color, and what can only be seen as smudges today were indicated as sections of text by the eighteenth-century illustrators who first saw these paintings.

When we consider the represented shape of this panel against locations in the forum, its size becomes both exceptional and familiar. If the panel were placed in the colonnade in the forum, it would be no less than 9 meters long and 30 centimeters wide. With letters 3.5 centimeters tall, all seven routes would comfortably fit onto the panel. At the same time, the most famous map to come down through copies from antiquity, the Peutinger map,[534] would also fit comfortably

---

[534] I follow Talbert (2010) in calling this document a map rather than the traditional term, table.

Figure 7.4 Forum painting, fragment 14. Image courtesy of Riccardo Olivitio.

into this painted space. Moreover, the flattened representation of space on the Peutinger map demonstrates not only that Romans could condense a cartographic presentation in this way but also that they might well expect such a linear format. If a map rather than an itinerary were made of Pompeii's traffic system, it too, like the Peutinger map, would likely have been based upon earlier maps and the textual information from itineraries. These legacy data certainly would have influenced our imagined map's cartographic and information design, such as the conventions representing space as text, which in our case means a few street names and the directional indications. Compared to a textual itinerary, a map could represent the information of the traffic system more efficiently and completely, as it could avoid the repetitions necessary in itineraries. For example, the names of especially long streets, such as via Campaniensis or via Pompeiana, would be written only once, as would the direction of those streets that intersect multiple routes. Finally, the system of counting a relative number of *angiporta* from one point to the next would be unnecessary since all the streets, their relative number from a gate, and their connections to other streets would be explicit in the line work of the map.

To be clear, the map and itinerary just described are artifacts only of my imagination. No such objects from Pompeii have yet been recovered, nor are they likely to be in the future. That does not mean, however, they did not exist, and in light of the archaeological evidence it is hardly an outlandish claim to suggest that the might have once existed. Still, the purpose of this extended discussion is not to argue that a public presentation of the directional information for Pompeii's traffic system did actually exist but rather to linger in the imagining of what forms such objects of information transfer might have taken.

Excursus 3: One Master a Day

Sabinus followed the lost driver to the forum area and watched him tie his mules to the curb. With a sudden drop, Sabinus's attention was brought uncomfortably back to his own path as both of his front wheels fell into the holes in the pavement left by the removal of a pair of stepping stones (fig. 7.1, H).[535] *An ironic jolt*, thought Sabinus, because had the stones been in place his mules would have walked through gaps between them and guided his wagon over the outside stepping stone, only slightly grazing it with the rear wheel.[536] As the rear wheels dropped into the same holes and his too high stack of amphorae strained against their leather lashings, Sabinus looked ahead. A stream of carts was turning onto his street from the north and another wagon, blocking his lane, waited to turn to the north. Waiting was required because even with the stepping stones removed here (fig. 7.1, I), the intersection was too narrow for two vehicles to use at once.[537] Narrower still was the next section of street to the north, which meant that once he reached the stalled cart Sabinus would have to wait just to take another detour. Still, waiting gave Sabinus time to commiserate with the other driver about how things have changed.

"Used to be the other way around here," the other driver said over his shoulder. "We used to go right up the crooked Sarina street and everybody going south had to take the long way round.[538]

[535] All the stepping stones but one were removed from via delle Terme and via Consolare. The absence of filling materials and the odd remaining stone might suggest they were in the process of removal in the days before the eruption. Harris (2007, 179) claimed that these were removed for the pope's visit in 1849, but without further evidence.

[536] The remaining stepping stone here is particularly deeply worn.

[537] There are few other instances of the space of removed stepping stones having been filled in with stone: vicolo Storto, vicolo delle Terme.

[538] A guard stone, now partially embedded in the western curb, shows a diagnostic overriding mark of previous northbound traffic. On the name Sarina, see Farkas 2006, 212–13.

"That was before the Fabii bought the right[539] to install that ramp[540] across the intersection (fig. 7.1, J)," replied Sabinus, pointing to the west. "They must have had to bribe Clemens to keep it."[541]

"Fortunes change fast in Pompeii," said the other driver, pointing with his thumb to his right. "Nigidius Maius's house used to be a great *domus* in the north, but now it's been broken into pieces since the earthquake. There's even a bakery!"[542]

As the last southbound cart cleared the intersection and the driver started off, Sabinus saw the first thing to lift his mood for the day: in the distance two men were trying to harness their donkeys to back of a cart, which was stuck on the curb and leaning precariously on one wheel. Before that Fabii blockage, Sabinus recalled that this particular kind of incident occurred often enough that the old-timers called this spot "calamity corner."[543] Inexperienced drivers would hug the western curb trying to avoid the oncoming traffic and not notice the curbstones getting higher and higher. With the hubs rolling over the curbs, the cart's momentum would pull the entire axle up onto the curb and leave the outside wheel hanging above the pavement. This is precisely what these two had managed to accomplish. Now came the tricky task of pulling the cart off the curb without destroying it, no simple task with the huge millstone resting on its bed.[544] *Sure, I did that in my first year,* Sabinus conceded to himself. But, as he told Cerylus, he never damaged his vehicle.

Taking the route north past Nigidius's bakery[545] and then west back to the same narrowed street, now wide enough for two-way traffic, Sabinus winced at the sound of his back wheel grinding against the edge of the street. He'd forgotten that since the old curbstone was worn so deeply they had to put in this damned new guard stone (fig. 7.1, K).[546] Next time, he thought, he'll go farther forward into the intersection and swing a wider turn to miss that edge.

Once clear of the intersection, the top of the great Salt Gate (fig. 7.1, L; fig. 7.5), largest in the city, could be seen up ahead. As Sabinus climbed this street, the three passages of the gate appeared: two pedestrian passages for people entering and leaving the city and a roadway through the gate wide enough for two large wagons to pass each other.[547] Just

---

[539] In an analogous situation, M. Holconius Rufus and G. Egnatius Postumus (*duoviri*) were able to pay 3,000 HS for the right to "block the light" when their expansion of the Apollo Sanctuary overtook the southern portion of vicolo Storto Nuovo; CIL X 787.

[540] Poehler 2012, 103, n. 40.

[541] T. Suedius Clemens recovered much public space lost to private use, but this blockage was not one of those things; CIL X 1018; see also Cole 2009, 57–64.

[542] CIL IV 138.

[543] To borrow from Plautus *Epid.* 591.

[544] McCallum 2010.

[545] VI 6, 17–21.

[546] Chapter 5, 133–34.

[547] Chapter 2, 51; 8, 240–1.

Figure 7.5 Porta Ercolano.

inside the gate, in fact at the very first door inside the city, a broad and shallow ramp paved in the same manner as the street offered entry to a stable area for visitors. Sabinus smiled at the painted calls of his fellow *muliones* for Pansa and Polybius adorning the walls near the gate. And he was very much in agreement with his own name painted in support of Polybius—he really did bring good bread.[548] Standing on his ramp, an innkeeper made his own offer explicit by calling out "Beds! Breakfast! Room to park!"[549] *There's better food in the city, sure, better beds too*, thought Sabinus, *but why drive your wagon across town for a meal? If you arrive in the evening, spend the night, get directions from the innkeep, and start fresh in the morning.*

It's morning now,[550] however, and Sabinus thought the man should save his breath. Few arriving now needed a bed, and if they needed directions, they probably already got them just beyond the gates. Indeed, once outside the city, Sabinus saw the familiar sight of carts lined up against the western curb and the men and boys who drove them loitering among the tombs. Most sit on the bench built by Mamia,[551] but one boy was haggling over the price to lead a man and his wagon carrying pigments through the city to the Palestra of the theater.[552] Sabinus was out of earshot by the time they worked out a price, but the conversation

[548] CIL IV 429.

[549] On the shouts in the street, Aus. *Ep.* 6.19–26.

[550] Because Pompeii had a traffic system and because this Lex Iulia Municipalis names only Rome, I have not applied the ban on daytime travel in Sabinus's story. The emperor Claudius's edict, however, I assume, was not optional.

[551] CIL X 998.

[552] Poehler and Ellis 2012, 9.

lightened his mood again. *This trip might take all day*, he thought, *but it's better than days without a trip, when Cerylus sends me outside the southern gate to wait, like these men, to do deliveries for hire. Better to have only one master a day*, thought Sabinus, as the slopes of Vesuvius, dotted with vineyards and villas, rose up ahead.

Digressus 3

Nuisances abounded in the Pompeian street. As Sabinus's journey illustrates, cart drivers had to navigate a number of small annoyances, from parked carts and lost drivers to narrowed intersections and ongoing street repairs. Pedestrians, property owners, and the street architecture dedicated to them—high curbs, guard stones, and especially stepping stones—were often given precedent and the right of way. As the scores of overriding marks on stepping stones show, carts rode up and onto these objects repeatedly during the course of a trip through the city. Sometimes this was due to poor driving, but the sheer number of impacts indicate that most often the cause was the combination of other vehicles in the street and the fixed width between the wheels. In order to avoid one object with one wheel, the opposite wheel was forced into confrontation with another object. Even when removed, stepping stones caused difficulty, as did other large holes in the street, such as the collapses of cesspits that were built under the sidewalks and the edges of the street. One such collapse occurred on vicolo del Fauno even before the street paving was complete.[553] Certainly, most carts were strong enough to withstand the force of these jolts, but carts with full loads broke their axles and collapsed drainage structures often enough for ancient authors to remark upon these events, even turning them into a euphemism for calamity: "the cart is overturned."[554]

The border of the street was no less hazardous for cart drivers. Guard stones pushed vehicles away from the edge of the street, likely to protect pedestrians, who were themselves pushed to the edge and even into the street by impediments on the sidewalks.[555] In a few examples, these guard stones also prevented vehicles from getting stuck on elevated curbs. In his survey of the city, Hartnett has found "at least forty-five places where the sidewalk was elevated more than 50 cm above the roadbed and thus threatened to make contact with the axles."[556] In twelve of these examples, a house owner ramped his curbs upward to elevate

---

[553] It is possible the collapse occurred after the eruption.

[554] Chapter 1, 16.

[555] For guard stones, chapter 3, 97–100; on pedestrians ceding sidewalk space, see Hartnett 2011, 141, n. 19.

[556] Hartnett 2011, 154–55.

the stature of his home, but in only one case would associated guard stones have
deflected a vehicle before the curb rose above the axle height.[557] In these cases,
even if drivers avoided getting hung up on the rising curb, they often still hit the
curb with their wheel hubs, carving long lines in the curbstones. The most egre-
gious examples can be found at the Porta Nocera and along the north side of via
di Nola at the so-called Casa dei Gladiatori (V 5, 3).[558]

Although restricted largely to the edges of the city, there was at least one
street feature that was not a nuisance to wheeled traffic: the broad, paved ramps
that allowed vehicles into and out of the insulae. Mostly these ramps signaled
the existence of a parking area within an inn, but they also were found at commercial properties that required a constant supply of materials. Such ramps
also suggest that the property owner likely owned a vehicle, which is not true
of some industries—bakeries in particular—that chose to create a wide pull-off
area in front of their buildings.[559] Taking over the space of the sidewalk, these
side ramps became an impediment to pedestrians when carts were unloaded
but would have been a benefit to wheeled traffic using that street. In his detour
around the narrowed section of via Consolare, Sabinus passes the bakery beside
the Domus of Cn. Alleius Nigidius Maius (Casa di Pansa), which surprisingly
had no ramp. The curbstones bordering the service entrance are disturbed
and certainly could have allowed vehicles onto the sidewalk. It is also possible
that this bakery received all its supplies via mules and panniers. If neither were
true, the delays at this intersection would have caused significant congestion,
encouraging northbound vehicles to push through the narrowed section of via
Consolare and undermining the value of the detour around it.

The wide, paved ramps just inside the city (and some outside)[560] were also
locations where information about the traffic system was transferred between
the local and the visitor. As Sabinus sees while leaving the city, an innkeeper was
a likely source of directions, but he might also have commoditized that information, giving it out only if one were to stay at his inn, eat at his counter, or park
in his stable. We know for certain that the skilled labor of a muleteer was often
hired with or without mules or vehicles.[561] While many legal cases tend to focus
on the driver's competence in packing loads, it is fair to assume that knowledge
of the local routes, inside the city and in the region, was also part of this competence. In fact, drivers hired to make a round-trip delivery could be made liable

[557] VI 17, 10.

[558] Hartnett 2011, 154, fig. 5.8.

[559] Saliou 1999, 163, fig. 3; Poehler 2011a, 197–201.

[560] On via dei Sepolcri ramps lead into the villa of the Mosaic Columns and to the reburied Villa
of Cicero. The Villa of Mysteries also had a paved ramp within it.

[561] Martin 1990. Note also a mule sold in the archive of Jucundus, CIL IV 3340.

for the customs duties on their return trip, even if the cart was empty, since it was expected they should know about the route.[562] The driver should have included the customs cost into his fee, found an alternative route, or taken on another contract to deliver goods back to the origin.

With Pompeii's traffic system in place, locals would have had both an advantage over visitors to the city and an additional economic opportunity. Inscriptions relating to the *muliones* indicate that drivers could be found and hired near the city gates at most Roman cities, and a station of the *cisarii* is attested outside the Porta Stabia.[563] These drivers offered services for those without the means of haulage or personal transport as well as guiding services for those who were arriving (or leaving) with their own animals or vehicles. At Pompeii, the organization of traffic into a system was a further pressure point that a driver might use to convince a potential client of the need for his services. Doubtless reminding visitors of Claudius's ban on all but pedestrian traffic in cities would help make the services of a *cursor* to lead the vehicle seem all the more necessary. Indeed, one wonders if *muliones* and *cursores* might not have reported or even blocked those who refused their services.[564] Such economic pressures, beyond the legal authority of the magistrates, also may have contributed to the consistency of driving behavior seen in the archaeological record. These same economic opportunities were not lost on those wealthy enough to stable their own carts within their urban residence. Like those who saw opportunity in building dedicated commercial complexes or in subdividing their own properties to cater to the demand of a rental market, leasing one's cart when not serving his own transport needs simply made good economic sense.[565] By one measure, a cart owner could clear a 150% profit by hiring out his own driver and vehicles.[566] By another measure, that of facile forms of self-flattery, a cart owner who would name his servants Sabinus and Cerylus might simply enjoy dabbling, like the emperor Vespasian, in the world of the *mulio*.

[562] D.19.2.60.7–8.

[563] Campedelli 2014, 146; CIL X 1064. Beyond Pompeii, see Van Tilburg 2007, 47, nn. 406–8.

[564] On cursors, see Smith 1890, *Cursores*; van Tilburg 2007, 139; Kaiser 2011b, 96, n. 84.

[565] Pirson 1993, 1997; Craver 2010.

[566] Poehler 2011a, 205–6.

8

Traffic in the Roman World

Where does Pompeii's traffic system fit in the history of Roman urbanism? Is it, like so many other artifacts found at Pompeii, unique only for its preservation, or might the traffic system at Pompeii actually be unique in Roman history? If the former, if Pompeii is but one of many cities to have had some directional system imposed on the circulation of vehicles, one must ask: was Pompeii a forerunner, or was it late to the game of traffic organization? If the traffic system was unique, why should Pompeii be so special? Such questions of context obviously cannot be answered at Pompeii. It is possible, however, that the method for studying traffic developed there could be exported to other Roman cities and used to evaluate whether those urban sites actively managed their traffic. These questions and the pursuit of their answers is the subject of this chapter. To approach these issues, the evidence for traffic found at two dozen sites around the Mediterranean is considered against two primary questions: were there two-way streets organized by driving on a particular side, and were there streets restricted to a single direction? The comparison with Timgad in particular offers an important window onto how Romans at the end of the first century BCE in Italy and at the beginning of the second century CE in North Africa approached issues of urban design and infrastructural management. The comparison also serves as a springboard into a brief history of traffic management in the Roman world, into which Pompeii's system of traffic is situated.

Traffic and the Roman City

Until the industrial revolution Rome was the greatest urban society in the West, and her cities were the great multifunctional arms of empire.[567] Cities were the physical footprint of Roman imperialism and the laboratories of Roman cultural

---

[567] Woolf 1997, 6.

colonization. They provided the complex governmental organs and personnel that the Imperial system lacked and served as both producers and markets for a globalized Mediterranean trade. Perhaps most important of all to the experience of any Roman city was its function as an architectural tableau. On this landscape the fast-turning historical cycles of elite competition and benefaction would help to create its standard forms—arches and amphitheaters, baths and basilicas—and experiment with new expressions of Roman urban life. The most far-reaching of these innovations were infrastructural, such as the institution of or retrofitting for underground sewage systems, particularly in the second century CE. Sewerage not only changed one's daily relationship to waste but also could literally elevate the city, as street levels and the surrounding floor levels of buildings were raised to accommodate the conduits.[568] For many cities, the benefits of sewer systems were obviously worth the changes. Although it will be harder to recognize archaeologically or historically, we must ask this same question of traffic systems: were they worth the trouble of instituting and maintaining?

Of course, this wide urban world of Rome is larger than any question that can be put to it. In Italy alone nearly six hundred higher-order settlements existed in antiquity.[569] The search for traffic in Roman cities, therefore, necessarily is possible only at a small sample of such sites in Italy and beyond. There are simply too many to examine in total, and even in the fraction of those excavated, the focus was on exposing monumental, funerary, and domestic spaces over streets, intersections, and infrastructure. Additionally, as comparanda to Pompeii, most cities outside of Italy that can be studied tend to be different in size, later in chronology and have very different cultural legacies. Each of these factors would influence a given city's approach to (or avoidance of) traffic management, further isolating Pompeii's potentially unique infrastructural history.

With these caveats acknowledged, the results of the urban surveys I conducted over the last fifteen years are presented in table 8.1 and figure 8.1. These data represent only those sites at which directional data were found. Nondirectional wearing was ubiquitous. The data are arranged by object and wearing type, by the count, certainty, and strength of the evidence, whether they represent driving on the right or left side of the street, and if they document one-way traffic. The sites are listed by country, with those sites with the most information listed first. What is immediately clear is that the evidence for direction is rare: the total amount of evidence discovered at these sites is only 37% of that recovered at Pompeii. Undoubtedly, the expansive use of stepping stones at Pompeii had much to do with the imbalance of directional evidence found

---

[568] Wilson 1935, 53–55.
[569] Sewell and Witcher 2015.

Table 8.1 **Traffic evidence from the Roman world.**

Site	Objects Worn	Wearing Type	Count, Certainty of Evidence	Count of Evidence of Right-Side Drive	Count of Evidence of One-Way Street
Italy					
Paestum	CS (12), Gate (1), GS (4)	O (6), S (11)	17/43 (2.53)	15 (88%)	
Alba Fucens	CS (12), SS (3)	O (3), S (12)	15/46 (3.07)	6 (75%)	6
Minturnae	CS (7), GS (4)	O (7), S (4)	11/33 (3.00)	2 (50%)	8/24 (3.00)
Rome	CS (1), Gate (6)	O (5), S (2)	7/21 (3.00)	1 (100%)	6/19 (3.17)
Egnazia	GS (7)	O (3), S (4)	7/17 (2.43)	3 (43%)	
Herculaneum	CS (5), GS (2)	O (1), S (6)	7/17 (2.43)	2 (100%)	3
Ostia	CS (2), Gate (2), GS (1)	O (3), S (2)	5/18 (3.6)	4 (80%)	
Tharros	CS (3), GS (1)	O (2), S (3)	5/14 (2.80)		5/14 (2.80)
Saepinum	CS (2), SS (1)	O (2), S (1)	3/10 (3.33)	2 (100%)	
Algeria					
Timgad	CS (90)	O (30), S (57), C (3)	90/259 (2.88)	58 (65%)	
Madaure	Gate (2)	O (1), S (1)	2/7 (3.50)	2 (100%)	
Khamissa	CS (2)	S (2)	2/3 (1.50)	1 (50%)	
Djemila	Gate (1)	O (1)	1/3 (3.00)	1 (100%)	
Thibilis	CS (1)	S (1)	1/2 (2.00)	0 (0%)	
France					
Glanum	CS (4)	O (3), S (1)	4/15 (3.75)	1 (25%)	
Ambrussum	Bedrock (1), CS (2)	O (3)	3/9 (3.00)	2 (67%)	

Table 8.1 **Continued**

Site	Objects Worn	Wearing Type	Count, Certainty of Evidence	Count of Evidence of Right-Side Drive	Count of Evidence of One-Way Street
Greece					
Isthmia	Architecture (2)	O (1), S (1)	2/7 (3.5)		
Turkey					
Perge	CS (21), Gate (3)	O (16), S (9)	24/81 (3.38)	13/23 (57%)	
Ephesus	Architecture (3), CS (2), Gate (3), PS (1)	O (5), S (4)	9/32 (3.56)	7 (100%)	
Sardis	CS (8)	O (6), S (2)	8/30 (3.75)	1 (13%)	
Laodiceia	CS (3)	O (1), S (2)	3/11 (3.67)	3 (100%)	
Heliopolis	Gate (1)	S (1)	1/4 (4.00)	1 (100%)	
Sagalossos	CS (1)	S (1)	1/3 (3.00)		
Side	PS (1)	O (1)	1/2 (2.00)		

there: a third of all evidence was recorded on these objects. Stepping stones and guard stones are rare at other Roman cities, but where they existed, vehicles tended to contact them at almost the same rate.

Nearly all evidence for traffic comes from curbstones (77.4%), but the piers of gates occasionally (8.4%) record a direction of travel because many wide streets were compressed into a single lane to pass through them. The forms of evidence preserved on these features—overriding and sliding wear—were identified at most (75%) of the sites visited. On the other hand, only three examples of cyclical wearing were found anywhere outside of Pompeii (where only fifteen exist). The absence of this form is a consequence of the wider streets and lower curbs at most other sites, which meant carts were less frequently near the curb, and when interactions did occur, the space (i.e., the vertical plane of the curbstone) upon which that interaction could be recorded was much smaller. The data on this are clear: lower curbs were overridden 24% more often than the higher curbs at Pompeii and Timgad. One the other hand, no new forms of evidence were found, which leads to two conclusions regarding the study of ancient

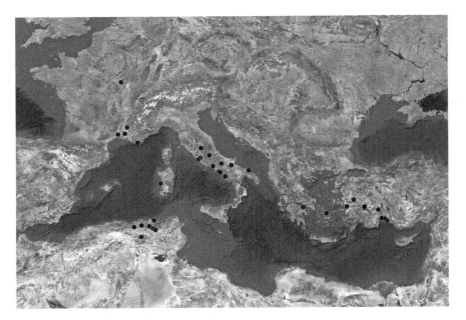

Figure 8.1 Distribution of sites surveyed.

traffic. First, the similar behaviors of ancient cart drivers, as constrained by the similar street architectures that contained them, produced similar interactions within environments throughout the Roman world. Therefore, the three classes of evidence described in Chapter 5 are the best forms of evidence available so far for the study of traffic and they are not solely a Pompeian phenomenon. Second, and descending from this, the wide availability of these three shapes demonstrates that the method described in this book offers the ability to identify and interpret these remnants of behavior in nearly all classical cities and beyond.

Two-Way Streets

Even with the appropriateness of this method and evidential forms, no other complete system of traffic can be observed outside of Pompeii. On the other hand, all the elemental building blocks of that system—two-way streets, right-side driving, and one-way streets—are identifiable. Indeed, that the wide streets were two-way rather than two-lane in a single direction was very clear from the surveys. Similarly, that drivers throughout the empire preferred to drive on the right-hand side of the street was also observable, though its practice was not as consistent as at Pompeii. From Timgad to Side, nearly two-thirds of the evidence for driving on either side of the road demonstrates right-side driving. This fraction is significantly lower than was found for Pompeii. As the detailed examination of Timgad will show, however, much of the evidence for regularly hitting the left curb is a reflection of larger streets that are not limited to a single direction. Indeed, the evidence for hitting the left curb in the rest of the Roman world underscores how the control of behavior within an organized system of one-way streets produced the absence of similar evidence at Pompeii.

One of the widest streets encountered during the survey was the roughly 15.5-meter breadth, not including the colonnaded sidewalks, of the Roman Avenue at Sardis.[570] Despite its width, the presence of rutting across its entire surface, and obvious signs of recent repair, the most unusual feature of the Roman Avenue is a paved area on its south side approximately 3 meters wide, slightly elevated by a low curb from the rest of the street.[571] The directional evidence worn into this curb shows that both eastbound carts driving on the right-hand side and west-bound carts driving on the left were overriding this curb and climbing onto the paved area. The evidence here, however, overwhelmingly documents left-side driving. In fact, at its eastern end, the curb is cut down to form a ramp designed to facilitate access to the paved area, specifically from left-side driving vehicles. It is possible that Sardis went its own way and chose driving on the left as the most basic traffic rule.[572] Still, although the evidence for left-side driving occurs at more than one location and possibly from more than one period, it seems more likely that it is the unusual nature of the paved area itself that explains the movement of traffic. Based on the purpose-built access to the space and the bidi-rectionality of the traffic evidence along it, the paved area appears to have been a parking area for vehicles to load and unload their wares. Functioning like the side ramps of Pompeii, this paved area was perhaps originally a sidewalk that remained elevated as the south side of the street was enlarged for a colonnade.

One-Way Streets

At only three other sites, all of them in Italy, was evidence found for traffic on a street having been restricted to a single direction. Two of these cities, Alba Fucens and Minturnae, were founded or became Roman colonies around 300 BCE and were established along with Rome's earliest roads: via Valeria Tiburtina and via Appia. The evidence for one-way streets, however, comes from the Imperial period. At Alba Fucens (fig. 8.2), a long, narrow street descends from the amphi-theater toward the main excavated *cardo*. No fewer than five short paved ramps are

---

[570] I am deeply grateful to Nick Cahill, Marcus Rautman, and Bahadir Yildirim for giving me a tour of Sardis.

[571] The original excavators called this area a sidewalk; Sardis Plan B34, 1961.

[572] E.g., doorways were entered mostly on the right in the Roman world, but Ellis (2018, 205) documents cases of cities that were mostly on the left.

Figure 8.2 Alba Fucens.

found on the east side of the street, three of which have unmistakable evidence for northbound vehicles turning onto the ramps and then turning out again to continue northward. In the excavated portion of the city, only one other street is narrow enough to carry a single lane of traffic, and it is therefore impossible to know if the next parallel street to the east was equally limited, perhaps to southbound traffic toward the amphitheater.

At Minturnae (fig. 8.3) the evidence is equally unequivocal and limited to a single street but interestingly provides the only confirmed reversal of direction on a one-way street outside of Pompeii. Between the Republican forum to the west and the *temenos* of Temple B to the east, a narrow street records abundant evidence for southbound traffic replacing northbound traffic. Farther east, this street encircles the Augustan-era theater but takes a sharp jog where the *cava* meets the scene building.[573] In navigating these difficult turns, carts cut overriding marks into a curbstone diagnostic of southbound traffic. These were matched by wearing at the street's farther end, on the northeast corner where it meets via Appia. Even stronger evidence for vehicles turning northbound off via Appia and onto this eastern theater street exists on this same stone, which is supported by additional northbound evidence farther up the same street.

That the southbound pattern replaced the northbound pattern is clear from the interruption of the wear at the northeast corner of the intersection with via

---

[573] Johnson 1935, 5.

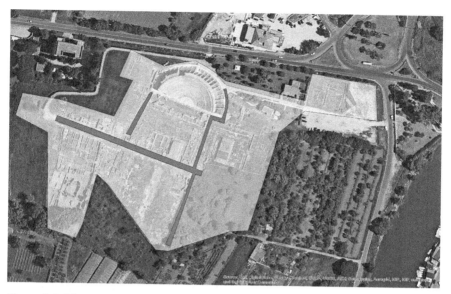

Figure 8.3 Minturnae.

Appia (fig. 8.4). Here an inscribed base (datable to ca. 116–17 CE) stands in the place of the previous corner curbstones and blocks the sliding wear found on the next curbstone east that is characteristic of approaching a right-hand turn, in this case to the north.[574] The reversal of the direction on this street is strongly suggested by the placement of the base, itself unworn, which removed the rest of the evidence for a west-to-north turn at the corner. Like Alba Fucens, not enough of Minturnae is accessible to determine if a complex system like Pompeii's was in place. The reversal of Minturnae's eastern theater street, however, does demonstrate both the interest to control traffic by restricting travel to a single direction and the ability to institute and communicate changes to those restrictions.

Another set of evidence for one-way traffic comes from Rome itself. Near the Porta San Sebastiano is the so-called Arch of Drusus (fig. 8.5), a tripartite monument that carries the Aqua Antoniana but which may be Trajanic rather than Severan in origin.[575] Within each of these three archways is convincing evidence— six sliding and overriding marks—of vehicles moving exclusively northbound and into the city. Despite the deep wear across the entire bottom of the monument, no trace of southbound traffic was found. That this directional wear

[574] Johnson (1935, 46, fig. 22) shows the base is in situ immediately after excavation. On the inscription, see AE 1935.26; Bremmer 1998, 17, n. 56. I am indebted to Rex Wallace for his help with this inscription.

[575] Platner and Ashby 1929, 32.

Figure 8.4 Statue base of Pompeia Sosia Falconilla, Minturnae.

occurred in antiquity rather than in later periods is almost certain. Procopius tells us that the via Appia was still in excellent shape in 535 CE, but sometime later the Arch of Drusus was incorporated into the surrounding walls, leaving only the central archway open until the mid-nineteenth century.[576]

The wearing on the Arch of Drusus thus demonstrates one-way movement at Rome 150 years after the Lex Iulia Municipalis was instituted and 50 years after the destruction of Pompeii. While it is intriguing to speculate on Rome's traffic in the later empire—were some one-way streets instituted throughout the city? did they alternate in direction? was the ban on daytime travel superseded?— at this point we lack the evidence to do any more than that. Indeed, my very brief survey in the capital found only one other piece of directional evidence at

---

[576] Procop *BG* 1.14; See Piranesi 1748, pl. 8; Duruy 1884, Getty image 84.XA.760.14.48, "Arch of Drusus at the Porta S. Sebastiano."

Figure 8.5 Arch of Drusus, Rome.

Rome: an overriding mark (on the right-hand side of the street) at the southwest corner of the Temple of Caesar's precinct in the Forum Romanum. If Rome introduced traffic control measures later in its life, it likely did so only because of the transformation of its physical frame after the fire of 64 CE and through the incubation of new ideas about traffic control in the many cities of her empire.

The most tantalizing evidence for the circulation of traffic comes from Paestum (fig. 8.6), where no fewer than twenty-one directional wearing patterns were identified.[577] Excavations along the *decumanus maximus* uncovered five intersections to the west of the *cardo maximus*, four of which are still visible. At these intersections there is strong evidence for traffic driving along the right side of the *decumanus* and for traffic turning on to and off of the four crossing *cardines*.[578] Turns to the north are evident along the north side of the street at each intersection, but only on *cardo* III can any southbound traffic be detected. Similarly, along the south of the *decumanus*, two streets (*cardo* I and *cardo* II)

---

[577] Only Pompeii, Timgad, and Perge preserved more evidence.
[578] By count, 83%; certainty for right-side evidence is 3.4.

Figure 8.6 Paestum.

reveal southbound turns, but in two cases (*cardo* II and *cardo* IV) also show northbound vehicles using these streets.

With vehicles traveling on the right and mostly making only right-hand turns northward or southward off the *decumanus*, it appears that Paestum might have had a diverging system of traffic, as Pompeii did in the decades preceding the Augustan era. What prevents us from making this determination with confidence is the inability to place the few examples of contrary evidence chronologically. That is, were these contradictory patterns created concurrently, thus undermining an argument for directional control? Or also like Pompeii, did Paestum later institute a system of alternating direction on adjacent streets that replaced the diverging system? The evidence at the southern ends of these excavated streets, where we would expect the southbound traffic to turn off each *cardo*, only complicates that question further by documenting traffic northbound on *cardo* I and both northbound and southbound on *cardo* II, but with southbound being more likely the later, not original, pattern. Given the exceptional length of these parallel streets (273 m), it would seem very likely that head-on encounters (and a long and difficult reversal) would have been a regular occurrence in the absence of some systemic control.[579] Too little of Paestum's street grid is exposed to determine for certain whether it had a traffic system or systems like those at Pompeii

---

[579] Pedley's (1990, 123) length of these streets is accurate but also curiously coincidental to the Roman colony's date of foundation.

or whether, despite the abundant evidence of preferred directions, drivers in Paestum simply managed the problems of congestion as they occurred, without any larger plan for their management. It seems now, however, that in Roman Italy, the latter hypothesis is less likely.

Pompeii and Timgad

For its size, the completeness of its excavation, and the similarities in its street architecture, no site compares as favorably to Pompeii in issues of traffic as Timgad (fig. 8.7). Founded by Trajan two decades after Pompeii's destruction, the Colonia Marciana Ulpia Traiana Thamugadi was established against a low hill into which were cut a theater and a platform for the forum. The new city's purpose was both to settle Roman veterans and to use them as a defensive bulwark at the southern edge of the empire. The rigid, military-camp-like design of Timgad mirrors these purposes and orders the city along two primary axes— the *cardo maximus* and *decumanus maximus*. For traffic, the checkerboard grid plan made navigation beyond these primary routes a simple matter: every street stretched uninterrupted across at least half the breadth of the city. One needed only to reach the end of the block and turn in a new direction if he found himself lost or on the wrong course.[580] Yet for all the utility of this rectilinear grid plan, "when it was laid out in the year 100 it was almost an anachronism."[581] By the plan alone, one could easily forget Timgad was a Trajanic rather than Augustan or even Republican foundation.[582]

If the shape of the street network was anachronistic, the sheer volume of space given over to it was not. Fully one-third of Timgad is streets, which is nearly two-and-one-half times the space given over to streets at Pompeii. The average street is easily more than 15 Roman feet across, and the broad colonnaded avenue approaching from the west was at least 50 Roman feet wide.[583] The choice of Timgad's particular street architectures—including a durable paved surface covering an underground sewage system and a continuous curb that elevated an often colonnaded sidewalk space on many streets—were also second-century urban phenomena. That these pedestrian spaces were needed is suggested by the evidence for a large volume of wheeled traffic at Timgad. Despite being paved

---

[580] Chapter 6, 165–77.

[581] MacDonald 1986, 25.

[582] Compare Aosta, Trier, or Turin for Augustan colonies and Italica, Luni, or Paestum for Republican foundations.

[583] MacDonald (1986, 36) gives a figure of ca. 33% streets for Timgad. My calculations are higher, as much as 40% of the total excavated area.

Figure 8.7 Timgad. Street network in gray, colonnaded sidewalks in crosshatch, transport properties in dark gray.

in dense materials (large rectangular limestone blocks) laid out in a particularly durable arrangement (set diagonally to the street direction), the effect of many wheeled vehicles can be seen on several streets (fig. 5.5).[584] Indeed, despite Timgad's wider streets, more durable pavements, and its lack of stepping stones, years of high traffic volume produced ruts over the center of the *decumanus maximus*, showing drivers in Timgad, like Pompeii, generally kept to the middle of the street.

The volume of traffic can also be surmised by the internal space of city blocks given over to it: there are forty-seven ramps leading off the street and into stable areas, sixteen more stables without ramps, and twelve additional likely stables with unknown entrance types.[585] Across Timgad, ninety-two stone troughs used for watering animals were also documented in stables, filling out more of their

---

[584] Chapter 5, 113–14.

[585] Three types of ramps were identified: ramps paved in stone (7%), ramps that cut a slanted surface through a curb (11%), and those that simply wore ruts through it (45%).

transportation infrastructure.[586] Comparing only the stables with ramps to those at Pompeii, there are 50% more transport properties at Timgad, and these are compressed into an area almost three-and-one-half times smaller.[587] Although most of its city blocks are only a fraction of the size of Pompeii's, eight insulae at Timgad contain more than one stable, compared to three at Pompeii. These statistics show the prevalence of private investment in traffic infrastructure at Timgad, though the original design of the city seems to have set the example on providing ample space for movement throughout the city. From the outset, the entire city was designed to have only two-way streets, which, combined with the regularity of the grid plan, facilitated navigation and eliminated the kinds of congestion recognized in the archaeology of Pompeii and the literature of Rome. Indeed, the absence of one-lane, thus one-way, streets was a decision consciously made by those Romans who founded Timgad.

Because of the choice to create comparatively wide thoroughfares, we can expect that forms of traffic organization based on limiting streets to a single direction, such as diverging or alternating one-way street systems, would not be present. The evidence worn onto the curbstones in fact shows this to have been the case. At Timgad, there are ninety examples of directionally interpretable wearing patterns with an average certainty of 2.91, or just below the diagnostic category. While this gives high confidence in the interpretations made, the distribution of the evidence is uneven across the city. These eighty-nine observations are found at only 35 intersections of 153 surveyed and represent only twenty-two of fifty-one streets (fig. 8.7). Still, none of the eight streets with more than one piece of directional evidence indicates that street was limited to a single direction. Additionally, for the streets with directions established by one or more forms of evidence, no alternation of direction could be determined, nor were batches of diverging directions observed leaving either the *decumanus maximus* or the *cardo maximus*.

Vehicular traffic at Timgad was therefore never governed by directional rules other than the rule of driving on the right side of the street. As at Pompeii, the evidence that recorded this rule's application is not evenly distributed across the breadth of Timgad's urban street network. Also like Pompeii, it is clear that right-side driving was the norm, though at Timgad its contravention occurred with surprising regularity. For example, although 81% of the wearing patterns along the *cardo maximus* show right-side driving, less than half of the evidence (46%) on *cardo* West IV shows driving on the right. Two other streets, the *decumanus*

---

[586] I am grateful to S. Ellis and S. Hay for their partnership in the trough survey.

[587] Pompeii: 36 stables with ramps, 110 insulae, excavated area ca. 45.8 ha; Poehler 2011a. Timgad: 47 stables with ramps, 107 insulae, excluding suburban areas, ca. 13.4 ha. Stables without ramps are not included in this comparison as they have not been systematically identified at Pompeii.

maximus and *cardo* West III are split almost evenly (56% and 59% for right-side driving, respectively). How should we understand these results? What does it mean that there was no restriction on direction at Timgad other than right-side driving and that even this rule seems to have been often ignored? In the first instance, these results put Pompeii's system of traffic into clearer light, making that city's administrative response to an urban infrastructural problem both more remarkable and particular. The 153 intersections at Timgad—42 more intersections than are accessible even at Pompeii—represent the single largest data set available for the study of traffic in the Roman world. Moreover, Timgad offers a nearly complete ancient street grid. If a system of traffic were in place, the evidence for it should have been found. With only two decades separating Timgad's birth from Pompeii's spectacular extinction, it is perhaps even likely that Timgad's urban planners were aware of the solution to traffic congestion instituted at Pompeii. By contrast, Timgad's architects—even before the first stone was laid for the colony—had decided to apply an urban design that antici- pated many infrastructural concerns. Specifically, they gave far more city space over to movement, making traffic freer by undercutting the potential for con- gestion. Pedestrians were given dedicated sidewalk space, regularly covered by great porticos, and wheeled traffic had wide and durable streets, uninterrupted by the architecture (blockages) or the accessories (stepping stones) of surface drainage.

Such broad streets also gave additional room for turning, allowing both the vision to plan for and the space to execute long, low-angled turns. Compared to Pompeii, where one needed to bring his vehicle almost into the intersection because of the offset relationships of streets and encroachment of buildings, drivers in Timgad regularly could see traffic at an intersection well before reach- ing it, allowing them to begin their turn while still approaching that intersection. The effect of this difference was to record the greater number of left-hand turns that seemed to indicate left-side driving.[588] That these data are not evidence for driving on the left or for there having been no preference for either side is revealed by two facts. First, in thirteen of the fifteen examples of left-side driving, a pattern of right-side driving is found on the very same stone, indicating (as at modified corners in Pompeii) that certain intersections were more important in the street network and therefore witnessed and recorded a wider array of driving behaviors. Indeed, over half of all left-side examples come from the *decumanus maximus*, arguably Timgad's most important street. Moreover, in the remaining two examples, the shallow angle of the wearing shows vehicles were taking long, shallow turns across the *decumanus*. Conversely, the only examples of cyclical

---

[588] Wide left turns were also recognized at Glanum.

Figure 8.8 Cyclical wearing at Timgad.

wearing demonstrate right-side driving and reveal that vehicles were moving along that curb for some distance before beginning the turn (fig. 8.8).

These broad left-hand turns also suggest, supported by the ruts showing the preference for center lane driving, that the volume of traffic was insufficient to prevent left-turning drivers from making such long arcs. Moreover, when compared to Pompeii and many other Republican-era cities of Italy that had to institute administrative systems or a retrofit or had to radically change their urban frames in the face of traffic congestion, the space available that permitted such sweeping left turns demonstrates Timgad's approach was decidedly one of prevention. As part of the city's original design, urbanistic, infrastructural, martial, and aesthetic choices were intermingled and expressed in larger public spaces, particularly in the size of streets. Despite having more than double the number of transport properties, Timgad never developed a system of traffic because it never needed one. It is this capaciousness, despite the grid-like shape, that put Timgad at 100 CE in the vanguard of Imperial urban design. Indeed, we should see Timgad as having a new conception of urban space draped over an older urban frame. Although later cities will reject the formal grid pattern, they will keep the primary thoroughfare (the so-called *decumanus maximus*) and continue to grow that street in size and importance. The Plateia as a concept—perhaps best represented at Perge—was designed to collect and concentrate urban movement into dedicated spaces, while also neatly bifurcating it into pedestrian and vehicular zones. By 200 CE, cities had given up the rectilinear grid of Timgad, but embraced its idea of facilitating movement on every street and refocused it onto single, practically and aesthetically ideal route. In this light, at 100 CE, we should see Timgad as one of the best examples of first century urbanism, not the worst example of second and third century urbanism.[589]

A Brief History of Traffic Management

From their very first legal formulations in the Twelve Tables to some of their last codifications in the Codex Theodosianus, Romans were concerned with issues of traffic. In that millennium traffic was never a major concern, yet the width and condition of thoroughfares, the size and weights of vehicles and animals, and even the time, type, speed, and direction of travel were all addressed in statutes, decrees, municipal charters, and local systems. Moreover, as the singularity of traffic organization in Pompeii and Roman Italy demonstrates, we have lost a great deal of what the Romans established for themselves in attempts to control vehicles and pedestrians. The preceding discussion of cities across Rome's empire with evidence for traffic complements what we know from literary, historical, and epigraphic sources, offering both general conclusions about Roman movement practices and highlighting some of the unique circumstances known only to archaeology. Together these sources permit a brief and basic history of Roman traffic, in both law and practice, to be written.

The Early Republic

By the middle of the fifth century BCE, Rome had established in the laws of the Twelve Tables a minimum width of 8 Roman feet (2.36 m) for a street or a road to be called a *via* and twice that dimension on a bend (4.72 m). It is likely that this regulation was in place earlier still, as the Twelve Tables codified extant laws and customs.[590] The need for such a law suggests that many thoroughfares of the archaic city were not sufficiently wide for public use.[591] At the same time,

---

[589] This urban transformation raises another question: where are transport properties located in the third century and after?

[590] Crawford 1996, 555–75.

[591] van Tilburg 2007, 128.

however, this prescribed width for all *viae* was a minimum, not a set dimension. Many streets were larger, and exceptions of narrower streets, especially for private streets, surely did exist. Other types of paths, such as *actus* (4 RF) and *iter* (2 RF), were simply defined differently.[592] It is surprising that following its declaration in the Twelve Tables there is no mention of the regulation of street width for seven hundred years.[593] Later still, only in the fourth or early fifth century CE, the Codex Theodosianus records that the distance between private buildings was set to 10 Roman feet (15 RF where public buildings were involved).[594] Perhaps no change to the law was ever desired or required, because it had little practical impact on urban life. Since *viae* could be and usually were wider than the minimum 8 RF and streets not termed *via* could be narrower, there was a very limited range for the law's application.[595] Whether one attributes the subsequent silence on street width to the law's effectiveness or its meaninglessness, one thing is clear: in the earliest codification of Roman law the free movement of people and vehicles was written into the responsibilities of government.

The Middle and Late Republic

Throughout the Republic, concern for movement was focused on the condition of the surface of the streets rather than merely their width. At Rome, the paving of roads traditionally begins with via Appia in 312 BCE, but within the city the *clivus publicius* was the first street that we know of to have been paved (238 BCE). Neither route is said to have been paved in stone, and later, more explicit statements further complicate the issue.[596] Thus, in 174 BCE two censors, Q. Fulvius Flaccus and A. Postumius Albinus, claimed to have paved all the streets of Rome in stone (*vias sternedas silice*) and all the roads outside the city in gravel (*glarea*). Scholars continue to doubt, as do I, whether all streets were actually paved in silex,[597] and later authors continued to complain of muddy streets in the capital.[598] Although the Lex Iulia Municipalis is not explicit about the use of silex, it does say to cover the footpaths with stone, and by the first century BCE, it seems likely that many streets had been given a stone pavement.[599]

[592] van Tilburg 2007, 27; Kaiser 2011b, 32.
[593] Kaiser (2011b, 56, n. 51) cites Gaius, D.8.3.8; Celsus, D.8.6.6.1d.
[594] *Cod. Theod.* 4.24.
[595] van Tilburg (2007, 27–31) and Macaulay-Lewis (2011, 266–68) review measured street widths; Chapter 6, 149.
[596] van Tilburg (2007, 7, n. 81) gives lines by Festus and Varro, who describe the street only as *munierunt* or *aedificarunt*, respectively.
[597] van Tilburg 2007, 7.
[598] Juv. 3.247; Mart. 7.61; Sen. *Ira.* 3.35.5.
[599] Ll. 53–55.

Outside of Rome, the condition of urban streets was naturally far more variable, as is our record of their maintenance. Recently, however, Campedelli has compiled the epigraphic record of municipal actions concerning roads in Italian towns. Her research on the creation, paving, and repair of streets reveals that during most of the second century BCE, paving in stone was still rare in Italian cities. These inscriptions also demonstrate an intensification of interest in the condition of the street at the end of the Republic that continued throughout the first century CE.[600] The epigraphic record thus elides perfectly with the archaeological evidence at Pompeii, where the first silex pavements appeared before the installation of the colony (80 BCE) and proliferated with the arrival of the Serino aqueduct (ca. 20 BCE).[601] These pavements then spread across nearly all of the western half of the city by 79 CE but had yet to cover most of the eastern streets.

The chronology of these inscriptions led Campedelli to conclude that in the wake of the Social War, as many cities throughout Italy were coping with their new status as *coloniae*[602] or *municipia*, road building was one common need that the new governmental and administrative structures could address.[603] Rome was the model for such actions and in some cases was the direct source of the legal language regarding the condition of the street.[604] Municipal charters from the late second and mid-first century BCE to the late first century CE (the Lex Tarentina, Lex Coloniae Genetivae, and Lex Flavia Irnitana, respectively) as well as legislation from this same period (Lex Iulia Municipalis) and from the second century CE (Papinian) consistently describe the rights and responsibilities of both citizens and magistrates. These city charters use nearly identical language to assign the rights and duties of the quattuorvir, triumvir, duumvir, or aedile to public infrastructure.[605] "Whatever roads, ditches or drains a IIvir or aedile shall wish publicly to construct, to introduce, to change, to build or to pave within those boundaries which shall be those of the colonia Iulia, whatever of that shall be done without damage to private individuals, it is lawful for them to do that."[606] Though a single sentence, the scope of the magistrate's charge is remarkable, covering nearly all Roman urban infrastructure, from the primary form of public space, the street, to the primary form of public good, water management.

---

[600] Campedelli 2014, 47.

[601] Like the *clivus publicius*, the *via pumpaiianeis* is not claimed to have been paved in stone; Campedelli 2014, 148–49. Poehler and Crowther 2018, 591–93.

[602] E.g., Cic. *Sul.* 61; Laurence 1994, 22–23.

[603] Campedelli 2014, 66.

[604] Rome, however, seems to have borrowed at least some of its legal language from Hellenistic sources; Campedelli 2014, 39.

[605] The IIIvir at Tarentum and its status as a *municipium* (Orso was a *colonia*) are the only substantive distinctions in the language of these two texts.

[606] Translation by Crawford (1996, 308), who notes similarity in texts (311, 439).

More specifically, the inclusion of a specific provision to permit the paving of a street can be taken to indicate an expectation of a patchwork of different street-surface types not unlike the variety demonstrated at Pompeii and elsewhere.[607] As late as the early third century CE (and undoubtedly later still), it was still necessary for inhabitants to be legally barred from digging holes in the street, which might suggest the absence of stone pavements on many streets. Excavations of the beaten ash streets at Pompeii demonstrate the need for such regulation.[608] It is unclear if these pits were the cause of these resurfacings or if the impending repair permitted them to be cut. Whatever the case, the history of paving and repaving at Pompeii suggests that soon the entire city would have been paved in silex, making such pits more difficult to create. In the context of Pompeii's trajectory in 79 CE, it is interesting to note the omission of the magistrate's right to pave a street from the Lex Flavia Irnitana, the text of which is otherwise nearly identical to that of the Lex Tarentina and the Lex Coloniae Genetivae. By 91 CE, the date of the Lex Flavia Irnitana's inscription, it seems that paving a street was an act of the magistrate so common and so well-expressed in other legal mandates that it was no longer necessary to mention within a civic charter.[609]

The most famous and most discussed traffic regulation comes from twelve lines of the Lex Iulia Municipalis in which daytime travel for vehicles at Rome was banned (ll. 56–61), with a few important and perhaps expansive exceptions (ll. 62–67). While this law was discussed in Chapter 1, what has yet to be explored is how it fits into the history of Roman traffic management. Certainly, it is not the first ban on a particular kind of movement: the Oppian law (215 BCE) forbade women from riding in vehicles drawn by animals inside the city. Yet the Oppian law was a specific measure intended to address issues other than the movement itself. The Lex Iulia Municipalis is the first known attempt to control the circulation of traffic and the first legal reflection of traffic congestion as a problem of such magnitude that it had become a governmental concern. As Rome became the capital of an empire and the largest city in the world, its transportation needs grew exponentially. At some point before the middle of the first century BCE, Rome's urban requirements outstripped the capacity of her infrastructure, and traffic congestion became intolerable. No longer could magistrates be concerned only with the width and condition of the streets, now they had to worry about the volume and variety of the streets' users.

---

[607] Laird 2015, 235–72.

[608] Chapter 3, 60, fig. 3.3.

[609] González and Crawford, 1986. For example, Papinian (D.43.10.1) notes in the second century CE (in language reminiscent of the Republican charters) that city officials are to prevent individuals from digging in the streets.

In the context of the scale of the problem—bringing order to Rome's thousands of narrow, winding streets[610]—and its importance, the daytime ban on vehicular traffic is elegant in its simplicity. The Lex Iulia Municipalis was a temporal and typological knife cutting across an impossible geographical problem. A broad and blunt instrument, to be sure, the law simply divided all traffic into two categories—vehicular and pedestrian—and restricted the circulation of one in order to improve the movement of all. In the context of enforcing this bifurcation, the choice of using the sun as a signal had a number of benefits. Of course, the sun did not actually stop anyone from driving illegally, but it did universally and independently put the law in effect. Throughout most of the day and all night the rule was clear, and those who chose to flaunt the law would have to do so in broad daylight. The crepuscular light before dawn offered warning and perhaps a "grace period" to exit the city. The time when the prohibition on wheeled traffic ended each day, at the tenth hour, was at once more precise and equally unspecific. Necessarily, the sun was still up, but it was low in the sky. Perhaps this calculation was intended to give two hours of natural light to cart drivers, which might have been sufficient time to at least make their deliveries, even if they then left the city in the dark. The tenth hour was also the end of the public day, when many Romans—or at least elites and their retainers—were meant to be home, leaving the streets less congested.[611]

The model of traffic control the text of the Lex Iulia Municipalis describes for Rome is essentially that of a (solar-powered) light switch: traffic was either on or off, but when permitted, we know of no other rules on how driving would be conducted. At Pompeii at about the same time, another species of traffic control was being adopted. Like Rome, Pompeii experienced its own growing pains throughout the late second and first centuries BCE, and like Rome, it seems to have concluded that it needed to give order to the flow of vehicles on its streets. It isn't clear if the institution of a traffic system was because of Pompeii's own problems of congestion, because it wished to mimic the capital, because an edict of the capital had been forced upon the city,[612] or due to some combination of the three. While the archaeological evidence can say little about the time of day or night that traffic circulated at Pompeii, it is clear that the Pompeians understood that their model of traffic control could be more complex and be instituted geographically rather than only temporally. Undoubtedly it was the difference in scale between Rome and Pompeii that permitted the Pompeians to even attempt a different system, but it was the regular shapes of its orthogonal grid that most influenced its design.

---

[610] Tac. *Ann.* 15.37.

[611] Laurence 1994, 122–32.

[612] Although the Lex Iulia Municipalis was found at Heraclea, the text is specific to Rome.

The Age of Augustus

By the end of the Republic, therefore, there were at least two cities with different systems of traffic control. With the advent of the empire, the economic boom it permitted, and the consequent transformation of Roman urban landscapes, many cities would have come to need, like Rome and Pompeii, some means of managing the flow of vehicles. As the epigraphic record of Italy demonstrates, there was a growing appetite for public works relating to traffic, at least street paving, at the beginning of the Imperial period. Many cities also had responsibilities to supply wagons and animals in Augustus's *vehiculatio*, the Imperial travel and communication system that codified the Republican system of requisitions and later became the *cursus publicus*.[613] Although these cities would be compensated financially, it was up to them to supply and manage the required transportation materials. Direct experience with state control of traffic, at very least the means of travel, therefore would not be unusual for many municipal magistrates.

Additionally, Italian elites were witness to the Augustan administration's vast expansion of the number of public slaves, contracted skilled laborers, and officials it employed in its many public programs. Whether by the *cura aquarum*, with its 240 public slaves,[614] the *cura annona*, with its thousands of men employed as public officials and private contractors,[615] or the *opera publica*, with its head officials culled from the senatorial and, occasionally, consular ranks,[616] Augustus not only expanded the state's administrative capabilities and responsibilities but also "professionalized" many forms of knowledge, opening leadership roles to a wider segment of Roman Imperial society.[617] Indeed, he gave the top post of the *vehiculatio* to his own freedman,[618] while Agrippa headed the *cura aquarum* and repaved Rome's streets. Wherever one drove and whenever one drank from a fountain, they had Agrippa and the new Augustan regime to thank. What most Romans might have been less aware of was the larger transformation of how cities were governed, with power vested in institutions rather than individuals.

> The city known and displayed, measured by professional surveyors, listed by census-officials, is a city (unlike that of the late Republic) under control. The cohorts of the City Prefect or the Prefect of the Firewatch depended for their effectiveness on this detailed information, and on the willing collaboration of the local officials of the *vici*. The manifest 'rationality' of the

---

[613] Kolb 2001, 95–98; Gentry 2015.
[614] Frontin. *Aq.* 117.1.
[615] Aldrete and Mattingly 1999.
[616] Robinson 1992, 54.
[617] Wallace-Hadrill 2005, 58.
[618] Smith 1890, "Cursus Publicus."

system makes us ask why such measures were not introduced before. But it is not a mere exercise of rationality and administrative efficiency; it is part and parcel of a paradigm shift, from a knowledge conceived in traditional and ritual terms to the professionalized knowledge under imperial surveillance.[619]

Given Augustus's cultivation of an image of himself for emulation, it is not unreasonable to expect that local magistrates would have recognized a path to prominence in the expansion of local infrastructural systems. In fact, inscriptions from Aesernia, Allifae, Ostia, and Sora show that Augustan Rome was indeed the model of Imperial administration: cities in Italy appointed *curators viarum* in precisely the same way. It is easy enough to imagine a candidate for municipal office promising to solve local traffic congestion by creating rules of the circulation of vehicles and adding additional public slaves to the aedilican staff to administer those rules. Pompeii seems to prove this assumption. Not only is a traffic system documented archaeologically; so too is a unique official who might administer it—the *aedile v(iis) a(edibus) s(acris) p(ublicus) p(rocurandis)*—which is first attested in 14 BCE, the heart of the Augustan age.[620]

The Early Empire

The Augustan era was a time of exceptional growth in physical infrastructure as well as the necessary administrative systems to govern it. While there remains no compelling direct evidence that systems of traffic like Pompeii's were prevalent in Roman cities, the balance of the evidence suggests that they would not be unknown or unwanted. Moreover, by the mid-first century CE the condition of the streets and roads, at least in Rome, had become a state responsibility. Not only did emperors, following the example of Agrippa, repair and repave streets, from the time of Claudius they paid for the work as well.[621] By the reign of Antoninus Pius, there is even an Imperial official (*procurator ad silices*) in charge of the street surfaces.[622] Beyond maintaining serviceable roads, Roman emperors throughout the later first and second centuries also took action against problems of traffic congestion and harmful behaviors. Claudius banned all travel through Italian cities except on foot or while being carried in a litter.[623] The prohibition

---

[619] Wallace-Hadrill 2005, 77.

[620] Campedelli 2014, 61–63; Chapter 7, 196.

[621] Campedelli (2014, 30–31) lists Agrippa, Claudius, Nero, Vespasian, Domitian, Marcus Aurelius, and Caracalla; Salway 2007, 195.

[622] CIL 6.1598.

[623] Suet. *Cl.* 25; Robinson 1992, 74–76; van Tilburg 2007, 123.

seems to have been difficult to enforce, as Hadrian would repeat the ban on riding on horseback—though he excluded only overloaded wagons—before Marcus Aurelius reinstated the ban on all riding and driving.[624] It is unclear if these laws were intended to protect pedestrians, but Flavian emperors in particular took action to ensure that pedestrians had the right of way at least when on the sidewalks. Famously, Domitian cleared the sidewalks that had been taken over by private use.[625] But again, it seems, old rules needed reinforcement: the same prohibition is found 140 years earlier in the Lex Iulia Municipalis.[626] The problem of private encroachments was so bad at Pompeii that Vespasian had sent down T. Suedius Clemens to restore "to the citizens of Pompeii public places illegally appropriated by private persons."[627]

If the traffic law of the Lex Iulia Municipalis was a solution to a problem at Rome in the Republic, these edicts of the emperors were attempts to redress a common problem across a deeply urban empire. Like that earlier law, the Imperial bans on riding, driving, and overloaded vehicles were at once relatively narrow in scope but exceptionally broad in effect. Rather than solve traffic congestion by dividing types of traffic by time, these proclamations were aimed at dissolving the differences in speed and size among those types. The impact of these Imperial edicts was not merely to institute a speed limit and slow traffic to a safer pace (i.e., walking) but also to create a more homogeneous flow. Consider our modern highways. We have maximum speed limits mainly for reasons of safety, but we also have minimum speed limits to create a common relative pace for all road users. When traffic is moving at roughly the same speed, vehicles can react to one another without the abrupt changes in speed that have reverberating effects on still other vehicles. The bunching and stretching we experience on modern highways is a problem not only of total volume of traffic but also of variability in speed, as one car drives slowly in the left lane and another merges onto the highway from the right. It isn't known if the Romans understood the relationship between speed differential and traffic congestion, but the reiteration of this rule for at least a century does suggest they understood the rule's positive effect on congestion.[628]

It is also unknown how long the ban on daytime travel remained in effect, though the complaints of Juvenal might suggest it was still in force in the later first

---

[624] van Tilburg 2007, 134. Note the word used now is *vehicula* to describe both edicts.

[625] Mart. 7.61.

[626] Ll. 68–72.

[627] CIL X 1018; Cole 2009, 57–64.

[628] I am grateful to an anonymous reviewer who reminds me that there were other, nonfunctional motivations for repeating such edicts, such as symbolic and legitimating connections to earlier emperors or the opposite, to claim the benefits of these acts as their own.

century.[629] Certainly, there is no contradiction between the Republican-era law on time and type of traffic and the Imperial proclamations on its speed and size. Moreover, if enforced together, these two sets of regulations would have been a simple but powerful system of control for the ancient world. Again, an analogy to our driving practice is instructive. Our systems of traffic control are essentially massive campaigns of communication between the state and the driver to instruct one on the place (lanes), direction (one-way streets), and times (parking signs and stop lights) in which driving is permitted. Communication with drivers in the ancient world could not rely on their literacy or on the uniformity of local systems and therefore required that information be simple and enforceable by mere observation. In 100 CE, a farmer driving his wagon overflowing with produce through Rome at noon would have been obvious to everyone.

At the same time that the emperors were establishing and repeating those regulations, individuals and town councils around the empire were making architectural and urbanistic choices that would improve those cities both ornamentally and functionally. In the early empire, these choices were manifest in two areas of urban construction: larger city gates and arches with more passages connected to wider streets. The changes to portal architecture up to the first century CE can be traced in three gates from Pompeii, beginning with the Porta Stabia, which in its current form dates mostly to the third century BCE. Designed to be wide enough only for one lane of traffic to enter or to exit at once, the Porta Stabia received its first sidewalk around 100 BCE.[630] In the same period, the reconstruction of the Porta Marina ensconced the division between pedestrians and wheeled traffic architecturally by the creation of a dedicated pedestrian passage beside the paved street. Undoubtedly, the difficulty encountered by the wheeled traffic using the steep slope of via Marina gave pedestrians good reason to stay out of the road. During the Social War the northern Porta Ercolano was destroyed in the bombardment by the Roman forces and seems to have been rebuilt in (as early as) the Augustan era (fig. 7.5).[631] The new gate was built in a tripartite form, with covered sidewalks along either side of a central entrance wide enough for two lanes of traffic. The newest and largest gate at Pompeii thus not only divided traffic by type, pedestrian and vehicular, it also made it possible for that traffic to be divided by direction, so that entering and exiting traffic would not interrupt each other.

Though not comprehensive, van Tilburg's brief sketch of city gates (mostly from the Western Empire) illustrates the same trajectory of change from narrow

---

[629] Chapter 7, 193–4.

[630] Van der Graaff and Ellis, 2018.

[631] Maiuri 1929, col. 132–39, table I; Richardson 1988, 48; van der Graaff 2013, 110–13, 188–91; cf. Frohlich 1995.

one-lane gates to massive structures with as many as four passages. Considering the late Republican date for the physical and legal separation of traffic by type, it is perhaps not surprising that other bipartite and tripartite gates can be dated, respectively, as early as 44 BCE at Frejus and 25 BCE at Aosta. The design of the Porta Ercolano can thus be seen as the logical outcome of the urbanistic (the gradual addition of sidewalks throughout the city) and legal (Lex Iulia Municipalis's temporal and typological division) developments over the preceding century to address traffic congestion by separating vehicles and pedestrians. The value of these tripartite gates and arches both to traffic and to the ornament of a city is clear from their continued adoption at new foundations such as Timgad and Colchester and at extant cities like Antalya, Hieropolis, and Spello in the first and early second centuries CE. It was likely in the third century CE that Colchester changed the Balkerne Gate into a four-passage portal, like the gates at Autun, with two distinct openings for both wheeled traffic and pedestrians.[632]

These larger gates, however, needed to meet larger streets on the interior to create the congestion-relieving functions expressed in their designs. For cities newly founded in the late first and second centuries CE, the width of streets was simply a matter of design. That every street at Timgad, for example, was wider than 5 meters demonstrates that urban planners of the era appreciated the elegance and understood the importance of broad thoroughfares. And while the colonnades along many such streets speak to the aesthetic interests of those planners, the particularly durable diagonal arrangement of the paving stones reveals their simultaneous concern for urban infrastructure. By the second century CE, many issues of traffic congestion in new Roman cities were solved before they started by decompressing the space allotted to movement within the larger urban aesthetic design. Centers like Timgad were thus the inheritors of four hundred years of Roman urban experience in which sparsely populated towns grew into densely packed cities that encroached upon their own passage architectures and managed the resulting congestion through simple mechanisms of traffic segregation and complex systems of traffic control.[633]

Extant cities, however, could not as easily widen their streets to solve problems of traffic congestion. At Ostia, changes to the street network began under Domitian and were done with considerable effort, whether for aesthetic or infrastructural reasons. The creation of the enlarged *cardo maximus* under Hadrian, for example, was accomplished as a single project, erasing almost any trace of the earlier architecture. Once completed, Ostia had a wide boulevard connecting the river to the forum, equipped with colonnades and shops, rivaling those

---

[632] MacDonald 1986, 74–99; van Tilburg 2007, 94–104.

[633] Van Tilburg (2007, 30, n. 262) cites Hoepfner and Schwander (1994) for a similar widening of urban streets between the Classical and Hellenistic periods.

pedestrian thoroughfares of contemporary provincial cities. And like those other cities, Ostia closed the street to wheeled traffic near the city's monumental center.[634] Many other streets were altered by having their surfaces raised significantly (ca. 1.5 m) in order to implant an underground sewage system. Doing so meant that the floor level of surrounding buildings had to be elevated as well, leaving those who could not or would not participate literally a few steps below their neighbors.[635] Putting water below the street made the streets drier and more amenable to pedestrians, which resulted in lower curbs and narrower sidewalks, where they existed at all.

Perhaps the best opportunity that Romans had to radically alter the structure of their cities was in the wake of catastrophe. The great fire of Rome in 64 CE is the obvious and paramount example. Tacitus tells us that Nero's architects, Severus and Celer, oversaw the reconstruction and implemented an urban plan that included long, wide streets fronted by colonnades, open spaces, and aqueduct-fed fountains. They also enacted building codes that restricted the height of buildings, their relationship to other buildings, and the materials of their construction. Most Romans found the look of their new city appealing and appropriate whether or not they recognized the infrastructural improvements in traffic flow, water supply, and fire prevention embedded in that aesthetic.[636]

The reconstruction of Pompeii following the earthquake(s) of post-63 CE offers another example of how aesthetics and infrastructure intermingled, albeit in a far more constrained expression and with a different outcome. Rather than widen their streets, the Pompeians chose to update their public amenities, especially in the forum, which was finally transformed into a closed pedestrian zone.[637] To accomplish this, several streets that once accessed the forum were interrupted by new or expanded architectures, which repurposed these newly vestigial appendages in the street network within the surface drainage system.[638] The new Imperial aesthetic for the forum, however, completed the exclusion of vehicles and reduced traffic circulation in the southwest of the city to only a handful of streets. Unlike Rome, Pompeii's reconstruction made the potential for traffic congestion worse, not better. Why Pompeii did not take the opportunity to radically reshape its urban frame as Rome did is unknown. Perhaps the destruction at Pompeii wasn't as complete as at Rome,[639] perhaps the politics

---

[634] Meiggs 1973, 135.

[635] Wilson 1935, 53–55.

[636] Tac. *Ann.* 15.42–43.

[637] Forum paintings, however, depict both vehicles and animals; Olivito 2013, fragments 1–2, 7–8.

[638] Poehler 2011b.

[639] Anderson (2011) has shown many Pompeian homes were occupied during their reconstruction.

were more complicated or finances insufficient,[640] or perhaps people just didn't want such a dramatic change. It is also possible that Pompeii's remarkable system of traffic made such a change more manageable.

The High Empire

Tacitus's reports of Rome's revival are illustrated by the remaining fragments of the Severan marble plan.[641] These inscribed slabs show that into the third century CE the streets of Rome were wide and regularly arranged, though not orthogonal, and many were provided with sidewalks and colonnades. Immediately following the completion of the marble plan by Septimius Severus, his son Caracalla would change the city again with the addition of the via Nova to connect his great baths to the Circus Maximus. Thought to be one of the widest boulevards in Rome at a reported 100 Roman feet, Caracalla's via Nova paralleled and superseded the via Appia, the greatest road of its time. The via Nova was built near the apogee of a long-gestating tradition in Roman urban architecture to turn important streets into public showcases. These streets also eventually began to shed their transportation roles, shunting vehicles onto secondary routes that were often older, smaller, and took more circuitous routes to the important locations in the city. William MacDonald described the emphasis on these new streets and their articulation in Imperial cities as the Roman armature, consisting "minimally of a high street wider than the other streets, plazas [. . .], civic buildings, and open structures marking junctions or intersections, or providing amenities, along the way."[642] The shift in emphasis away from the rigidity of the grid represents "an emphasis on experiential space, in which the seemingly unplanned or disorderly arrangement of monuments in terms of geometry has a spatial logic that was based on movement along an armature or major street and the connectivity between monuments."[643]

The origins of this second-century-CE phenomenon can be traced back more than a century to its gestational forms preserved in the Vesuvian cities. At Pompeii, via dell'Abbondanza had long been one of the primary thoroughfares and one of its most ornamental and architecturally coherent streetscapes, but by 79 CE it was blocked in two places, and its western section had become especially isolated in the street network. Via Marina, extending across the forum from via dell'Abbondanza, was already completely a pedestrian zone, equipped

[640] Dobbins 1994, 693; Franklin 2001, 1.
[641] See Slab n. XI–6 (Stanford n. 1abcde), Stanford Digital Forma Urbis Romae Project.
[642] MacDonald 1986, 3.
[643] Laurence, Esmonde Cleary, and Sears 2011, 116.

Figure 8.9 Colonnaded street, Perge.

with a broad silex street, tessellated with white marble pieces, and bordered by wide cocciopesto and pebble sidewalks.[644] The northern sidewalk led westward beyond the pedestrian area to one of only three colonnaded sidewalks in all of Pompeii.[645] Ironically, the creation of the platform for the colonnade took over the earlier sidewalk and pedestrian passage though the Porta Marina. At Herculaneum, colonnaded sidewalks were more common but still piecemeal additions and apparently mostly of private initiative. The closure of the colonnaded *decumanus maximus* transformed its length into a transverse axis of a grand public monument, extending the space of the so-called Basilica Noniana and connecting it with monumental structures along and on either end of the *decumanus*.

While Herculaneum's and Pompeii's main streets either lost or had their transport functions greatly reduced in favor of monumentality, the great colonnaded street at Perge made movement a centerpiece of its second-century-CE design (fig. 8.9). Created as part of a great Hadrianic expansion, the street was more than 20 meters wide and 300 meters long, connecting the Hellenistic gate and new monumental arch to a nymphaeum at the base of the acropolis. The waters of this fountain flowed the length of the street within a decorative water canal,

[644] Chapter 3, 75.
[645] Two others are on via del Foro and on via dell'Abbondanza, east of vicolo del Anfiteatro.

which firmly separated it into two lanes.[646] Each lane, however, was paved in the polygonal style of Roman Imperial highways and could carry three vehicles abreast at once. Evidence from the eastern side of the Hellenistic gate and from the farthest southwestern curb demonstrates that in its first phase, the great colonnaded street used its central division to split wheel traffic by direction based on the rule of right-side driving. Both northbound traffic on the east side and southbound on the west moved around the outside of the gate and oval courtyard, leaving these monuments to pedestrians only.

For seventy years the great colonnaded street put Perge at the pinnacle of contemporary Roman urban tradition. By the Severan period, however, that tradition was changing. Around 200 CE the Pergeans decided to create a new plaza at the city's entrance, which, accompanied by a nymphaeum and the South Bath, blocked the western route of the colonnaded street for vehicular use. The western lane was subsequently given over to pedestrians and built over by monuments, while the eastern side was made to carry both directions of traffic. These facts indicate it was not a decline in traffic volume—in fact, the western lane had recently been repaired prior to its closure—but a desire to push wheeled traffic to one side that precipitated the change. A similar history can be seen in the great colonnaded street at Sagalassos (fig. 8.10). Precociously early, the pavement on Sagalassos's grand street preserves traces of ruts from a time before the steps to the Lower Agora and Severan Nymphaeum forced all wheeled traffic to use a winding one-lane street to continue farther into the city, eventually reaching the Upper Agora.[647] Like a microcosm of via Nova leading to the Septizodium and the via Appia to the Forum Romanum, these streets at Sagalossos paralleled one another for a time, offering two different functions and experiences for both residents and visitors. In Septimius Severus's hometown of Lepcis Magna, the emperor commissioned a colonnaded street to lead from the harbor to his new forum (planned as a double forum) and nymphaeum and to continue still farther along the river. The ambitious design attempted to recenter the city by pulling people down a grand artery toward a new monumental heart and shifted the focus for regional travel to the original *decumanus*, though still embellishing this route architecturally with a tetrapylon linking three gates to the port.[648]

Neither the planned street nor second forum was ever finished at Lepcis Magna, but this was a failing of resources, not a change in urban fashion.

---

[646] Özgür 1989, 69–73.

[647] Waelkens 2005.

[648] I owe much here to Laurence, Esmonde Cleary, and Sears's (2011, 127–31) discussion of Lepcis Magna.

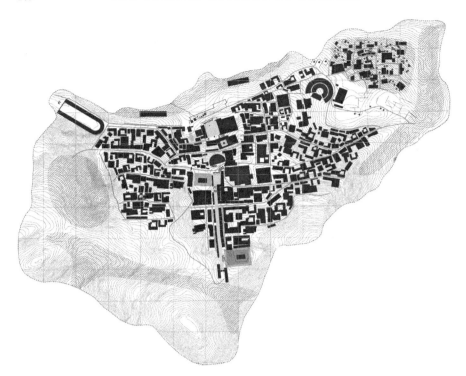

Figure 8.10 Sagalassos, second century CE. After Sagalassos Archaeological Research Project, city map.

Elsewhere in North Africa and as far afield as Germania, the broad, monumental street—the platea—would continue to grow in fashion and importance, bringing ambiguity between the street and the square.[649] Similar grand boulevards were created into the early fifth century, such as the Arcadiane at Ephesus, which was said to have been lit by lamps between the harbor and the theater.[650] While the Arcadiane was being built, the Embolos, Ephesus's main thoroughfare, was encroached upon by private buildings. The problem was severe enough, as at Pompeii and at Rome three centuries earlier, that a new law and demolitions were required. Also like Pompeii, there is evidence for a traffic route through the public square,[651] though in the Upper (State) Agora at Ephesus this route likely relates to the deconstruction of pagan architectures such as the Temple of Rome and the deified Julius Caesar and the Prytaneum. Spoliation of the latter was used to construct the Baths of the Scholasticia.[652] Wearing from vehicles on

[649] Triflió 2013.
[650] Foss 1979, 56–59.
[651] Chapter 2, 50–51.
[652] Foss 1979, 78–83.

Figure 8.11 Wearing on column bases in Upper Agora, Ephesus.

the columns of the southeast propylon and on the easternmost columns of the basilica demonstrate the movement of vehicles into and out of the Upper Agora and its colonnades (fig. 8.11). Moreover, the damage these vehicles caused to the columns suggests both a significant traffic volume with sufficient freedom to move through architectures that would normally be closed to wheeled traffic. Though closer scrutiny of the chronology here is needed, the study of traffic certainly will have a role to play in understanding the history of Ephesus as a Roman city in transition during the late antique period.

Conclusion

The history of traffic management in the Roman world is in truth but one small slice through the larger history of Roman urbanism. From the foundation of Rome, the concern for traffic—both its freedom and its constraint—has been bound up in the width and condition of streets as well as the largely architectural means by which different species of urban movement could be

organized. In the fifth century BCE the Twelve Tables established the minimum width of a *via*, reflecting issues of archaic Rome's form. Never again,
however, would too small streets trouble inhabitants of Roman cities; by 100
CE they were redesigning cities around boulevards of unsustainable dimensions. Instead, it is the surface of their city streets that Romans will devote
attention to from the third century BCE onward. The first stone-paved streets
appear early in this century and then are adopted slowly and unevenly across
and within Roman cities over the next four hundred years. Pompeii serves as
a representative example. Arriving before the institution of the colony, the
first silex pavements at Pompeii were given to the major streets—at least to
via Stabiana. Within a century silex surfaces covered almost every street in the
western half of the city, and even as streets around them were being repaired
or replaced, some routes remained (though durable and perhaps even preferable) in beaten ash. Epigraphic evidence tells a similar story across the Italian
peninsula.

Over the same period Pompeii and other Roman cities developed sidewalks.
Evolving first in a piecemeal fashion as a means for individuals to elevate and
accentuate their homes, the architecture of the sidewalk and curb became institutionalized by the first century CE as a means to separate pedestrians from
vehicles and from water. The idea of physical separation was ensconced in the
Lex Iulia Municipalis as a solution to Rome's intolerable congestion and became
a legal segregation of traffic types. The sheer size of Rome and its population
made this the only possible solution, but the concomitant physical growth of
other Roman cities—and indeed the creation of sidewalks—encroached upon
the space of the street, making legal systems of separation both more practical
and appealing. It is here that the traffic system at Pompeii, an ingenious administrative response to the city's own successes, fits. Other Roman cities moving
between Republican and Imperial forms, such as Alba Fucens, Minturnae, and
Paestum, have hints of similar systems to regulate traffic, but every city preserved
some evidence of traffic circulation.

In the first and second centuries CE emperors' edicts cut across all cities
to slow the flow of traffic and dissolve the differences among its types and
sizes. Their solutions were powerful when followed, but the need to repeat
these rules perhaps demonstrates their unpopularity. Cities in this period
took on the challenge to improve the situation in the street but did so not
primarily to improve traffic but rather to reconceive urban space around a set
of aesthetic principals. These redesigns and retrofits privileged certain parts
of the city and gave pedestrians prominence on many major thoroughfares.
The wide streets and colonnades at Timgad illustrates how, through the suffi-
ciency of space, high volumes of traffic could be accommodated with only the
most basic of traffic regulation. By the third century CE, Roman cities were

built around pedestrian movement and their experience of place. Changes to Perge, Sagalossos, Lepcis Magna, and Rome itself show vehicular traffic was shunted onto secondary routes, even as those routes were once the primary urban thoroughfares of their age. In sum, later Romans did not change their traffic, they changed their cities.

9

Conclusion

Having situated the traffic systems known from Pompeii within the larger history of Roman traffic and Roman urbanism, one can now say that its system was neither unique nor successful in the longue durée. The building blocks of this system—right-side driving and one-way streets—are found in many urban environments of the early empire, but no later cities appear to have adopted, adapted, and improved upon it. On the other hand, what can be said about Pompeii's traffic is remarkably complex and subtle. Indeed, the traffic system at Pompeii appears at once elegant in its simplicity and realistic in its imperfections. Like all of the city's infrastructure it was urban in scale but was neither comprehensive nor applied equally everywhere. Thus, just as the design of Pompeii's fourth-century urban plan adjusted from the ideal to accommodate the realities of topography, so too were traffic rules instituted and adapted where and as needed. Sometimes the plan and rules were simply ignored. Similarly, like the unfinished eastward expansion of silex street surfaces, so too was the idea of alternating one-way directions incompletely enacted, at least in the northeast. For this reason, much can be said about the circulation in the western half of the city, but in the east—even in the excavated areas of the city—the evidence for traffic fades away the farther one goes from via dell'Abbondanza. And like the Augustan-era surface-drainage system, the management of traffic was done with minimal intervention. On the largest streets, evidence points to the rule and the norm: drivers were required to use the right side of the road but would, whenever possible, try to stay in the middle of the street. One-way streets were instituted, but the evidence reveals they would not all stay flowing in the same direction. Over time, the Pompeians revised their system to the changing needs of their urban life, shifting from the simplest of regulations—"north for northbound, south for southbound" off the main street—to more complex alternations of directions and detours to relieve pressure from those few intersections where nearly all carts must eventually go. Finally, in extraordinary circumstances the system could sustain significant change as formerly important routes were blocked and the direction of detours, as well as their accompanying through routes, were reversed.

Pompeii's traffic system was thus neither monolithic in its design nor mechanical in its operation. Instead, our image of Pompeii's traffic system is one of overlapping and incomplete yet simultaneously complementary systems adjusting to local interventions and greater historical events. Such alterations and exceptions tend to impact scholars' confidence in ascribing a systemic cause to the less than perfectly symmetrical patterns observed. It must be remembered, however, that there is nothing incompatible between the absence of mathematical precision or geometric symmetry and the systematic organization of urban behaviors. Again, just as it can be demonstrated that a city block's shape does not have to be identical for it to have been planned with the differently shaped blocks around it (Chapter 2), so too can a system of traffic exist without unanimity in the data at a particular location or perfect patterns in its expression across a sequence of locations. In one sense, these are but the muddled realities of urban life inscribed in their multitudes and in their exceptions upon the infrastructure of the city. Our own experience with traffic systems tells us that there is nothing incongruous with following rules of the road and accepting change: a town turning its center (e.g., the forum or, later, a colonnaded street) into a pedestrian zone, a wealthy home owner co-opting a one-way street into a private drive (e.g., vicolo del Labirinto), or an industrial space choking another street with its activity and debris (e.g., vicolo IX 11–IX 12).

In another sense, the apparent messiness of these realities is often an illusion of their apparent synchronicity. Because Pompeii's immediacy comes as a moment frozen in time, it can be difficult to disentangle the last day from the preceding decades and centuries. It is harder still to imagine what parts of that final moment were works in progress, the incomplete future of a people and their city. Pompeii is an unfinished painting on a reused canvas. Regarding traffic, some of these issues of evolution and afterlife are more easily identified than others. For example, the project to replace the city's beaten ash surfaces with silex pavements was left undone by the eruption (Chapter 3). Similarly, at the same time that the use of stepping stones and guard stones had proliferated across these silex pavements, localized adaptations in the surface drainage system were testing their obsolescence (Chapter 4). Forms of "soft" or administrative infrastructure, like the traffic system, are more difficult to ascertain because their physical manifestations are fewer, more widely dispersed, and often indirect. We also simply have less experience in their interpretation. Thus, while silex covers vast stretches of Pompeii and its edges are defined by the stones still in place, traffic patterns are but the absences formed by equally absent vehicles and are found only in specific yet disconnected locations across the city.

One of the goals of this book therefore has been to address this method-ological gap between the evidence available to us and our ability to recognize and interpret it (Chapter 5). Along with the greater underlying argument that a system of traffic did exist, there is also a question: how do we know that it did—or didn't? Archaeologically speaking, what does a system look like, how do we understand its operation, and how do we identify change over time? Indeed, distinguishing between change over time and a lack of control becomes a fundamental step in identifying a system or its absence. Close examination of and reflection on individual wearing patterns have shown that we do have the stratigraphic tools to make such determinations. Just as we can tell the differ-ence between two people simultaneously filling a pit, bucket by bucket, from opposite sides versus a single person filling that pit half from one side and then half from the other, so too can we recognize when carts were simultaneously or sequentially converging on the same corner.

Archaeologically, it is clear that the city government was responsible for the origin, maintenance, and modification of Pompeii's traffic systems. In the first instance, the intent of the Pompeian driver to follow a set of complementary regulations is undeniable in the constancy of the wearing patterns that reflect his behaviors. That such intent is present across the entire city echoes the reg-ular expression of the municipal authority's will equally evident in the format of streets throughout the city, the patterns of their repair, and the restrictions on their replacement. Similarly, the systematic control of the drainage of waste water also demonstrates the Pompeian facility in the administration of citywide infrastructural systems. What's more, these systems—the structure of the street, the drainage of runoff, and the circulation of traffic—all occupy the same linear spaces of the city.

Still, the administration of traffic is different from that of laying pavements or preventing flooding: stones stay put until worn out, and water runs only where gravity and architecture permit. Vehicles, however, must constantly be kept on course by human action. With the silence of traditional source material directly related to the subject—ancient literature, epigraphy, and legal documents—the process by which drivers learned (and initially learned of) the rules of the road must be imagined rather than discovered. But what one imagines must be both functional and Roman; it must be both possible and plausible. Fortunately, in the maps and itineraries that express Roman perceptions of space and in the hierarchical structure of Roman society, there are indications of how the traffic system could have been represented visually and widely shared verbally.

Schematic rather than scale maps, like the Peutinger map or the Cadaster of Orange and public inscriptions of itineraries, like that from Patara, offer a format and a formula for how directional information might have been shared visually. The remarkable forum paintings from the Praedia of Julia Felix even show how such a set of information might have been displayed in the heart of Pompeii itself. These documents also illustrate how information is transmitted among people of different social statuses. Among the porticos children receive instruction, a scribe takes dictation, men consult documents, and one of the men standing before the long painted inscription may be reading it aloud for the benefit of others.[653] Verbal transmission of traffic rules also likely radiated out of the forum through the web of social relations that connected magistrates to drivers. In a few cases, though multiplying in effect over years, magistrates could simply inform their own drivers of the rules. Most drivers, however, would be less directly connected to the traffic regulations and receive instructions through their professional associations, business contacts, and social relations. Between the magistrates and elites of the city and the slaves and freedmen who drove the carts were individuals and groups—*Augustales* and collegia in particular—who mediated the relations between these distant statuses and communicated their intentions. Incentives to follow the rules also cascaded down these lines of social relations in the forms of economic and political partnerships: the same aediles responsible for ordering traffic also let building contracts that put a portion of the transport industry on the public payroll.

For a visiting driver, hiring a knowledgeable guide or following the actions of others and asking for direction could have allowed him to navigate Pompeii's traffic system. Once outside his own city, the Pompeian driver became the visitor, and his navigation of other Roman cities was likely governed (depending on the time period) by only a very few laws and customs. Like Rome, towns could have segregated wheeled traffic and foot traffic into night and day travel. In this context, it is important to note that although the text of the Lex Iulia Municipalis refers specifically to Rome, the tablets were found hundreds of miles away at Heraclea. For those towns that deemed it necessary or desirable, the ban on daytime carts would have been easy to institute. On the other hand, the pronouncements of the emperors that limited travel through towns to foot traffic and banned overloaded vehicles were not optional. However far our Pompeian driver went, he was subject to these edicts even if those edicts needed to be repeated.

Once outside of Italy and beyond the first century CE, the likelihood that this fictive Pompeian driver would encounter a regulated pattern of urban circulation like Pompeii's dropped considerably (Chapter 8). Instead, he would likely have been astounded by the space afforded to movement in the broad colonnaded boulevards of Vaison la Romaine or Empúries, Timgad or Lepcis Magna, Gerash or Palmyra, Side or Sardis, or scores of other urban centers around the Roman

---

[653] Olivito 2013, 68–72.

empire. By the second century CE cities had solved many of their traffic problems, at least on main thoroughfares, by embedding infrastructural improvements in great aesthetic changes. In this process the segregation of traffic by type
was further institutionalized as the space given over to pedestrians increased
from narrow and crowded sidewalks to wide, porticoed passages and finally to
the transformation of primary routes into dedicated pedestrian boulevards that
shunted vehicles onto side streets.

The cities of Italy, however, did not experience this revolution of urban space
in the same way as the provinces witnessed it. While many impediments to such
change (and a few exceptions) may be cited, the broader historical reality was
that Italian cities did not relieve whatever problems of traffic congestion they
experienced through urbanistic choices. How, then, were such problems solved?
Although still relatively sparse, the directional evidence for traffic in Italy (not
including Pompeii) is stronger than anywhere else in the Roman world. Only at
Alba Fucens, Minturnae, and Rome can streets limited to a single direction be
observed. Only at Minturnae is there another street that can be shown to have
had its one-way street reversed. Only at Paestum can a series of four intersections hint that there once existed a system of diverging directions like that of
Pompeii. As a group, these cities suggest that beginning in the early Imperial
era, Pompeii was not alone in possessing systematic traffic regulation and that
such solutions were a reflection of the particular urban conditions of peninsular
Italy. Pompeii's now well-documented system of traffic is especially valuable in
support of this claim. As an example and a model, Pompeii offers an evidentiary
tether to the interpretation of other sites, not only demonstrating in the heart
of the Roman world that a traffic system was possible but also showing how it
functioned and evolved.

Only further investigation—and likely excavation—can substantiate the
existence of traffic systems beyond Pompeii. Still, the analyses above offer a
starting point and at least one Roman cultural universal. Despite all the local
institutions, Imperial legislation, and changes to the urban environments, one
thing remained constant in vehicular traffic: Romans drove on the right. There
is much room yet to test this hypothesis, to build on this observation, and to
employ the methods developed in this book. For example, my survey of Roman
cities was limited to a representative sample of the best street networks in
Algeria, Greece, Italy, southern France, and western Turkey. This leaves most of
the western empire, Hispania in particular, as well as a number of North African
cities unstudied. Similarly, as the evidence from Ephesus demonstrates, there is
much to gain from traffic in the study of late antique cities and their transforma-
tions. I hope this book will inspire further work on traffic in the Roman world
specifically and on urban infrastructure more generally.

For Pompeii, I also hope this book might contribute to a renaissance in city-wide studies of Pompeii's extant architectures by demonstrating how much we still overlook in that ancient city. The focus of research at Pompeii since the mid-1980s has rightly been on diachronic questions of the city's evolution with excavations of greater and greater scope—from individual buildings or building types to whole city blocks to multiple insulae to entire urban regions. These projects have genuinely rewritten the history of Pompeii. Indeed, the evolution of the street grid, its surfaces, and its architectures recounted in this book would have been impossible without those investigations. Still, there remains much to be gained by walking the city with fresh eyes and novel questions. Consider the "discovery" of the cyclical wearing into the curbstone at via Consolare and vicolo di Mercurio: although the stone had been exposed for 250 years and tens of millions of visitors had walked past it in that time, it was not until 1999 that someone seized upon its significance and, *crucially*, attempted to apply it to an archaeological landscape 45.8 hectares in area. The traffic systems at Pompeii are only one of many such discoveries that still await the patient observer.

BIBLIOGRAPHY

Adams, C. 2001. "'There and Back Again': Getting Around in Roman Egypt." In R. Laurence and C. Adams, eds., *Travel & Geography in the Roman Empire*, 138–66. London: Routledge.

Aldrete, G. S., and D. J. Mattingly. 1999. "Feeding the City: The Organization, Operation, and Scale of the Supply System for Rome." In D. S. Potter and D. J. Mattingly, eds., *Life, Death, and Entertainment in the Roman Empire*, 171–204. Ann Arbor: University of Michigan Press.

Allison, P. M. 2006. *The Insula of the Menander at Pompeii*. Vol. 3, *The Finds: A Contextual Study*. Oxford: Oxford University Press.

Anderson, M. 2011. "Disruption or Continuity? The Spatio-Visual Evidence of Post-earthquake Pompeii." In E. E. Poehler, M. Flohr, and K. Cole, eds., *Pompeii: Art, Industry and Infrastructure*, 74–87. Oxford: Oxbow Books.

Anderson, M. 2015. "Public Buildings and Private Opportunities: Some Dynamics in Pompeii's Urban Development." *JRA* 28, 71–95.

Anderson, M., et al. 2012. "Via Consolare Project: 2007–2011 Field Seasons in Insula VII 6." *Fasti Online* 247, 1–31.

Anniboletti, L. 2007. "Testimonianze Preromane del Culto Domestico a Pompei. I: Compita Vicinalia sulla Facciata di Abitazioni." *Fasti Online* 83, 1–10.

Anniboletti, L. 2008a. "Aspetti del Culto Domestico di Epoca Tardo-Sannitica: I Sacelli sulle Facciate di Abitazioni Pompeiane." In P. G. Guzzo and M. P. Guidobaldi, eds., *Nuove Ricerche Archeologiche nell'Area Vesuviana (Scavi 2003–2006)*, 209–22. Atti del Convegno Intern., Rome, 1–3 February 2007. Studi della Soprintendenza Archeologica di Pompei, 25. Rome: L'Erma di Bretschneider.

Anniboletti, L. 2008b. "Il Sacello VIII 4, 24: Un Culto Collegiale a Pompei." *Fasti Online* 104, 1–9.

Anniboletti, L., V. Befani, R. Cassetta, C. Costantino, M. Antolini, T. Cinaglia, P. Leone, and R. Proietti. 2007. "Pompei: Progetto 'Regio VI': I Primi Secoli di Pompei, Aggiornamento 2007." *Fasti Online* 84, 1–12.

Aoyagi, M. 1977. *La Casa della Nave Europa a Pompei*. Facoltà di Lettere, Università di Tokyo, Mena. 1. Tokyo: Institute for the Study of Cultural Exchange.

Aristotle. 1913. *A Treatise on Government [Politics]*. Trans. W. Ellis. London: Dent.

Arthur, P. 1986. "Problems of the Urbanisation of Pompeii: Excavations 1980–1981." *Antiquaries Journal* 66, 29–44.

Ashby, T., S. Le Pera Buranelli, and R. Tuchetti. 2003. *Sulla Via Appia da Roma a Brindisi: Le Fotografie di Thomas Ashby: 1891–1925*. Rome: L'Erma di Bretschneider.

Attema, P. A. J., F. Gennaro, J. F. Seubers, B. Belelli Marchesini, and B. Ullrich. 2014. "Early Urbanization at Crustumerium (9th–5th c. B.C.)." In E. Robinson, ed., *Papers on Italian Urbanism in the First Millennium b.c.*, 175–96 *JRA Suppl*. 97. Portsmouth, RI.

Baldassare, I., ed. 1990–99. *Pompei: Pitture e Mosaici*, vols. 1–11.

Ball, L. 2002. "How Did the Romans Install Revetment?" *AJA* 106, 551–73.

Ball, L., and J. J. Dobbins. 2013. "Pompeii Forum Project: Current Thinking on the Pompeii Forum." *AJA* 117, 303–51.

Beard, M. 2008. *Pompeii: The Life of a Roman Town.* London: Profile.

Befani, V. 2008. "Progetto 'Rileggere Pompei': Lo Scavo nel Tratto Meridionale del Vicolo del Fauno." *Fasti Online* 113, 1–13.

Berg, R. P. 2008. "Saggi Stratigrapfici nei Vicoli a Est a Ovest dell'Insula dei Casti Amanti (IX, 12). Materiali e Fasi." In P. G. Guzzo and M. P. Guidobaldi, eds., *Nuove Ricerche Archeologiche nell'Area Vesuviana (Scavi 2003–2006)*, 363–75. Atti del Convegno Intern., Rome, 1–3 February 2007. Soprintendenza Archeologica di Pompéi, 25. Rome: L'Erma di Bretschneider.

Bisel, S. C., and J. F. Bisel. 2002. "Health and Nutrition at Herculaneum: An Examination of Human Skeletal Remains." In W. M. F. Jashemski and F. G. Meyer, eds., *The Natural History of Pompeii*, 451–75. Cambridge: Cambridge University Press.

Bjur, H., and B. Santillo Frizell, eds. 2005. *Via Tiburtina: Space, Movement and Artefacts in the Urban Landscape.* Rome: Svenska Institutet di Rom.

Bogdan, C. 2011. "A Quantitative Study of Cart Traffic in Pompeii through Wear Analysis." Thesis, University of Massachusetts–Amherst.

Bonasia, V., and A. Oliveri del Castillo. 1968. "Average Density of Stratigraphic Sequences at Vesuvius and Phlaegraean Fields at Different Heights." *Bulletin Volcanologique* 32, 415–23.

Bonghi Jovino, M., ed. 1984. *Ricerche a Pompei: L'Insula 5 della Regio VI dalle Origini al 79 d.C. (Campagne di Scavo 1976–1979).* Rome: Bretschneider.

Branting, S. 2004. "Iron Age Pedestrians at Kerkenes Dag: An Archaeological GIS-T Approach to Movement and Transportation." Diss., University of Chicago.

Bremmer, J. N. 1998. "Aspects of the Acts of Peter: Women, Magic, Place and Date." In J. N. Bremmer, ed., *The Apocryphal Acts of Peter: Magic, Miracles, and Gnosticism*, 1–20. Leuven, Peeters.

Broneer, O. 1973. *Topography and Architecture (Isthmia).* Athens: American School of Classical Studies at Athens.

Brun, J.-P. 2008. "Un Stile Zero? Andron e Decorazione Pittorica Anteriore al Primo Stile nell'Insula I 5 di Pompei." In P. G. Guzzo and M. P. Guidobaldi, eds., *Nuove Ricerche Archeologiche nell'Area Vesuviana (Scavi 2003–2006)*, 61–70. Atti del Convegno Intern., Rome, 1–3 February 2007. Soprintendenza Archeologica di Pompei, 25. Rome: L'Erma di Bretschneider.

Bustamente, M., I. Escriva, A. Fernandez, E. Huguet, P. Iborra, D. Quixal, A. Ribera, and J. Vioque. 2010. "Pompeya. Alrededor de la Vía 'degli Augustali': El Macellum (VII, 9, 25) y la Casa del 'Forno a Riverbero' (VII, 4, 29). Campaña de 2009." *Fasti Online* 210, 1–32.

Cahill, N. 2002. *Household and City Organization at Olynthus.* New Haven, CT: Yale University Press.

Campbell, B. 2000. *The Writings of the Roman Land Surveyors.* London: Society for the Promotion of Roman Studies.

Campedelli, C. 2014. *L'Amministrazione Municipale delle Strade Romane in Italia.* Bonn: Rudolf Habelt.

Capasso, L. 2001. *I Fuggiaschi di Ercolano: Paleobiologia delle Vittime dell'eruzione Vesuviana del 79 d.C.* Rome: L'Erma di Bretschneider.

Carafa, P. 2007. "Recent work on early Pompeii." In J. J. Dobbins and P. Foss, eds., *The World of Pompeii*, 63–72. London: Routledge.

Carafa, P. 2011. "Minervae et Marti et Herculi Aedes Doricae Fient (Vitr. 1.2.5). The Monumental History of the Sanctuary in the Triangular Forum." In S. Ellis, ed., *The Making of Pompeii: Studies in the History and Urban Development of an Ancient Town*, 89–111. *JRA* Suppl. 85. Portsmouth, RI.

Carocci, F., E. De Albentiis, M. Gargiulo, and F. Pesando. 1990. *Le Insulae 3 e 4 della Regio VI di Pompei: Un'Analisi Storico-Urbanistica.* Archaeologica, 89. Rome: Bretschneider.

Carrillo, A., C. M. B. Lloris, and J. L. Jiménez Salvador. 1998. "Region I, Insula 8: The Spanish Project." In J. Berry, ed., *Unpeeling Pompeii*, 41–47. Milan: Electa.

Carrington, R. C. 1936. *Pompeii*. Oxford: Clarendon Press.

Carroll, M. 2010. "Exploring the Sancturary of Venus and Its Sacred Grove: Politics, Cult and Identity in Roman Pompeii." *PBSR* 78, 63–106.

Castagnoli, F. 1971. *Orthogonal Town Planning in Antiquity*. Cambridge, MA: MIT Press.

Castrén, P. 1975. *Ordo Populusque Pompeianus: Polity and Society in Roman Pompeii*. Rome: Bardi.

Castrén, P., R. Berg, A. Tammisto, and E.-M. Viitanen. 2008. "In the Heart of Pompeii: Archaeological Studies in the Casa di Marco Lucrezio (IX, 3, 5.24)." In P. G. Guzzo and M. P. Guidobaldi, eds., *Nuove Ricerche Archeologiche nell'Area Vesuviana (Scavi 2003–2006)*, 331–40. Atti del Convegno Intern., Rome, 1–3 February 2007. Soprintendenza Archeologica di Pompei, 25. Rome: L'Erma di Bretschneider.

Chevallier, R. 1976. *Roman Roads*. Berkeley: University of California Press.

Chiaramonte, C. 2007. "The Walls and Gates." In J. J. Dobbins and P. Foss, eds., *The World of Pompeii*, 140–49. London: Routledge.

Chiaramonte Treré, C. 1986. *Nuovi Contributi sulle Fortificazioni di Pompei*. Quaderni di Acme, 6. Milan: Cisalpino-Goliardica.

Ciarallo, A., and E. De Carolis. 1999. *Pompeii: Life in a Roman Town*. Milan: Electa.

Ciprotti, P. 1961. "Contributo allo Studio della Disciplina della Circolazione Stradale nell'Antichità: Roma e Pompei." *Rivista Giuridica della Circolazione e dei Transporti* 15.3, 262–77.

Coarelli, F., and F. Pesando. 2011. "The Urban Development of Northwest Pompeii: The Archaic Period to the 3rd C. B.C." In S. Ellis, ed., *The Making of Pompeii: Studies in the History and Urban Development of an Ancient Town*, 37–58. *JRA Suppl.* 85. Portsmouth, RI.

Coarelli, F., A. Zaccaria Ruggiu, F. Pesando, and P. Braconi. 2001–2002. "Pompei: Progetto Regio VI. Relazione Preliminare degli Scavi nelle Insulae 10 e 14." *RStPomp* 12, 223–28.

Codrington, T. 1918. *Roman Roads in Britain*, 3rd ed. New York: Macmillan.

Cole, K. 2009. "Reading the Walls of Pompeii: A Diachronic Analysis of Urban Development in the Vicinity of the Forum and the Negotiation of Public and Private Space." Diss., University of Virginia.

Cooley, A., and M. G. L. Cooley. 2014. *Pompeii and Herculaneum: A Sourcebook*, 2nd ed. New York: Routledge.

Coulston, J. 2001. "Transport and Travel on the Column of Trajan." In R. Laurence and C. Adams, eds., *Travel & Geography in the Roman Empire*, 106–37. London: Routledge.

Cozzi, S., and A. Sogliano. 1900. "La Fognatura di Pompei." *Notizie degli scavi di antichità*, 588–99.

Craver, S. 2010. "Patterns of Complexity: An Index and Analysis of Urban Property Investment at Pompeii." Diss., University of Virginia.

Crawford, M., ed. 1996. *Roman Statutes. BICS Suppl.* 64. London: Institute of Classical Studies, School of Advanced Study, University of London.

Crawford, M. 2005. "Transhumanence in Italy: Its History and Its Historians." In W. V. Harris and E. Lo Cascio, eds., *Noctes Campanae: Studi di Storia Antica ed Archeologia dell'Italia Preromana e Romana in Memoria di Martin W. Frederiksen*, 159–80. Naples: Luciano.

Crawford, M. H., L. Keppie, and M. Vercnocke. 2005. "Excavations at Fragellae, 1978–84: An Interim Report on the Work of the British Team, Part II." *PBSR* 53, 21–35.

Crouwel, J. 2012. *Chariots and Other Wheeled Vehicles in Italy before the Roman Empire*. Oxford: Oxbow Books.

Curle, J. 1911. *A Roman Frontier Post and Its People: The Fort of Newstead in the Parish of Melrose*. Glasgow: Maclehose.

Curti, E. 2008. "Il Tempio di Venere Fiscia e il Porto di Pompei." In P. G. Guzzo and M. P. Guidobaldi, eds., *Nuove Ricerche Archeologiche nell'Area Vesuviana (Scavi 2003–2006)*, 47–60. Atti del Convegno Intern., Rome, 1–3 February 2007. Soprintendenza Archeologica di Pompei, 25. Rome: L'Erma di Bretschneider.

D'Amore, C., M. Carfagna, and G. Matarese. 1964. "Definizione Antropologica della Popolazione Adulta di un Commune della Provincia di Napoli," 4. *Reale Accademia delle Scienze Fisiche e Matematiche di Napoli*, Lettere ed Arti in Napoli.

Davies, H. 2002. *Roads in Roman Britain*. Charleston, SC: History Press.

De Caro, S. 1985. "Nuove Indagini sulle Fortificazioni di Pompei." Istituto Universitario Orientale. Dipartimento di Studi del Mondo Classico e del Mediterraneo Antico. *Annali di Archeologia e Storia Antica* 7, 75–114.

De Caro, S. 1991. "La Città Sannitica: Urbanistica e Architettura." In F. Zevi, ed., *Pompei*, 23–46. Naples: Banco di Napoli.

De Caro, S. 1992. "Lo Sviluppo Urbanistico di Pompei." In Atti e Memorie della Società Magna Grecia, ser. 3, vol. 1, 67–90. Rome.

De Certeau, M. 1984. *The Practice of Everyday Life*. Berkeley: University of California Press.

De Franciscis, A. 1988. "La Casa di C. Iulius Polybius." *RStPomp* 2, 15–36.

Della Corte, M. 1929. "Excursus II: Epigrafi della Via fra le Isole VI e X della Reg. I." *Notizie degli scavi di antichità*, 455–76.

Devore, G., and S. Ellis. 2005. "New Excavations at VIII.7.1–15, Pompeii: A Brief Synthesis of Results from the 2005 Season." *Fasti Online* 48, 1–10.

Devore, G., and S. Ellis. 2008. "The Third Season of Excavations at VIII.7.1–15 and the Porta Stabia at Pompeii: Preliminary Report." *Fasti Online* 112, 1–15.

Dickmann, J.-A., and F. Pirson. 2002a. "Die Casa dei Postumii in Pompeji und Ihre Insula. 5th Vorbericht." *Römische Mitteilungen* 109, 243–316.

Dickmann, J.-A., and F. Pirson. 2002b. "Wohnen und Arbeiten im Antiken Pompeji: Die Erforschung der Casa dei Postumii zwischen Archäologie und Denkmalplege." *Antike Welt* 33, 81–94.

Dicus, K. 2014. "Resurrecting Refuse at Pompeii: The Use-Value of Urban Refuse and Its Implications for Interpreting Archaeological Assemblages." In H. Platts, J. Pearce, C. Barron, J. Lundock, and J. Yoo, eds., *TRAC 2013: Proceedings of the Twenty-Third Annual Theoretical Roman Archaeology Conference*, 56–69. Oxford: Oxbow Books.

Dietler, M., and I. Herbich. 1998. "Habitus, Techniques, Style: An Integrated Approach to the Social Understanding of Material Culture and Boundaries." In M. Stark, ed., *The Archaeology of Social Boundaries*, 232–63. Washington, DC: Smithsonian Institution Scholarly Press.

Dobbins, J. J. 1994. "Problems of Chronology, Decoration and Urban Design in the Forum at Pompeii." *AJA* 98, 629–94.

Dobbins, J. J. 2007. "The Forum and Its Dependencies." In J. J. Dobbins and P. Foss, eds., *The World of Pompeii*, 150–83. London: Routledge.

Dobbins, J. J., L. Ball, J. Cooper, S. Gavel, and S. Hay. 1998. "Excavations in the Sanctuary of Apollo at Pompeii, 1997." *AJA* 102, 739–56.

Duruy, V. 1884. *History of Rome*. London: K. Paul, Trench.

Dunkelbarger, J.S. forthcoming. "Drain Outlets and the Pompeian Street: Evidence, Models, and Meaning," D. Rogers, T.J. Smith, and C.J. Weiss (edd.), in A Quaint & Curious Volume: Essays in Honor of John J. Dobbins (Archaeopress).

Dwyer, E. J. 2010. *Pompeii's Living Statues: Ancient Roman Lives Stolen from Death*. Ann Arbor: University of Michigan Press.

Dybkjaer Larsen, J. 1982. "The Water Towers in Pompeii." *Analecta Romana Instituti Danici* 11, 41–67.

Ellis, S. 2004. "The Distribution of Bars at Pompeii: Archaeological, Spatial and Viewshed Analyses." *JRA* 371–84.

Ellis, S. 2011. "Pes Dexter. Superstition and the State in the Shaping of Shopfronts and Street Activity in the Roman World." In R. Laurence and D. Newsome, eds., *Rome, Ostia, Pompeii: Movement and Space*. Oxford: Oxford University Press, 160–73.

Ellis, S. Forthcoming. *Retailing in the Roman World: Food and Drink Outlets in the Urban Network*. Oxford: Oxford University Press.

Ellis, S., and G. Devore. 2006. "Towards an Understanding of the Shape of Space at VIII.7.1–15, Pompeii: Preliminary Results from the 2006 Season." *Fasti Online*, 71, 1–15.

Ellis, S., A. Emmerson, K. Dicus, G. Tibbott, and A. Pavlick. 2015. "The 2012 Field Season at I.1.1–10, Pompeii: Preliminary Report on the Excavations." *Fasti Online* 328, 1–21.

Ellis, S., A. Emmerson, A. Pavlick, and K. Dicus. 2011. "The 2010 Field Season at I.1.1–10, Pompeii: Preliminary Report on the Excavations." *Fasti Online* 220, 1–17.

Ellis, S., A. Emmerson, A. Pavlick, K. Dicus, and G. Tibbott. 2012. "The 2011 Field Season at I.1.1–10, Pompeii: Preliminary Report on the Excavations." *Fasti Online* 262, 1–26.

Eschebach, H., and L. Eschebach. 1995. *Pompeji vom 7. Jahrhundert v. Chr. bis 79 n. Chr. Mit Beiträgen von Erika Eschebach und Jürgen Müller-Trollius.* Cologne: Böhlau.

Esposito, D., P. Kastenmeier, and C. Imperatore. 2011. "Excavations in the Caserma Dei Gladiatori: A Contribution to Our Understanding of Archaic Pompeii." In S. Ellis, ed., *The Making of Pompeii: Studies in the History and Urban Development of an Ancient Town,* 112–37. *JRA Suppl.* 85. Portsmouth, RI.

Etani, H. 1998. "Preliminary Reports: Archaeological Investigation at Porta Capua, Pompeii, Fifth Season, Sep.–Jan. 1997–98." *Opuscula Pompeiana* 8, 111–34.

Etani, H. 2010. *Pompeii: Report of the Excavation at Porta Capua, 1993–2005.* Kyoto: Paleological Association of Japan.

Etani, H., S. Sakai, Y. Hori, and V. Iorio. 1999. "Rapporto Preliminare: Indagine Archeologica a Porta Capua Pompei: Sesta Camagna di Scavo di Scavo, 26 ott.–11 dic. 1998." *Opuscula Pompeiana* 9, 119–35.

Etani, H., S. Satoshi, and K. Ueno. 1996. "Preliminary Reports: Archaeological Investigation at Porta Capua, Pompeii, Third Season, Sep.–Dec. 1995." *Opuscula Pompeiana* 6, 51–65.

Farkas, N. 2006. "Leadership among the Samnites and Related Oscan-Speaking Peoples between the Fifth and First Centuries BC." Diss., Kings College London.

Favro, D. 1996. *The Urban Image of Augustan Rome.* Cambridge: Cambridge University Press.

Feil, D., L. Pedroni, and B. Tasser. 2005. "Regio VII, Insula 2, Pars Occidentalis. L'Attività dell'Instituto di Archeologia Classica e Provinciale Romana dell'Università di Innsbruck a Pompei." *RStPomp* 16, 256–58.

Fiorelli, G. 2001 [1875]. *La Descrizione di Pompei.* Ed. Umberto Pappalardo. Naples: Massa.

Fiorelli, G., and C. Sorgente. 1858. *Tabula Coloniae Veneriae Corneliae Pompeis.* Naples.

Flohr, M., and A. Wilson. 2011. "The Economy of Ordure." In G. C. M. Jansen, A.-O. Koloski-Ostrow, and E. M. Moormann, eds., *Roman Toilets: Their Archaeology and Cultural History,* 147–56. Babesch Annual Papers on Mediterranean Archaeology, 19. Leuven: Peeters.

Foss, C. 1979. *Ephesus after Antiquity: A Late Antique, Byzantine and Turkish City.* Cambridge: Cambridge University Press.

Frakes, J. 2009. *Framing Public Life: The Portico in Roman Gaul.* Vienna: Phoibos.

Franklin, J. L. 2001. *Pompeis Difficile Est: Studies in the Political Life of Imperial Pompeii.* Ann Arbor: University of Michigan Press.

Freud, S. 1907. *Der Wahn und die Träume in W. Jensens "Gradiva".* Leipzig: Fischer-Taschenbuch-Verlag.

Fröhlich, T. 1995. "La Porta di Ercolano a Pompei e la Cronologia dell'Opus Vittatum Mixtum." In *Archäologie und Seismologie,* 153–59. Munich: Biering & Brinkmann.

Fulford, M. 1998. "Regio I, Insula 9. Il Progetto Britannico." In J. Berry, ed., *Sotto i Lapilli,* 49–68. Milan: Electa.

Fulford, M., A. Wallace-Hadrill, G. Clark, A Clarke, H. Eckardt, A. Locker, A. Powell, M. Rendeli, D. Richards, J. Robinson, M. Robinson, and J. Timby. 1999. "Towards a History of Pre-Roman Pompeii: Excavations beneath the House of Amarantus (I.9.11–12), 1995–8." *PBSR* 67, 37–144.

Gallo, A. 2005. "Indagini Stratigrafiche nella Domus IX, 1, 22–29 (cd. di M. Epidio Sabino)." *RStPomp* 16, 207–11.

Gallo, A. 2008. "Nuove Ricerche Stratigrafiche nella Casa di M. Epidio Sabino (IX,1,29) a Pompei." In P. G. Guzzo and M. P. Guidobaldi, eds., *Nuove Ricerche Archeologiche nell'Area Vesuviana (Scavi 2003–2006),* 321–29. Atti del Convegno Intern., Rome, 1–3 February 2007. Soprintendenza Archeologica di Pompei, 25. Rome: L'Erma di Bretschneider.

García y García, L. 2006. *Danni di Guerra a Pompei.* Rome: L'Erma di Bretschneider.

Garnsey, P. D. A., and R. Saller. 1987. *The Roman Empire: Economy, Society and Culture.* Berkeley: University of California Press.

Garzia, D. 2008. "Pompei. Regio VI, Insula 2: Aggere. Relazione di Scavo Settembre 2007." *Fasti Online* 122, 1–3.

Gautier, T. 1890. "Arria Marcella." In *One of Cleopatra's Nights, and Other Fantastic Romances*, trans. L. Hearn, 17–25. New York: Worthington.

Geertman, H. 1998. "Lo Sviluppo Urbanistico della Città e la Sua Storia." In J. Berry, ed., *Sotto i Lapilli: Studi nella Regio i di Pompei*, 17–25. Milan: Electa.

Geertman, H. 2007. "The Urban Development of the Pre-Roman City." In J. J. Dobbins and P. Foss, eds., *The World of Pompeii*. London: Routledge, 82–97.

Gentry, R. 2015. "The Vehiculatio in Roman Imperial Regulation: Particular Solutions to a Systematic Problem." *Madison Historical Review* 12, 1–14.

Gerkan, A. von. 1940. *Der Stadtplan von Pompeji*. Berlin: Archäologisches Institut des Deutschen Reiches.

Gesemann, B. 1996. *Die Strassen der antiken Stadt Pompeji: Entwicklung und Gestaltung*. Frankfurt am Main: Lang.

Giddens, A. 1984. *The Constitution of Society: Outline of the Theory of Structuration*. Cambridge, MA: University of California Press.

Giglio, M. 2005. "Scavi nelle Case IX, 7, 22; IX, 7 25 e Lungo la Viu Mef[iu]." *RStPomp* 16, 202–4.

Giglio, M. 2008. "Indagini Archeologiche nell'Insula 7 della Regio IX di Pompei." In P. G. Guzzo and M. P. Guidobaldi, eds., *Nuove Ricerche Archeologiche nell'Area Vesuviana (Scavi 2003–2006)*, 341–48. Atti del Convegno Intern., Rome, 1–3 February 2007. Soprintendenza Archeologica di Pompei, 25. Rome: L'Erma di Bretschneider.

González, J., and M. H. Crawford. 1986. "The Lex Irnitana: A New Copy of the Flavian Municipal Law." *JRS* 76, 147–243.

Gottdiener, M. 1993. "A Marx for Our Time: Henri Lefebvre and the Production of Space." *Sociological Theory* 11, 129–34.

Grénier, A. 1934. *Manuel d'Archéologie Gallo-Romaine. II: L'Archéologie du Sol. 1: Les Routes*. Vol. 2. Paris: Picard.

Grimaldi, M. 2014. *Pompeii: La Casa di Marco Fabio Rufo*. Vol. 2. Naples: Valtrend.

Guzzo, P. G. 2007. *Pompei: Storia e Paesaggi della Città Antica*. Milan: Electa.

Guzzo, P. G. 2011. "The Origins and Development of Pompeii: The State of Understanding and Some Working Hypotheses." In S. Ellis, ed., *The Making of Pompeii: Studies in the History and Urban Development of an Ancient Town*, 11–18. *JRA* Suppl. 85. Portsmouth, RI.

Hanell, K. 1962. "San Giovenale." In A. Boëthius, N. G. Sahlin, and Gustav, King of Sweden, eds., *Etruscan Culture: Land and People: Archaeological Research and Studies Conducted in San Giovenale and Its Environs by Members of the Swedish Institute in Rome*. Malmö: Columbia University Press.

Harris, H. A. 1974. "Lubrication in Antiquity." *Greece & Rome* 21, 32–36.

Harris, J. 2007. *Pompeii Awakened: A Story of Rediscovery*. London: I.B. Tauris.

Harris, W. V. 1993. "Between Archaic and Modern: Problems in Roman Economic History." In W. V. Harris, ed. *The Inscribed Economy: Production and Distribution in the Roman Empire in the Light of Instrumentum Domesticum*, 11–30. *JRA* Suppl. 6. Portsmouth, RI.

Hartnett, J. 2008. "Si Quis Hic Sederit: Streetside Benches and Urban Society in Pompeii." *AJA* 112, 91–119.

Hartnett, J. 2011. "The Power of Nuisances on the Roman Street." In R. Laurence and D. Newsome, eds., *Rome, Ostia, Pompeii: Movement and Space*. Oxford: Oxford University Press, 135–59.

Haverfield, F. J. 1913. *Ancient Town-Planning*. Oxford: Clarendon Press.

Hillier, B., and J. Hansen. 1984. *The Social Logic of Space*. Cambridge: Cambridge University Press.

Hobson, B. 2009. *Latrinae et Foricae: Toilets in the Roman World*. London: Duckworth.

Hoepfner, W., and E. L. Schwandner. 1994. *Haus und Stadt im Klassischen Griechenland. Wohnen in der Klassischen Polis*, 1. Munich: Deutscher Kunstverlag.

Hopkins, K. 2000. *A World Full of Gods: The Strange Triumph of Christianity*. New York: Free Press.

Humphrey, J. W., J. P. Oleson, and A. N. Sherwood, eds. 1998. *Greek and Roman Technology: A Sourcebook*. London: Routledge.

Jacobelli, L. 2006. "Su un Nuovo Cippo L.P.P. Trovato nell'Area nelle Terme Suburbane di Pompeii." *RStPomp* 17, 67–68.

Jacobs, J. 1961. *The Death and Life of Great American Cities.* New York: Random House.

Jansen, G. C. M. 2011. "Interpreting Images and Epigraphic Testimony." In G. C. M. Jansen, A.-O. Koloski-Ostrow, and E. M. Moormann, eds., *Roman Toilets: Their Archaeology and Cultural History,* 165–75. Babesch Annual Papers on Mediterranean Archaeology, 19. Leuven: Peeters.

Jensen, W. 1918. *Gradiva: A Pompeiian Fancy.* Trans. H. Downey. New York: Moffat, Yard.

Johnson, J. 1935. *Excavations at Minturnae.* Vol. 1, *Monuments of the Republican Forum..* Philadelphia: University of Pennsylvania Press.

Jones, R., and D. J. Robinson. 2005. "Water, Wealth, and Social Status at Pompeii: The House of the Vestals in the First Century." *AJA* 109, 695–710.

Jones, R., and D. J. Robinson. 2007. "Intensification, Heterogeneity and Power in the Development of Insula VI.1." In J. J. Dobbins and P. Foss, eds., *The World of Pompeii,* 389–406. London: Routledge.

Jones, R., and A. V. Schoonhoven. 2003. "The Story of a Street: The Vicolo di Narciso and the Urban Development of Pompeii." In P. Wilson, ed., *The Archaeology of Roman Towns,* 128–36. Oxford: Oxbow Books.

Kaiser, A. 2011a. "Cart Traffic Flow in Pompeii and Rome." In R. Laurence and D. Newsome, eds., *Rome, Ostia, Pompeii: Movement and Space,* 174–93. Oxford: Oxford University Press.

Kaiser, A. 2011b. *Roman Urban Street Networks.* New York: Routledge.

Kastenmeier, P., G. di Maio, G. Balassone, M. Boni, M. Joachimski, and N. Mondillo. 2010. "The Source of Stone Building Materials from the Pompeii Archaeological Area and Its Surroundings." *Periodico di Mineralogia,* special issue, 39–58.

Keenan-Jones, D. 2010. "The Aqua Augusta. Regional Water Supply in Roman and Late Antique Campania." Diss., Macquarie University.

Keenan-Jones, D., J. Hellstrom, and R. Drysdale. 2011. "Lead Contamination in the Drinking Water of Pompeii." In E. E. Poehler, M. Flohr, and K. Cole, eds., *Pompeii: Art, Industry and Infrastructure,* 131–48. Oxford: Oxbow Books.

Kellum, B. 1999. "The Spectacle of the Street." In B. Bergmann and C. Kondoleon, eds., *The Art of Ancient Spectacle,* 283–99. New Haven, CT: Yale University Press.

Killgrove, K. 2010. "Migration and Mobility in Imperial Rome." Diss., University of North Carolina, Chapel Hill.

Killgrove, K. 2014a. "How Long Was the Average Roman Stride?" *Powered by Osteons.* http://www.poweredbyosteons.org/2014/07/how-long-was-average-roman-stride.html. Accessed July 18, 2014.

Killgrove, K. 2014b. "How Long Was the Average Roman Foot, and What Was Their Shoe Size?" *Powered by Osteons.* http://www.poweredbyosteons.org/2014/07/how-long-was-average-roman-foot-and.html. Accessed July 22, 2014.

Købke, C. S. 1841. *The Forum, Pompeii, with Vesuvius in the Distance.* J. Paul Getty Museum, 85. PA.43.

Koga, M. 1991. "The Surface Drainage System of Pompeii." *Opuscula Pompeiana* 2, 57–72.

Kolb, A. 2000. *Transport und Nachrichtentransfer in Römischen Reich.* Berlin: Akademie Verlag.

Kolb, A. 2001. "Transport and Communication in the Roman State: The Cursus Publicus." In R. Laurence and C. Adams, eds., *Travel & Geography in the Roman Empire,* 95–105. London: Routledge.

Koloski-Ostrow, A.-O. 2015. *The Archaeology of Sanitation in Roman Italy.* Chapel Hill: University of North Carolina Press.

Kronenberg, L. 2015. "The Rise of Sabinus: Sexual Satire in Catalepton 10." *Classical Journal* 110, 191–212.

Laird, M. 2015. *Civic Monuments and the Augustales in Roman Italy.* Cambridge: Cambridge University Press.

Láng, O. 2003. "New Data concerning the Diagonal Road between Aquincum and Brigetio." In Zs. Visy, ed., *Proceedings of the XIXth International Congress of Roman Frontier Studies, Pécs, Hungary. September 2003*, 657–66. Pécs: University of Pécs.

Langdon, J. 1986. *Horse, Oxen, and Technological Innovation.* Cambridge: Cambridge University Press.

La Regina, A., I. Insolera, and D. Morandi. 1997. *Via Appia: Sulle Ruine della Magnificenza Antica.* Milan: Leonardo Arte.

Laurence, R. 1994. *Roman Pompeii: Space and Society.* London: Routledge.

Laurence, R. 1995. "The Organization of Space in Pompeii." In T. J. Cornell and K. Lomas, eds., *Urban Society in Roman Italy*, 63–78. London: Routledge.

Laurence, R. 1998. "Land Transport in Roman Italy: Costs, Practice and the Economy." In H. M. Parkins and C. Smith, eds. *Trade, Traders and the Ancient City*, 129–48. London: Routledge.

Laurence, R. 1999. *The Roads of Roman Italy: Mobility and Cultural Change.* London: Routledge.

Laurence, R. 2008. "From Quarry to Road: The Supply of Basalt for Road Paving in the Tiber Valley." In F. Coarelli and H. Patterson, eds., *Mercator Placidissimus: The Tiber Valley in Antiquity, Rome*, 705–30. Rome: Quasar.

Laurence, R., S. Esmonde Cleary, and G. Sears. 2011. *The City in the Roman West c. 250 BC–c. AD 250.* Cambridge: Cambridge University Press.

Laurence, R., and D. Newsome, eds. 2011 *Rome, Ostia, Pompeii: Movement and Space.* Oxford: Oxford University Press.

Laurence, R., and A. Wallace-Hadrill, eds. 1997. *Domestic Space in the Roman World: Pompeii and Beyond. JRA Suppl.* 22. Portsmouth, RI.

Lauristen, T. 2013. "The Form and Function of Boundaries in the Campanian House." In A. Anguissola, ed., *Privata Luxuria: Towards an Archaeology of Intimacy*, 95–114. Munich: Utz.

Lazer, E. 1995. "Human Skeletal Remains in Pompeii." Diss., University of Sydney.

Lazer, E. 2007. "Victims of the Cataclysm." In J. J. Dobbins and P. Foss, eds., *The World of Pompeii*, 607–19. London: Routledge.

Lefebvre, H. 1991. *The Production of Space.* Oxford: Blackwell.

Lefebvre des Noëttes, R. 1931. *L'Attelage: Le Cheval de Selle à travers les Âges: Contribution à l'Histoire de l'Esclavage.* Paris: Picard.

Levoy, M., and J. Trimble. 2002. "Stanford Digital Forma Urbis Romae Project." *Stanford Digital Forma Urbis Romae Project.* http://formaurbis.stanford.edu/index.html. Accessed November 15, 2015.

Ling, R. 1990. "A Stranger in Town: Finding the Way in an Ancient City." *Greece & Rome* 37, 204–14.

Ling, R. 1997. *The Insula of the Menander at Pompeii*, vol. 1. Oxford: Oxford University Press.

Liu, J. 2008. "Pompeii and Collegia: A New Appraisal of the Evidence." *Ancient History Bulletin* 22, 53–70.

Liveley, G. 2011. "Delusion and Dream in Théophile Gautier's Arria Marcella." In S. Hales and J. Paul, eds., *Pompeii in the Public Imagination from Its Rediscovery to Today*, 105–17. Oxford: Oxford University Press.

Longobardo, F. 2004. "Problemi di Viabilità in Campania: La Via Domitiana." In L. Petacco and S. Quilici Gigli, eds., *Viabilità e Insediamenti nell'Italia Antica*, 277–90. Rome: L'Erma di Bretschneider.

Lynch, K. 1960. *The Image of the City.* Cambridge, MA: MIT Press.

Macaulay-Lewis, E. 2011. "The City in Motion: Walking for Transport and Leisure in the City of Rome." In R. Laurence and D. Newsome, eds., *Rome, Ostia, Pompeii: Movement and Space*, 262–89. Oxford: Oxford University Press.

MacDonald, W. 1986. *The Architecture of the Roman Empire: An Urban Appraisal*, vol. 2. New Haven, CT: Yale University Press.

Maiuri, A. 1929. "Studi e Ricerche sulla Fortificazione di Pompei." *Monumenti Antichi* 33, 113–290.

Maiuri, A. 1940. "Pompei: Scavo della 'Grande Palestra' nel Quartiere dell'Anfiteatro (a. 1935–1939)." *Notizie degli scavi di antichità*, 165–238.

Maiuri, A. 1944. "Pompei: Isolamento della Cinta Murale tra la Porta Vesuvio e la Porta Ercolano." *Notizie degli scavi di antichità*, 275–94.

Maiuri, A. 1973. *Alla Ricerca di Pompei Preromana: Saggi Stratigrafici.* Naples: Società Editrice Napoletana.

Malmberg, S., and H. Bjur. 2011. "Movement and Urban Development at Two City Gates in Rome: The Porta Esquilina and Porta Tiburtina." In R. Laurence and D. Newsome, eds., *Rome, Ostia, Pompeii: Movement and Space*, 362–85. Oxford: Oxford University Press.

Martin, S. 1990. "Servum Meum Mulionem Conduxisti: Mules, Muleteers and Transportation in Classical Roman Law." *TAPA* 120, 301–14.

Martin, S. 2002. "Roman Law and the Study of Land Transportation." In J. J. Aubert and B. Sirks, eds., *SPECVLVM IVRIS: Roman Law as a Reflection of Social and Economic Life in Antiquity*, 151–68. Ann Arbor: University of Michigan Press.

Mau, A. 1875. "La Piazza Centrale di Pompei." *Bullettino dell'Instituto di Corrispondenza Archeologica*, 261–68.

Mau, A. 1882. *Geschichte der decorativen Wandmalerei in Pompeji.* Berlin: Reimer.

Mau, A. 1899. *Pompeii: Its Life and Art.* Trans. F. W. Kelsey. London: Macmillan.

McCallum, M. 2010. "The Supply of Stone to the City of Rome: A Case Study of the Transport of Anician Building Stone and Millstone from the Santa Trinita Quarry (Orvieto)." In C. D. Dillian and C. L. White, eds., *Trade and Exchange: Archaeological Studies from History and Prehistory*, 75–94. New York: Springer.

Meiggs, R. 1973. *Roman Ostia.* Oxford: Clarendon Press.

Michel, D. 1990. *Casa dei Cei (I 6, 15).* Häuser in Pompeji, vol. 3. Munich: Hirmer Verlag.

Miele, F. 1989. "La Casa a Schiera I, 11, 16: Un Esempio di Edilizia Privata a Pompei." *RStPomp* 3, 165–84.

Miniero, P. 1987. "Studio di un Carro Romano dalla Villa C." *Mélanges de l'École Française de Rome* 99, 171–209.

Miniero, P. 1991. "Stabia. Attività dell'Ufficio Scavi: 1991." *RStPomp* 5, 221–28.

Mithen, S. 2003. *After the Ice: A Global Human History, 20,00–5,000 bc.* London: Harvard University Press.

Mogetta, M. 2014. "From Latin Planned Urbanism to Roman Colonial Layouts: The Town-Planning of Gabii and Its Cultural Implications." In E. Robinson, ed., *Papers on Italian Urbanism in the First Millennium b.c.*, 145–74. *JRA Suppl.* 97. Portsmouth, RI.

Mouritsen, H. 1988. *Elections, Magistrates and Municipal Elite: Studies in Pompeian Epigraphy.* Rome: L'Erma di Bretschneider.

Nappo, S. C. 1997. "The Urban Transformation at Pompeii in the Late Third and Early Second Centuries b.c." In R. Laurence and A. Wallace-Hadrill, eds., *Domestic Space in the Roman World: Pompeii and Beyond*, 91–120. *JRA Suppl.* 22. Portsmouth, RI .

Nappo, S. C. 1998. "Insula I.4 and the House of the Lyre Player. The Italian Project." In J. Berry, ed., *Unpeeling Pompeii*, 27–39. Milan: Electa.

Nappo, S. C. 2007. "Houses of Regions I and II." In J. J. Dobbins and P. Foss, eds., *The World of Pompeii*, 347–72. London: Routledge.

Newsome, D. 2007. "Pompeii Analyses. 150 bc–ad 79." Thesis, University of Birmingham.

Newsome, D. 2009. "Traffic, Space and Legal Change around the Casa del Marinaio at Pompeii (VII 15.1–2)." *BABESCH* 84, 121–42.

Newsome, D. 2011. "Introduction." In R. Laurence and D. Newsome, eds., *Rome, Ostia, Pompeii: Movement and Space*, 1–54. Oxford: Oxford University Press.

Nilsson, M. 2014. "Vicolo delle Nozze d'Argento." *Insula V 1. The Swedish Pompeii Project.* http://www.pompejiprojektet.se/house.php?hid=19&hidnummer=9245489&hrubrik=S treet%20-%20Vicolo%20delle%20Nozze%20d%E2%80%99Argento. Accessed November 18, 2015.

Nishida, Y. 1991. "Measuring Structures of Pompeii." *Opuscula Pompeiana* 1, 91–102.

Ohlig, C. 2001. *De Aquis Pompeiorum—das Castellum Aquaein Pompeji: Herkunft, Zuleitung und Verteilung des Wassers*. Nijmegen: C. Ohlig.

Olivito, R. 2013. *Il Foro nell'Atrio: Immagini di Architetture, Scene di Vita e di Mercato nel Fregio dai Praedia di Iulia Felix (Pompei, II, 4 3)*. Bari: Edipuglia.

Ostrow, S. E. 1985. "The Augustales along the Bay of Naples: A Case for Their Early Growth." *Historia: Zeitschrift für Alte Geschichte* 34, 64–101.

O'Sullivan, T. 2011. *Walking in Roman Culture*. Cambridge: Cambridge University Press.

Özgür, M. E. 1989. *Perge*. Istanbul: NET Turistik Yayinlar A.S.

Parslow, C. C. 1998. "Preliminary Report of the 1997 Fieldwork Project in the Praedia Iulia Felicis (Regio II. 4), Pompeii." *RStPomp* 9, 199–207.

Patterson, J. R. 2006. *Landscapes and Cities: Rural Settlement and Civic Transformation in Early Imperial Italy*. Oxford: Oxford University Press.

Pedley, J. G. 1990. *Paestum: Greeks and Romans in Southern Italy*. London: Thames and Hudson.

Pedroni, L. 2011. "Excavations in the History of Pompeii's Urban Development in the Area North of So-Called "Altstadt." In S. Ellis, ed., *The Making of Pompeii: Studies in the History and Urban Development of an Ancient Town*,158–68. JRA Suppl. 85. Portsmouth, RI.

Pedroni, L., and A. Ribera i Lacomba. 2005. "Pompeii-Casa Arianna (VII, 4, 31–51). Verifiche Stratifiche." *RStPomp* 16, 258–59.

Pesando, F. 2006. "Il Progetto Regio VI. Campagna di Scavo 2005." *RStPomp* 17, 48–51.

Pesando, F. 2007. "Il Progetto Regio VI: 'I Primi Secoli di Pompei'—Campagna di Scavo 2006: Le Ricerche dell'Universita di Napoli 'L'Orientale.'" *RStPomp* 18, 111–13.

Pesando, F., and M. P. Guidobaldi. 2006. *Pompei, Ercolano, Oplontis, Stabiae*. Rome: Laterza.

Piganiol, A. 1962. *Les Documents Cadastraux de la Colonie Romaine d'Orange*. Paris: Centre National de la Recherche Scientifique.

Pike, G. 1967. "Pre-Roman Land Transport in the Western Mediterranean Region." *Man* 2, 593–605.

Piranesi, G. B. 1748. *Alcune Vedute di Archi Trionfali ed altri monumenti inalzati da Romani parte de quali se veggono in Roma e parte per l'Italia*. Rome.

Pirson, F. 1993. *Mietwohnungen in Pompeji*. Munich: Verlag Dr. F. Pfeil.

Pirson, F. 1997. "Rented Accommodation at Pompeii: The Evidence of the «Insula Arriana Polliana» VI 6." In R. Laurence and A. Wallace-Hadrill, eds., *Domestic Space in the Roman World: Pompeii and Beyond*, 165–81. JRA Suppl. 22. Portsmouth, RI.

Platner, S., and T. Ashby. 1929. *A Topographical Dictionary of Ancient Rome*. London: Oxford University Press.

Poehler, E. E. 1999. "Narrowing Stones and the Traffic System in Pompeii." Thesis, University of Chicago.

Poehler, E. E. 2003. "Romans on the Right: The Art and Archaeology of Traffic." Thesis, University of Virginia.

Poehler, E. E. 2006. "The Circulation of Traffic in Pompeii's Regio VI." *JRA* 19, 53–74.

Poehler, E. E. 2009. "The Organization of Pompeii's System of Traffic: An Analysis of the Evidence and Its Impact on the Infrastrucutre, Economy, and Urbanism of the Ancient City." Diss., University of Virginia.

Poehler, E. E. 2011a. "Where to Park? Carts, Stables, and the Economics of Transport in Pompeii." In R. Laurence and D. Newsome, eds., *Rome, Ostia, Pompeii: Movement and Space*, 194–214. Oxford: Oxford University Press.

Poehler, E. E. 2011b. "Practical Matters: Infrastructure and the Planning for the Post-Earthquake Forum at Pompeii." In E. E. Poehler, M. Flohr, and K. Cole, eds., *Pompeii: Art, Industry and Infrastructure*, 149–63. Oxford: Oxbow Books.

Poehler, E. E. 2012. "The Drainage System at Pompeii: Mechanisms, Operation and Design." *JRA* 25, 95–120.

Poehler, E. E. 2016. "Measuring the Movement Economy. A Network Analysis of Pompeii." In M. Flohr and A. Wilson, eds., *The Economy of Pompeii*. Oxford: Oxford University Press.

Poehler, E. E., and S. Ellis. 2012. "The 2011 Season of the Pompeii Quadriporticus Project: The Southern and Northern Sides." *Fasti Online* 249, 1–12.

Poehler, E. E., and B. Crowther. 2018. "Paving Pompeii: The Social History of an Infrastructural Practice." *AJA* 122.4, 579–609.

Poehler, E. E., J. van Roggen, and B. Crowther. 2019. "The Iron Streets of Pompeii." *AJA* 123.2, 237–262.

Pucci, G., E. Chirico, V. Salerno, and F. Mari. 2008. "Le Ricerche dell'Universita di Siena a Pompei." In P. G. Guzzo and M. P. Guidobaldi, eds., *Nuove Ricerche Archeologiche nell'Area Vesuviana (Scavi 2003–2006)*, 223–36. Atti del Convegno Intern., Rome, 1–3 February 2007. Soprintendenza Archeologica di Pompei, 25. Rome: L'Erma di Bretschneider.

Purcell, N. 1983. "The Apparitores: A Study in Social Mobility." *PBSR* 51, 125–73.

Quilici, L. 1990. *Le Strade: Viabilità tra Roma e Lazio*. Vita e Costumi dei Romani Antichi, 12. Rome: Quasar.

Quilici, L., and S. Quilici Gigli. 2002. *La Via Appia: Iniziative e Interventi per la Conoscenza e la Valorizzazione da Roma a Capua*. Rome: L'Erma di Bretschneider.

Raper, R. A. 1977. "The Analysis of the Urban Structure of Pompeii: A Sociological Examination of Land Use (Semi-Micro)." In D. L Clake, ed., *Spatial Archaeology*, 187–221. London: Academic Press.

Rega, L. 1991. "Il Progetto di Ricostruzione del Carro [di Stabia]." In *VIAE PUBLICAE ROMANAE X. Mostra europea del turismo artigianato e delle tradizioni culturali - Roma Castel Sant'Angelo 11 - 25 Aprile 1991*, 109–12. Rome: Leonardo – De Luca.

Ribera i Lacomba, A., M. Bustamente, P. Guillem, E. Huguet, P. Iborra, R. Martinez, R. Asunción, J. Salavert, and J. Vioque. 2009. "La Casa de Ariadna o dei Capitelli Colorati (Pompeya) (VII, 4, 51 Y 31) y Via degli Augustali: Excavaciones y Proyecto de Restauración. Campaña 2008. Informes y Trabajos." In *Excavaciones Enel Exterior 2008 Informes y Trabajos*, 93–103. Ministerio de Cultura. http://www.mcu.es/patrimonio/docs/MC/IPHE/Publicaciones/IT/N3/3_casa_de_ariadna.pdf. Accessed August 24, 2015.

Richardson, L. 1978. "Concordia and Concordia Augusta: Rome and Pompeii." *Parola Passato* 33, 260–72.

Richardson, L. 1988. *Pompeii: An Architectural History*. Baltimore: Johns Hopkins University Press.

Rispoli, P., and R. Paone. 2011. "Pompeii Scavi, Canale Conte di Sarno. Lavori di Sistemazione e Rifunzionalizzazione 2009–2011." *RStPomp* 22, 126–33.

Robinson, E. 2014. "Non-Greek Urbanism in Southern Italy in the 4th and 3rd c. B.C." In E. Robinson, ed. *Papers on Italian Urbanism in the First Millennium b.c.*, 197–204. *JRA Suppl.* 97. Portsmouth, RI.

Robinson, M. 2011. "The Prehistoric and Protohistoric Archaeology of Pompeii and the Sarno Valley." In S. Ellis, ed., *The Making of Pompeii: Studies in the History and Urban Development of an Ancient Town*, 19–36. *JRA Suppl.* 85. Portsmouth, RI.

Robinson, O. F. 1992. *Ancient Rome: City Planning and Administration*. New York: Routledge.

Rodríguez Morales, J. 2014. "Elementos Metálicos en las Vías Antiguas. Un Sistema Objetivo para la Datación de los Caminos Antiguos." In *Actas de las Novenas Jornadas de Patrimonio Arqueologico en la Comunidad de Madrid*, 51–62. Madrid: Comunidad de Madrid.

Rosen, J. November 10, 2014. "The Knowledge: London's Legendary Taxi-Driver Test, Puts Up a Fight in the Age of GPS." *New York Times Style Magazine*. http://nyti.ms/1LwpmPY. Accessed November 13, 2015.

Ross Taylor, L. 1914. "Augustales, Seviri Augustales, and Seviri: A Chronological Study." *TAPA* 45, 231–53.

Russell, B. 2014. *The Economics of the Roman Stone Trade*. Oxford: Oxford University Press.

Sagalassos Archaeological Research Project. http://www.sagalassos.be/. Accessed May 11, 2015.

Sakai, S. 1991. "Some Considerations of the Urbanism in the So-Called Neustadt of Pompeii." *Opuscula Pompeiana* 1, 35–57.

Sakai, S., and V. Iorio. 2008. "L'Indagine del J.I.P.S. nel Vicolo di M. Lucrezio Frontone: Un'Ipotesi sul Periodo dell'Urbanizzazione della Citta in Relazione agli Assi Stradali." In P. G. Guzzo and M. P. Guidobaldi, eds., *Nuove Ricerche Archeologiche nell'Area Vesuviana (Scavi 2003–2006)*,

399–408. Atti del Convegno Intern., Rome, 1–3 February 2007. Soprintendenza Archeologica di Pompei, 25. Rome: L'Erma di Bretschneider.

Salama, P. 1951. *Les Voies Romaines de l'Afrique du Nord.* Algiers: Impr. Officielle.

Saliou, C. 1999. "Les Trottoirs de Pompéi: Une Première Approache." *BABESCH* 74, 161–218.

Salway, B. 2007. "The Perception and Description of Space in Roman Itineraries." In M. Rathmann, ed., *Wahrnehmung und Erfassung Geographischer Räume in der Antike,* 181–209. Mainz: Von Zabern.

Sandor, B. 2013. "Jupiter's Finest Wheels." *JRA* 26, 693–700.

Seiler, F., H. Beste, C. Piraino, and D. Esposito. 2005. "La Regio VI Insula 16 e la Zona della Porta Vesuvio." In P. G. Guzzo and M. P. Guidobaldi, eds., *Nuove Richerche Archeologiche a Pompei ed Ercolano,* 216–34. Atti del Convegno Internazionale, Rome, 28–30 November 2002. Soprintendenza Archeologica di Pompei, 10. Naples: Electa.

Seiler, F., M. Märker, P. Kastenmeier, and S. Vogel. 2011. "Interdisciplinary Approach on the Reconstruction of the Ancient Cultural Landscape of the Sarno River Plain before A.D. 79." In H.-R. Bork, H. Meller, and R. Gerlach, eds., *Umweltarchäologie: Naturkatastrophen und Umweltwandel im Archäologischen Befund.,* 145–54. Tagungen des Landesmuseums für Vorgeschichte Halle (Saale), 6. Halle/Saale: Landesamt f. Denkmalpflege u. Archäologie Sachsen-Anhalt.

Sewell, J., and R. Witcher. 2015. "Urbanism in Ancient Peninsular Italy: Developing a Methodology for a Database Analysis of Higher Order Settlements (350 BCE to 300 CE)." *Internet Archaeology,* 40. http://intarch.ac.uk/journal/issue40/2/. Accessed November 18, 2015.

Shaw, B. 2007. "Sabinus the Muleteer." *Classical Quarterly* 57, 132–38.

Sigurdsson, H. 2007. "The Environmental and Geomorphological Context of the Volcano." In J. J. Dobbins and P. Foss, eds., *The World of Pompeii,* 43–62. London: Routledge.

Sillieres, P. 1983. "Ornieres et Voies Romaines." *Caesarodunum* 18, 37–45.

Sitwell, N. 1981. *Roman Roads of Europe.* New York: St. Martin's Press.

Smith, W. 1890. *A Dictionary of Greek and Roman Antiquities.* London: John Murray.

Sogliano, A. 1937. *Pompei nel suo Sviluppo Storico: Pompei Preromana (dalle Origini all'a. 80 av.C.).* Rome: Athenaeum.

Sommella, P. 1989. *Urbanistica Pompeiana: Nuovi Momenti di Studio.* Rome: Consorzio Neapolis.

Sorriento, A. 2008. "Vico del Fauno, Saggio 2." *Fasti Online* 105, 1–6.

Spinazzola, V. 1917. "Pompei. Continuazione degli Scavi in Via dell'Abbondanza." *Notizie degli scavi di antichità,* 247–64.

Spinazzola, V. 1953. *Pompei alla Luce degli Scavi Nuovi di Via dell'Abbondanza (Anni 1910–1923).* Rome: Libreria della Stato.

Staccoli, R. A. 2003. *The Roads of the Romans.* Los Angeles: J. Paul Getty Museum.

Stanford Digital Forma Urbis Romae Project. http://formaurbis.stanford.edu. Accessed December 10, 2015.

Stefani, G. 2003. *Menander: La Casa del Menandro di Pompei.* Milan: Electa.

Stöger, H. 2008. "Roman Ostia: Space Syntax and the Domestication of Space." In A. Posluschny, K. Lambers, and I. Herzog, eds., *Layers of Perception: Proceedings of the 35th International Conference on Computer Applications and Quantitative Methods in Archaeology (CAA), Berlin, 2–6 April 2007,* 322–27. Bonn: Habelt.

Stöger, H. 2011. "The Spatial Organisation of the Movement Economy: The Analysis of Ostia S Scholae." In R. Laurence and D. Newsome, eds., *Rome, Ostia, Pompeii: Movement and Space,* 215–42. Oxford: Oxford University Press.

Syme, R. 1958. "Sabinus the Muleteer." *Latomus* 17, 73–80.

Talbert, R. 2010. *Rome's World: The Peutinger Map Reconsidered.* Cambridge: Cambridge University Press.

Thomas, M., I. van der Graaff, and P. Wilkinson. 2013. "The Oplontis Project 2012–13: A Report of Excavations at Oplontis B." *Fasti Online* 295, 1–9.

Trifilò, F. 2011. "Movement, Gaming and the Use of Space in the Forum." In R. Laurence and D. Newsome, eds., *Rome, Ostia, Pompeii: Movement and Space*, 312–31. Oxford: Oxford University Press.

Trifilò, F. 2013. "Text, Space, and the Urban Community: A Study of the Platea as Written Space." In G. Sears, P. Keegan, and R. Laurence, eds., *Written Space in the Latin West, 200 B.C. to ad 300*, 169–84. London: Bloomsbury.

Tsujimura, S. 1991. "Ruts in Pompeii: The Traffic System in the Roman City." *Opuscula Pompeiana* 1, 58–86.

Tuccinardi, M., and F. Ruffo. 1987. "Saggi nel Vico dei Soprastanti." *RStPomp* 1, 135–40.

Twain, M. 1869. *The Innocents Abroad; or, The New Pilgrims' Progress: Being Some Account of the Steamship Quaker City's Pleasure Excursion to Europe and the Holy Land: With Descriptions of Countries, Nations, Incidents, and Adventures as They Appeared to the Author.* Hartford: American Publishing.

van der Graaff, I. 2013. "The City Walls of Pompeii: Perceptions and Expressions of a Monumental Boundary." Diss., University of Texas at Austin.

Van der Graaff, I. and S. J. R. Ellis, (2017). 'Minerva, Urban Defenses, and the Continuity of Cult at Pompeii', *Journal of Roman Archaeology* 30: 283–300.

van der Graaff, I., J. Muslin, M. Thomas, P. Wilkinson, J. R. Clarke, and N. Muntasser. 2016. "Preliminary Notes on Two Seasons of Research at Oplontis B (2014–2015)." *Fasti Online* 362, 1–14.

van der Poel, H. B. 1984. "Corpus Topographicum Pompeianum. Pars III. The RICA Maps of Pompeii." Rome: The University of Texas at Austin.

van Roggen, J. 2015. "Guard Stones: Street Infrastructure in Pompeii." *Aisthesis* 4, 54–78.

van Tilburg, C. 2005. *Romeins Verkeer: Weggebruik en Verkeersdrukte in het Romeinse Rijk.* Leiden: Primavera Press.

van Tilburg, C. 2007. *Traffic and Congestion in the Roman Empire.* London: Routledge.

Varone, A. 2008. "Per la Storia Recente, Antica, e Antichissima del Sito di Pompei." In P. G. Guzzo and M. P. Guidobaldi, eds., *Nuove Ricerche Archeologiche nell'Area Vesuviana (Scavi 2003–2006)*, 349–62. Atti del Convegno Intern., Rome, 1–3 February 2007. Soprintendenza Archeologica di Pompei, 25. Rome: L'Erma di Bretschneider.

Vigneron, P. 1968. *Le Cheval dans l'Antiquité Gréco-Romaine.* Nancy: Faculté des lettres et des Sciences humaines de l'Université de Nancy.

Vitale, F. 2000. *Astronomia ed Esoterismo nell'Antica Pompei e Ricerche Archeoastronomiche a Paestum, Cuma, Velia, Metaponto, Crotone, Locri e Vibo Valentia.* Padua: CLEUP.

Waelkens, M. 2005. "Test Trenches on the N–S Colonnaded Street: July 31–August 4, 2005." *Archaeology's Interactive Dig.* http://interactive.archaeology.org/sagalassos/field05/cstreet3.html. Accessed December 10, 2015.

Wagener, A. P. 1912. *Popular Associations of Right and Left in Roman Literature.* Baltimore: Furst.

Wallace-Hadrill, A. 1994. *Houses and Society in Pompeii and Herculaneum.* Princeton, NJ: Princeton University Press.

Wallace-Hadrill, A. 1995. "Public Honour and Private Shame: The Urban Texture of Pompeii." In T. Cornell and K. Lomas, eds., *Urban Society in Roman Italy*, 39–62. London: St. Martin's Press.

Wallace-Hadrill, A. 2005. "Mutatas Formas: The Augustan Transformation of Roman Knowledge." In K. Galinsky, ed., *Age of Augustus*, 55–84. Cambridge: Cambridge University Press.

Wallace-Hadrill, A. 2013. "Planning the Roman City: Grids and Divergence at Pompeii and Falerii Novi." In H. Eckardt and S. Rippon, eds., *Living and Working in the Roman World*, 75–93. *JRA Suppl.* 95. Portsmouth, RI.

Weiss, C. 2010. "Determining Function of Pompeian Sidewalk Features through GIS Analysis." In B. Frischer, J. W. Crawford, and D. Koller, eds., *Making History Interactive: Proceedings of the 37th CAA, March 22–26*, 363–72. Oxford: Archaeopress.

Weller, J. 1999. "Roman Traction Systems." http://www.humanist.de/rome/rts/index.html. Accessed November 7, 2015.

White, K. D. 1975. *Farm Equipment of the Roman World*. Cambridge: Cambridge University Press.

Wilson, A. "Timgad and Textile Production." In D. J. Mattingly and J. Salmon, eds., *Economies beyond Agriculture in the Roman World*, 271–96. London: Routledge.

Wilson, F. 1935. "Studies in the Social and Economic History of Ostia: Part I." *PBSR* 13, 41–68.

Woolf, G. 1997. "The Roman Urbanization of the East." In S. Alcock, ed., *The Early Roman Empire in the East*, 1–14. Oxford: Oxbow Books.

Zanella, S. 2014. "Pompéi: Maison des Mosaïques Géométriques VIII 2, 3–16." *Chronique des Activités Archéologiques de l'École Française de Rome*, 1–11.

Zarmakoupi, M. 2011. "Porticus and Cryptoporticus in Luxury Villa Architecture." In E. E. Poehler, M. Flohr, and K. Cole, eds., *Pompeii: Art, Industry and Infrastructure*, 50–61. Oxford: Oxbow Books.

Zevi, F. 1982. "Urbanistica di Pompei." In *La Regione Sotterrata dal Vesuvio: Studi e Prospettive*, 353–65. Atti del Convegno Internazionale, 11–15 November 1979. Naples: Università degli Studi di Napoli.

INDEX